To Mark & Jacquie

WHEN MEN THINK
PRIVATE THOUGHTS

Books by Gordon MacDonald
from Thomas Nelson Publishers

Christ Followers in the Real World
The Life God Blesses
Ordering Your Private World (Anniversary Edition)
Rebuilding Your Broken World
Renewing Your Spiritual Passion
When Men Think Private Thoughts

WHEN MEN THINK
PRIVATE THOUGHTS

GORDON MACDONALD

OLIVER
NELSON

THOMAS NELSON PUBLISHERS
Nashville • Atlanta • London • Vancouver

Published in Nashville, Tennessee, by Thomas Nelson, Inc., Publishers, and distributed in Canada by Word Communications, Ltd., Richmond, British Columbia.

Library of Congress Cataloging-in-Publication Data

MacDonald, Gordon.
    When men think private thoughts : exploring the issues that
captivate the minds of men / Gordon MacDonald.
        p. cm.
    ISBN 0-7852-7839-7
    1. Masculinity (Psychology)—Religious aspects—Christianity.
2. Masculinity (Psychology).   3. Men (Christian theology).
4. Intimacy (Psychology).   6. Identity (Psychology)—Religious
aspects—Christianity.   7. Identity (Psychology).   8. Self-perception
in men.   9. Men—Psychology.   I. Title.
BV4597.M33   1996
248.8'42—dc20   96-13844
                                                                      CIP

Printed in the United States of America.

1 2 3 4 5 6 — 01 00 99 98 97 96

To the new generation of "men" in my family
Who are just starting to think private thoughts of their own
My grandsons:
Lucas Gordon (b. 5 September 1993)
Ryan Mark (b. 22 June 1994)
There's a word to you both at the end of this book

And always a dedication to Gail, my dear wife,
Who shares the journey of every written word

CONTENTS

FOREWORD

Life has its peak moments that seem to stand separate from and above all others. Seeing this manuscript cross the finish line is such an occasion for me. I have had the privilege of being on-site while many of these thoughts have been germinating in my husband's heart and mind. Long and stimulating hours have been spent as we have talked our way through these chapters. Hearing Gordon spin these ideas in homes, in restaurants, and at conferences and watching the eager responses of both men and women have convinced me of their value. In fact, several women insisted after such conversations that I write to them (even though I don't know them personally) when this book came out because their interest had been piqued.

In a day when more and more scientific evidence is being accumulated about the differences in male and female brains, it should be less surprising that men "appear" to be from Mars and women from Venus. We are different—big time.

The thoughts Gordon discusses in *When Men Think Private Thoughts* have been beneficial both in our parenting and in our marriage as we seek to understand each other. Beyond that, we have been grateful to note the way others are being challenged and helped.

This has been a difficult book for Gordon to write. I have loved cheering him on as he has dealt with the material himself before writing it for others. After thirty-five years of observing this man, I realize that this is part and parcel of who he is—insisting his words wash over his own soul first.

It is my hope that both men and women will come to many "aha" moments as they read these pages together. There no doubt will be ideas with which you will disagree or thoughts that will need to be bracketed for a later time. But if you stick with them to the end, you can reach deeper levels of acceptance and partnership. Just ask us.

Gail MacDonald

Midnight Games

Last evening at the midnight hour
Two men, in different places,
Unknown to each other,
Sat pondering the same subject:
The significance
Of fifty-five years of life.

There are those moments
When a certain mood
Causes a man's mind to open and scan
The resume of personal existence,
Engaging in a ruthless game best called
What's-the-Point?

For losers, this midnight game can be harsh, perhaps dispiriting,
*   or even destructive.*
For winners, it can be satisfying, fortifying, vindicating to the soul.

For both men the time to play this midnight game had come.
A strange reverie, you see, had captured the hour.
And this contest in private thinking, which, sooner or later,
*   almost every man plays, began for them.*

See one player at a desk in a high-ceilinged, paneled den.
Mozart plays softly in surround-sound, but no one listens.
The Late Night Show glares out in the dimness, muted, but no one
*   watches.*
A whiskey glass frequently "freshened" gains increasing attention.

In another location of great contrast, a second player rests his elbows
*   on a scratched kitchen table.*
Decaf, grown cold, half fills a mug.
Here, in this simple place, there is silence except, that is, for the deep
*   breathing of sleeping children in the next room and a wife*
*   humming a familiar tune as she brushes her hair and*
*   prepares for bed.*

From somewhere deep within the two players, a voice, call it
*   the Keeper-of-the-Score, cries out,*

"Add everything up! Compute the value of these years!
Be frank; hold nothing back, you two men who live on different sides
      of the tracks, who are separated by square footage, horsepower,
      clout, and portfolios."

And so the first of the two reaches for his oft-used glass
and begins his private thinking.
"I can play this game," he says,
"and I can win . . . big."

There's my house, he notes for openers: three garages,
      pool (covered), great room, and closets large enough
      to be squash courts.
This spread has been featured in Architectural Digest.
The Republicans come here for fund-raisers.
And the folks in town call it an estate.
It's mine, and—case you're curious, it's paid for.
And when the market gets just right, I'm going to sell this sucker
      and triple my investment.

I own a business, no partners, no public stock.
Nope. All mine!
Oh, and so are the four hundred-plus people on the payroll.
Now, I say they're all mine because I tell them when to come to work,
      when to take a break,
I say how much they'll earn (I broke the union) and whether or not
      they'll even have a job next week (we call it downsizing).
To my face, those people call me "Mister"; some even call me
      "Sir."
Lots of respect in that arrangement. (No one crosses me.)

There's my wife, and for the purposes of this game, I might as well
      speak of her in business terms.
The woman's mine; I've bought her everything.
I've capped her teeth, paid for weight spas
I've imported Paris's finest, gotten her into the best clubs.
New York's best doctors have resculpted virtually every part of her body.
Yep! She's mine. She owes me everything.
She can't leave; she can't change . . . without my authorization.

The kids are mine, too, when you add up the costs.
I've paid the orthodontist, Harvard, and the Lexus dealer.

I've set them in motion with trust funds, abortions, European
        vacations, and front-page weddings.
Let's be blunt: in pure economic terms, they're mine!
They do what I say, come when I call, face a future I've designed.

Oh, and while you're tallying up the score, remember to record
        my investments, my directorships, and my recent invitation
        to a state dinner in the White House.
That's all mine, too.

And don't forget my reputation:
Mentioned last month in Fortune, noted as a patron in the symphony's
        annual report, and admired for my low golfing handicap.
Right! All mine! Earned! Deserved! Secure!

"What's the point?" demands the Keeper-of-the-Score.
"Yes," this first player answers.
"I was just asking that myself."

If, for example, everything and every person in my world is mine,
Why am I so drained of spirit as I play this midnight game?
Why do I have this feeling that everything belongs to me . . .
        but my soul?
And why do I sit here, glass in hand, wondering:
    Why my wife is not here tonight,
    Why my children chose colleges and jobs a thousand miles away,
    If my company will survive paradigm shifts,
    If my reputation is adequately protected,
    If there is anyone who likes me?
Why do I brood on these things, bothered by a nagging void within,
        when so much is mine?

Time! Switch playing fields, for it is
A second player's turn at the midnight game.

Leave that pretentious scene, cross the tracks to a block of homes as plain
        and indistinguishable as white bread.
Don't disturb, but quietly watch.
A second player takes his turn at play in the midnight game.
From a beaten-up thermos he refills his mug to the half.
Private thoughts begin.

Gee, this house is getting old, he sighs, looking around.
Will the furnace last the winter? he wonders.
I've got to paint that ceiling, he promises.
Crabgrass is getting out of control, he complains.
If we don't refinance the mortgage, he reasons, it will be ours
    in six years and seven months.
But, you know, in a way this place really does own me; it welcomes me
    each evening as I walk from the bus.
Every room contains memories of Christmases and birthdays, crises and
    conflicts, giggles and prayers.
Crazy, but I do belong to this place; I'm rooted here.
I wouldn't take a million for it.

My job . . . just a job . . . will never make me a millionaire.
But I might as well admit after these thirty years, the job kind
    of possesses me.
I must have known a thousand people because I've served them.
All over town folks use things I've made or fixed.
Everyone knows that my word is my bond:
    Call me, I say, and I'll be there on time.
    Deal with me, I promise, and I'll give you a fair price.
    Bill me, I assure them, and I'll pay in fifteen days.
    Trust me, I say all the time, and I'll never let you down.
I like what I'm doing and the way I'm doing it.

My wife, he thinks as he uses a fork to clean his nails, she wasn't
    a cheerleader when I met her, she didn't go to Vassar. and—
    please don't tell her I said this—she's probably not going
    to win someone's beauty contest.
But hey, I might as well say the honest truth—
    I belong to her.
    She's full of affection for me.
    She's wise; she's sensitive; she's caring.
    And she's tough, and she's smart; nothing gets by her, believe me!
    She doesn't ask for much; she gives everything.
I'd give her anything she asked for, beginning with myself included,
    nothing, nothing, nothing held back.

Then there's my kids, average students, reasonable competitors,
    great potential, though.
Everyone says that to me.

Shoot! When you get right down to it, I may be their father,
        but I belong to those guys.
I like giving them every second of time there is.
I love being spectator to their fun and games.
I glow as I watch their hearts enlarge with insight and character.
The birth certificates in our strong box upstairs say they are mine,
        but my heart says that I am theirs.

Assets? You kiddin'? Look! I own nothing Wall Street
        snorts about.
What we've got wouldn't make for a good yard sale.
The only holdings of value are my friends, my memories,
        and my faith in God.
I'm just glad to be alive,
Especially after that prostate scare (but the doc said it was benign;
        to come back in a year).

So when they bury me,
And that looks like a while yet, my estate will be little more than
        an insurance policy and a way of life passed on to my sons
        and daughters.

Reputation; connections? I don't care what Moscow
        or Washington thinks.
Now, by the way, there are a few buddies and their wives,
And I'd jump to their side (and they to mine)
Should the occasion of need arise.
With them
    I laugh; I cry
    I give; I get
    I play; I help.
I belong to those folks.
If I've got something they need, it's theirs.
I tell you: I may be broke here (he pats his wallet);
But I'm loaded here (he touches his heart).

Time! It's past midnight. Game is over!
Count up the scores.
Who is winner?
Are you as confused as I as we watch two men extinguish the lights
        and head for bed?

Look! One reaches for the hand of his wife as they start up the stairs.
The other has nothing to hold on to.
One grins at something said by his wife, pats her on the rear,
*   and you have this suspicion that the night is not yet concluded.*
The other hears only silence as he arms the security system,
*   takes a sleeping pill, and lurches toward an empty bed.*

It was a strange experience, this midnight game.
We thought such games were won by power and accumulation,
*   by beauty and skill, by being connected.*
But maybe we were wrong and didn't understand that midnight games
*   are won most often by players whose records include:*
*   generosity, care,*
*   simplicity, love,*
*   a full heart.*

INTRODUCTION

WHEN MEN THINK PRIVATE THOUGHTS

Sooner or later everyone plays some version of the "Midnight Games." *When* people play (it doesn't have to be at midnight) and *where* they play (it can happen anywhere) are irrelevant. The games can be played, and often are, in the shower, on the drive to work, in the midst of a boring meeting, while cutting the lawn, and in church if the sermon gets out of control and becomes incomprehensible.

There is one constant in all these games: I call them *private thoughts*. All men possess them. Women, too. But this book will limit itself to the private thoughts that captivate men.

Define *private thoughts*? That's hard, almost impossible to do! For the term *private thoughts* is not meant to be part of a scientific or psychological analysis of the working of the mind. Not from me anyway. No, it refers to something that all men and women know is there: an inner, personal world that carries on its own conversations and insists on a kind of scorekeeping that can leave us, for example, content or unsettled, determined or beaten.

Some would say that it's dumb to keep score. Or that it's not healthy, that it's arrogant, and that it can't be done accurately. True. But there's this thing in the minds of people that seems to insist on playing the games and tabulating the results.

So many kinds of thoughts scramble onto the field of play in the midnight games that it would be an absurdity to estimate the number. Infinite numbers of thoughts, always there, constantly forming and re-forming probably even during the hours of sleep. Some of them are mere impulses, a nanosecond long; others are profound and return again and again. Clear thoughts; vague thoughts; ugly thoughts; splendid thoughts. Thoughts that can be described; thoughts sometimes so deep that they cannot be captured by mere words. Thoughts capable of generating laughter, melancholy, rage, passion, and unvarnished joy.

Among all these are the private thoughts. They are the ones I hold on to most tightly for fear that, if exposed, they might show a side of me that almost no one knows or would understand: the side that includes thoughts of possibilities, failures, dreams, fears, desires, shame, beliefs, regrets, memories—both good and bad—and, well, the list goes on and on.

What if all these private thoughts could be exposed for everyone to see? What do I do with the promise of the biblical writers that there is coming a time when "he will bring to light what is hidden in darkness and will expose the motives of men's hearts" (1 Cor. 4:5)? I am not a little bothered by the possibility of who may be standing around and eavesdropping when this day comes and *He* discloses *my* inventory of private thoughts. I hope, at least, my mother will not be within earshot! Can you understand this concern?

The mind: always thinking, thinking, thinking.

Because the Scriptures of the Hebrew/Christian tradition care so deeply about the state of the human soul, they often dig into the private thoughts of men. For example, Israel's earliest king, Saul, was a man of beguiling private thoughts. Regal on the outside, he was consumed with an inner typhoon of fantasies that caused him to see other people, like the young David, as threats or competitors. Another biblical player, Amnon (son of Saul's successor), entertained private thoughts of raging lust for his half sister Tamar. If Saul's private thoughts eventuated in violence, Amnon's ended in rape.

On the other hand, Joseph of Egypt nursed private thoughts of life-saving destiny and determination. And his God-given imagination took him a long way. St. Paul's private thoughts nagged him until he capitulated to a vision of Christ on the road to Damascus and became a Christ-follower. St. John, the writer of several New Testament books, had private visions of heaven, and he gave us some of the most inspired apocalyptic literature ever written.

So this is a book about the private thoughts of men, written by a man who spends a lot of time with men. I've now had enough experience to become sure that a lot of private thoughts follow certain lines of commonality. And my chapters pick up some of the common themes.

It's no secret that most men are uncomfortable airing their private thoughts. Almost every man has an anguished tale to tell of a time when he confided one of those thoughts to a friend, a woman, a mother or father. And he perceives that he paid a terrible price: ridicule, betrayal, or estrangement. Get burned once, and the message lingers forever: be careful never to open the heart again.

We fear that if anyone eavesdrops on our private thoughts, we will be exposed as shallow, sleazy, ignorant, evil, or immature. Or we worry that people will think us arrogant, egotistical, selfish, or sentimental.

But private thoughts need to be identified. They need to be measured. They need to go somewhere. They need to be demythologized. They need to be translated into positive energy.

Many of the private thoughts of men center on *comparisons*. We are tempted to measure ourselves against the warrior who seems never to be afraid, the athlete who appears to have no limits, the business mogul who behaves as if he possesses unrestricted resources, the academic who conveys the impression of having all the answers. Why am I not like them? we ask a thousand times. What would it take to catch up? Where did I go wrong?

Then again there are the private thoughts of *personal grandeur*. A boy imagines himself an astronaut, a teenager ponders a date with Miss America, a young adult male thinks himself into a successful entrepreneur, and an older man, watching a couple kissing in the park, wonders what it would be like to be young again.

Among the first private thoughts in the male are ones that center on the issue of *feelings,* which, most of us are taught, should rarely, if ever, be acknowledged. The don't-cry-act-like-a-man message comes early in life. And a boy learns to master his tear ducts and force his face into an expression that would make a stoic proud. *The feeling may be unbearable,* he thinks, *but there's no way I'm going to let you know it.* From that point forward in the male life feelings and emotions are increasingly stuffed somewhere. Fear, sadness, anxiety, smugness, anger, joy, loneliness, disappointment: *don't let them be seen, deep-six them, make them disappear, so far away, so deep, so buried that no one, even I, will ever know they were around.* But feelings do not stay stuffed forever.

They eventually pop up like a cork in water after a heart attack, for example, or when a man is blindsided by some momentous event for which he had not prepared himself. Tears, melancholy, and rage suddenly surface. Who knew they were there?

Another private thought has to do with the various *"what-if"* scenarios. What if my mother turned her back long enough for me to get my hand into the cookie jar? What if the firefighter invited me to sit beside him on the way to the fire? What if I was blessed with an unusually remarkable throwing arm and the Boston Red Sox manager called me from the stands to save the game? What if I owned that . . . ? What if she . . . ? What if my father . . . ?

Some private thoughts focus on *shame* and *guilt*. Can I break this habit? What if I were seen? What would my father say? Could I be more productive, more competitive in my work? Why am I attracted to that woman? Why am I seized by sexual thoughts? Why do I have fantasies of escape—a canoe trip down the Yukon, a silver Corvette, friendship with the president, the applause of a ticker tape parade?

There are private thoughts about *self-value*. Have I anything to offer? Will anyone really know the real me? Is anything I do ever enough? The private thoughts about *death*. Not when I die, but how will I die? And the *religious thoughts*. Am I really only one piece of a massive coincidence way back there? Is there, could there be, a God who is more than just a Supreme Being or a Cosmic Force? Do my fathers have anything to say to me? Do they see me? And if yes, how do they feel about me?

If private thoughts do not ever get measured by standards external to themselves, they have a tendency to drift into something likely to be self-destructive. Delusions of grandeur or delusions of insignificance, one or the other. Fantasies: I am the best, or I am the worst. Perceptions: I am loved, or I am despised. Orientation: I am special, or I am worthless.

I know these private thoughts. Most of them have been mine at one time. Some were easily dismissed; others nagged at me ruthlessly. I have been a player in the midnight games. I have played them in the dark and in the light. I used to play them alone. Now I am more than comfortable playing a new and better version (a noncompetitive version) of them with my wife and with my close male friends. Better still, I have come to learn that I can play the midnight games in the presence of God.

During the past few years, I have had the chance to talk with groups of men at least once every month. Many of these talks were given at an event we call First Monday in Lexington, Massachusetts. On other occasions the talks were given in other parts of the United States and Canada, in Europe and Australia.

Many times, I have used the title of this book to identify the larger topic of the talks. Frequently, women have asked if they could join the group, admitting that they wanted to know something more about what men think: "I haven't the slightest idea what my husband is thinking about most of the time"; "He doesn't talk to me"; and "He can get as hard as stone when the pressure is on." Somewhere I remember a woman saying, "I want to rap on his heart and cry out, 'Hello, is anyone home?'"

I haven't the slightest idea how many people will read this book. But I have a strong suspicion (a fear?) that whatever the number, more women than men will read it. And that amuses me because most of the things I will write about are meant for a men-only audience. Thus a male-oriented vocabulary, male pronouns, and male stories. Having said that, let me add that women are welcome. As long as they don't grow frustrated and say somewhere along the line, "Oh, grow up!"

At First Monday, I think I've startled some men when I've said, "Let's just pretend that we're sitting in a locker room. No clothes; only towels. We're just a bunch of guys—some of us with bodies so well put together that people like me are green with envy; others of us with big stomachs and skinny legs losing their hair. Let's identify the private thoughts: the issues with which most of us wrestle at one time or another but don't think that anyone else bothers with.

"Let's talk about fathers, about sex and why some of us have made such jerks of ourselves because of it, about disappointment, about competition, about fear, about marriage, about jobs and ambition, about anger, about measuring up, and about failure. And let's not leave God and faith out because, sooner or later, we have to deal with the issue of the soul—every man has one—and God touches that part of us most intimately."

What has never ceased to amaze me is how the atmosphere changes. In the beginning of these sessions, more than a few men are sitting silently, arms crossed almost in a gesture of defiance or deference. I get the feeling that some are saying, "Let's get this over with so I can get on with more important things: the game of the week, my lawn, my computer, my nap."

The minutes go by as we talk about private thoughts. I watch the arms unfold. Men sit forward on the edge of their seats. It's not that the talk is so wonderful. Rather, it's the fact that they are discovering that their private thoughts aren't so unique and unusual after all. "You too? I always thought that I . . ."

When the talk is over, I usually ask men to stand, form groups of four, and spend five minutes with this one question: *What was the one most important thing you thought about in the past thirty or forty minutes?*

Minutes later everyone sits, and I seek feedback. "What did you talk about in your groups?" I ask. And for the next thirty or forty minutes, the discussion becomes riveting. Almost no one leaves. Younger men stand to talk about their fathers. Older men stand to say that if they'd had a chance to discuss some of these things years ago, their marriages, their perspectives, would be entirely different. And almost always, someone stands and says, "I thought I was the only one who struggled with these private thoughts. For the first time I'm discovering I've got some brothers to talk to."

When men play the midnight games and think private thoughts, anything—the worst- or the best-case scenario—can happen. I hope that this book makes a small contribution in the direction of the best.

Gordon MacDonald
Lexington, Massachusetts
Canterbury, New Hampshire

CHAPTER 1

WHAT IT MEANS TO BE A "REAL MAN"

Once when I was young and idealistic, I wrote an angry, faultfinding article for a local religious publication. The piece inflamed more than a few readers, and one of them was sufficiently outraged to confront me eyeball to eyeball.

Today, decades later, the subject of my foolish article is forgotten. But the point of view of my rebutter is not. I can still remember what he said and how he said it. And I can easily recall how his words rocked what little self-confidence I had as a young male adult. And that is what I think he hoped to achieve. I'd made him mad, and he was returning the favor with interest.

He said with disdain, "You ought to go into the army; it might make a real man out of you."

That challenge, exploding like a grenade in my inner being, left me disconcerted for a long time afterward. Now, to some men, such a comment would have meant nothing. They'd have laughed it off. Perhaps, one or two would have tried to punch his lights out. I did neither. I just sulked. For what I heard him saying was that I was perceived to be falling short of what it means to be a man and (this is where my imagination entered overtime) that other men did not regard me as acceptable, as one of them.

I do not expect women to understand this, but most men will empathize when I say that I carried the hurt of those words for some time. You can tell a man you don't like the color of his shirt, the make of his car, the players on his favorite team, and the taste of his drink. But don't question his manhood unless you're prepared for the possibility of a larger-than-life reaction.

In another century, men might have dueled to the death over words like those. Today in some neighborhoods, men might agree to meet in an alley where fists, knives, or guns would settle the score. "Those are fightin' words," we men sometimes like to say.

But I chose to remain silent, not to fight back. He was, after all, four inches and sixty pounds my senior. But something deep within me, not made of God, would have preferred the alley option. That's an example of when men begin to think private thoughts.

When men think private thoughts, the shadowy concept of manhood and masculinity is never far from the focus of contemplation. We're tempted to wonder how we measure up in the minds of other men. Am I perceived as strong or weak? Tough or feeble? A help or a hindrance? A friend or an enemy? Able or unable? Smart or stupid?

Maybe one of the first times we asked ourselves questions like these was on a ball field when we stood with other boys waiting to be selected to play on someone's team.

Remember the ritual? The two biggest and best players flipped a coin or tossed a bat to determine first choice from the players pool. Then the agonizing process began. You could read the faces of the two team captains when they got near the end where the nerds were. *Do I have to take him?* If you were among the first picks, you knew you were good, you measured up. You were a first-round draft choice, so to speak. But if you were last! Well, it hurt, and it hurt badly. You kind of wanted to die. And it was all driven further home when they assigned you the position of "long-fielder" ("you back up the outfielders").

Defining real manhood. Knowing what makes me a man. No simple matter.

Apart from some physiological distinctions, it is no longer always clear exactly what we mean when we call someone a man or suggest that someone else is less than a man. A woman says, "There's a *man* for you!" It has sort of a derisive tone to it, suggesting that being a man is something close to being a barbarian or a clown. On the other hand, "he's a *man's man*" means something else. This phrase is usually reserved for references to someone who is big, agile, tough, competitive. Someone the men like and want to be around.

"Watch out for the man!" may be a resentful statement about someone who has power to make another person's life miserable. The *man* in his comment may be oppressive and cruel. Or consider this alternative: "I find him to be a *fine* man." One gets the impression of manhood defined in terms of character and nobility. William Booth, founder of the Salvation Army, once wryly played with these words when he said, "Some of my best *men* are women." The emphasis seems to be on fearlessness and dedication.

Right or wrong, we all used to think we knew exactly *what* a man was and *what* a woman was. There were fairly strict lines of demarcation, and few were the people who strayed across the lines. But something's changed. If you feel like a man today, it's no guarantee that you will feel like one tomorrow. Why? Because the essence of manhood is being redefined in our culture. Men may not like this, but it is happening, and we do well to face it and come to terms with it.

Those of us fifty years of age and older have a definition of manhood that may not quite match the definition of those who are younger. We were raised on models of manhood such as the Lone Ranger, General Douglas MacArthur, Robert Mitchum, and Charles Lindbergh. The worst—the absolutely worst—thing you could ever call us was a *sissy*. That was a volatile word in my generation.

Not so with a new generation of males who seem to have embraced new models. Rock musicians, software entrepreneurs, and househusbands, among others, just might fill their bill. The former models had a kind of acceptable gruffness about them. The latter a sense of passion or gentleness.

All too often, manhood is superficially defined by certain stereotypes. Here are three, for example. We men sometimes allow manhood to be defined by work, what a man does: *a real man is a hunter and provider;* he brings home the bacon. Sometimes we permit manhood to be defined in terms of the ability to attract women: *a real man is a stud;* women can't resist him. And it's possible to get sucked into a third definition based on how well a man deals with his enemies or his competitors: *a real man is a fighter;* others better back off when he comes by.

All three of these cultural stereotypes can mix in strange ways and do not always lend themselves to convenient or exclusive categories of thought. But they give us a place to start.

A REAL MAN IS A HUNTER AND PROVIDER: HE FEARS FAILURE

For thousands of years, a man's identity has been tied to his work, something usually requiring a kind of physical agility, muscle, and strength.

In the beginning, we were the guys who brought something home for the pot. Later on, we brought home the paycheck. That's who we were: the hunters, the providers. It was a tough way of life, but it was satisfying. I well remember a day when a boy would say, "When I grow up, I'm going to get a job and support my family." That's what *men* did! And in its day it brought lots of honor. We were needed!

In North America we have molded much of our notion of man as the hunter and provider around the nineteenth-century rugged individualist who pushed westward digging for gold, killing buffalo, shooting it out with bandits, and homesteading the land. He knew no fear, and he didn't need anyone. That was the image. When the frontier closed, the myth reemerged in the world of vocational and professional achievement.

Most recently, the picture of man as hunter and provider has been seen in achievers like Lee Iacocca who walked into Chrysler some years ago as if it were Dodge City. He shot it out with the government, Japan, and the traditionalists. He turned things around. A couple of million copies of his biography later, we all know that a real man is someone who can save a company from bankruptcy. A real man can do deals. A real man can design great software, fly 757's, and reattach limbs. A real man is successful. He never comes home empty-handed.

This real man doesn't just bring home the bacon; he brings it home in style. He drives a BMW or a Jeep Cherokee. He wears clothes that fit every occasion, belongs to the right clubs, vacations in the right places, and knows the right people. His world is filled with symbols of his success at hunting and providing.

Be like or at least look and act like such a man, and you will be counted among the men. Fall short, and you take your place among the countless drones who are held in low esteem.

This, then, is why failure becomes such an unthinkable experience. For if one's manhood is tied up in achievement through hunting and providing, then a lack of achievement speaks for itself. One is a loser. And men are never allowed to be losers. So failure—and all the symbols of failure—becomes a man's worst enemy.

Former world heavyweight champion Floyd Patterson once told how he brought a sack of disguises to every fight. If, after the fight, he could not leave the locker room a winner, he would leave as another person. Being the loser was unthinkable. And being a loser in the world of work is unthinkable—if work defines who you are.

I am reminded of a man in our community who, a few years ago, was sacked from his job. He found it impossible to tell his wife, his children, or his friends what had happened. So each day he left his home at the same time as always. Instead of heading to the work site, he went to the library and idled away the time in the reading room. In the evening he would go home and give a false report of his workday. That went on for several months, as long as he could manipulate funds to maintain the fiction of a regular paycheck. When it became impossible to continue the fantasy, he shot himself. Failure as a provider was unthinkable.

A tale of extreme behavior? Of course. But it illustrates the hold a man's work can have on him as a definer of who he is and whether or not he has value. As long as men equate achievement and success with manhood, failure will always be the worst enemy. As will the notion of admitting failure. Or being associated with anyone else who is failing.

Because failure is repugnant to the man who defines himself as a hunter-provider, it will be difficult for him to identify with failure. To confess weakness or ignorance. To embrace an illness or a disease. To accept limitations (until the facts are forcibly in), to admit that there are simply lots of things in this world he cannot do.

When I brood on these things, I begin to understand why lots of good men trip over simple things like, well, the following:

- Don't expect a man to find it easy to ask directions when everyone else knows that he's lost.
- Don't expect him to find it easy to acknowledge that he's made a mistake and that he needs forgiveness.
- Don't expect him to rejoice at setting a doctor's appointment where he may hear bad news.
- Don't expect him to willingly admit that he's wrong, doesn't know his facts, or hasn't done his homework.

These are some of the downsides of manhood when a man's only value is computed on the basis of his success as hunter-provider.

A Real Man Is a Stud: He Fears Rejection

Another stereotypical view of masculinity is based on a man's ability to attract women. The not-so-subtle message has to do with perceived virility. The stud, the definition suggests, has what it takes. The evidence is that he is surrounded by women; they are young and lovely; each seems prepared to do anything to gain his favor.

We deal with these ideas of man-as-defined-by-woman from the earliest days of adolescence. It is not a new insight to point to the cheerleaders on the sidelines of football games and to note the parallel between their role and that of the women of the primitive tribes who waited for the warriors to return from battle. If the warriors were victorious, the women were there to cheer for them and reward them. If they were defeated, the women became the spoils of the conquering warriors.

Today, we have sophisticated this picture just a bit. But the theme is there for anyone to notice. By this definition the woman is seen as a trophy, like a fish, a moose head, or a bearskin on a wall. To the best, the toughest, and the most virile of men go the best and the most beautiful of women. And the logic works in reverse. If you can find a way to beg, borrow, or steal the most beautiful of women, then, you guessed it, the world will conclude that you are some kind of a man. No wonder we men make such fools of ourselves.

At a distance actor Rock Hudson always seemed to be a winner in races of this type. In almost every one of his movies, he was the one who wound up with the dazzling girl. His influential powers with women seemed boundless. All the more reason why the world was shocked beyond words when the news came that Hudson was gay and dying of AIDS. I guess we were fooled.

The private thoughts of most men contain a stream of notions about man-as-defined-by-woman from a rather early age.

I have a distinct recollection of attending a college band concert when I was a seventh grader. Up on stage, sitting in the front row of the wind instruments, was the most lovely (college) girl I had ever seen. Female beauty was a new thing for me.

Until the writing of this book I have not thought about this incident in forty-five years. But as I recall it now, I doubt I heard a musical note all afternoon. My mind riveted itself upon this clarinet player and the thought of being with her. I was barely at the age where anything sexual might have entered the scenario, but I guess I was on my way.

As the music played, my puberty-driven mind conjured up the fantasy of a sudden fire in the school auditorium. I saw myself rushing through the commotion to the stage, taking her by the hand, and leading her to safety. But that fantasy wasn't good enough. So in another, much better, version, the fire and the pandemonium became more intense. I leaped to the stage, picked her up, and *carried* her to safety (which is really a marvelous work of imagination because I think she was bigger than I was). So the scenarios went: over and over again until I had exhausted all the rescue possibilities and she had expressed her unbounded grate-fulness in whatever way a seventh grader might hope for (I forget now). The point is that my imaginative heroics and her gratitude were a first stab at defining my sense of manhood by a woman's acceptance.

Other imaginative scenarios of the mind soon followed, perhaps not as antiseptic as the one I've related. Many built upon the notion that women found me irresistible and sought my company. Fortunately or unfortunately, that was not the case in real life. But the life of the mind told it all: there was a tremendous temptation to assume that in the affections and attentions of the female gender was a man's evidence that he was of the ranks of real men. To twist a piece of holy Writ, it was a way of thinking that suggested "by their women ye shall know them."

To the extent that a man begins to identify himself as the stud, the notion that he could ever be rejected becomes almost unthinkable. This is the unfortunate result when a man defines himself in such a fashion. Without realizing the significance of his perspective, he becomes preoc-cupied with shaping his appearance, his personality, and his actions in life according to what wins female attention, admiration, and capitulation. He has got to conquer; he has got to demonstrate his power. And the more "successful" he is, the more likely he is to grow terrified of the encounter in which he is not successful.

A REAL MAN IS A FIGHTER: HE FEARS POWERLESSNESS

Men have often been tempted by the culture to define manhood in terms of their ability to fight. This means that they need adversaries—enemies or competitors. It also means a sense of combativeness in the genes. Put bluntly, it highlights the crude question: Is there anyone you can beat up? If so, then to that extent you are some kind of a man! You're a winner.

In primitive life, it was a simple matter. You knew who the enemies were. And that was a man's job: get to them and destroy them. That's what men did. Man-as-warrior was a fairly well-defined job. Man-as-athlete. Man-as-protector. A man's world in simpler days was the battle-field, the athletic field, the locker room, the workplace. Anyplace where muscle and physical power won the day.

These were not places, men said, where women belonged. These were dangerous places where dangerous activities were pursued. Men knew they might die or get injured. But that was part of the risk and the price. And it was acceptable. The great virtue was courage.

The fighter who won was handsomely rewarded. He might win the king's daughter, the choicest lands, the decorations of honor, or the promotions to high rank. Overcoming the enemy, winning, was all he had to do—or die a noble death in the attempt (which in the latter case left out the king's daughter).

If the hunter fears failing and the lover fears rejection, what does the fighter fear? Losing, of course. Being powerless.

Powerlessness is a strange but real issue to many modern men. Gone are the days when the enemy's identity was obvious and you could get your hands around his throat.

Today the enemy can be the large corporation whose officers send down layoff notices you can't defend against. The enemy can be a system that won't offer a job, make a loan, or protect a house. The enemy can be media that seem to care nothing about the souls of children. The enemy can be a government that creates one law and regulation after another that make life increasingly difficult. The enemy can be a persistent secularization of your life and the lives of loved ones, and you don't seem to be able do anything about it. Result: men feel more and more powerless. Enemies are hard to define and hard to fight.

Sometimes we find ourselves welcoming clearly defined adversaries simply because they offer a chance to test this old-time version of manhood.

You are driving in the passing lane of an interstate highway. A man moves up behind you and blinks his lights, demanding that you get out of the way so he can pass. You're already five miles per hour over the speed limit, but he wants to go faster. Moving over means that you'll have to join a slower line of traffic. This of course is unacceptable, and the fighter's instinct ignites. So you ignore him for a mile or two.

Finally, you move over, but you do it real slowly so that he has to wait a few more seconds. For those seconds *you* are in control, and as long as you are in control, you are the superior, the dominant fighter of the two. For the umpteenth time you have proved yourself.

But when he passes you, it is payback time. He glares in your direction; he mouths some words that are not difficult to comprehend; and underscoring it all, he offers an extended middle finger as his superpowered chariot leaps ahead. Now he's the man. You're really mad. If religious, you're a bit self-righteous. But most of all you feel diminished. Your manhood has shrunk for a moment. The fight has turned against you.

It is the twentieth-century version of a challenge as old as human history. He's the enemy! And everything in you wants to respond. You wish you had a car with enough "horses" to catch up. You may even daydream for a moment about confronting him at the next rest stop ("Hey, I'm the guy you passed back there. Tell me, what were you saying when you went by? I didn't quite catch the words!"). In your daydream you rehearse the sarcasm until you're sure it will bite real deep. You see him back off, maybe even apologize. But then you finally drop the whole notion, thinking, *He'd probably pull a gun on me or something like that.*

We are men, so the reasoning goes, if we are better than other men. Then we are winners. And winning is the most important thing.

AUTHENTIC MANHOOD

Now if manhood is merely a matter of testosterone and the possession of male genitals, there is no problem. But probably every male knows in his soul that there is a problem, for manhood is more than a hormonal or an anatomical matter. Manhood is a way of thinking, being, and functioning. It is a social statement of who I am and who others think me to be. It is an issue of role. What place do I have in the community, and how am I valued in that position? Who am I in contrast to women?

I suggest that men invest an inordinate amount of time worrying over the genuineness of their manhood. It is an aspect of self-confidence that may in fact gnaw at most of us until the day we die. What mental energy is expended on this one issue alone!

The search for and the defense of manhood begin at an early age. I can see it when my grandsons follow their dads around the yard, seeking to mimic each grown-up male action. Soon the boys are throwing the ball like their fathers, walking like their fathers, even grunting like their fathers. Here they are at the age of two and three-plus, already pursuing certification as men, which they assume might be possible if they can duplicate the characteristics they observe in their fathers.

Once defining manhood begins, the pursuit of reassurance never stops. At the other end of the age spectrum in my family, for example, is my dear father-in-law who, a few years before he died, faced the removal of his prostate. From that point forward he was never able to fully control his bladder and, like many senior adults, was forced to wear an adult version of a diaper. His character was strong, and it made it possible for him to joke about his predicament with his family.

But I will always remember the night he confided to me what this one cruel event had done to cripple his sense of manhood: "I can't even keep from peeing in my pants." Imagine this anxiety from a man nearly eighty who had raised and supported a family, had built a successful business, had produced beautiful furniture in his shop, and had been recognized as a community and church leader many times over. Seventy-eight and still concerned about his feelings regarding manhood. Three males, two of them in the first years of life and the other seventy-eight: essentially driven by the same private thoughts.

That men struggle with such thoughts has something to do with the cultural context in which we live. We are no longer grouped in tribes and clans where once highly defined initiation rites were handed down from generation to generation. In such communities, a boy was led by the men of the village through a process that included instruction, ceremony, circumcision, and stressful (even painful) experiences. When the ordeal ended, the boy knew what he had become: a man. Who said so? Not the women, but the men! The men said so. And everyone else, including the women, accepted their judgment. Counted now among the men, he chose to act and think like one.

In his book *Iron John*, Robert Bly describes the "welcoming" ceremony among the boys of the Kikuyu in Africa. At the appropriate age a boy is taken by his mother to the place of initiation designated by the men of the village. There he fasts for three days.

On the third night of his ordeal he is brought to a fire where the older men sit:

> He is hungry, thirsty, alert, and terrified. One of the older men takes up a knife, opens a vein in his own arm, and lets a little of his blood flow into a gourd or bowl. Each older man in the circle opens his arm with the same knife, as the bowl goes around, and lets some blood flow in. When the bowl arrives at the young man, he is invited to take nourishment from it.

Bly goes on to speak of the significance of this event:

> In this ritual the boy learns a number of things. He learns that nourishment does not come only from his mother, but also from men. And he learns that the knife can be used for many purposes besides wounding others. Can he have any doubt now that he is welcome among the other males?

As I read Bly I note that in this scenario we receive milk from the mother, but blood from the father and his friends. We men badly need both. The milk gives nurture and strength. The blood provides the courage and vision of one's father and the father's father.

Back in the village, girls have no need for such an experience. They know they are welcomed among the women. Unlike the boys who have to come to a moment of leaving their mothers, the girls are able to remain. Furthermore, as their bodies pass through puberty, reminding them every twenty-eight days of their capability to be childbearers, the consistent message of womanhood is reinforced. The facts tell the story. A girl is a woman; her body says so and the women echo the message. But a boy is a man only when the men say so.

Not so in our world. More than a few authors have pointed out the absence of such rites in Western culture. With the exception of the bar mitzvah among Jews, there is almost nothing of universal definition that will assist a male in knowing when he has passed into maturity. What the tribe conferred through initiation, the boy in our time must earn and re-earn. And he must earn it basically on his own or with his peer group. Because there is no officially acknowledged jury or judge to declare that the process is over, the earning goes on for a lifetime in the experience of many males.

In spite of all the (questionable, I think) efforts made in our time to raise and educate boys and girls in a fashion that is free of gender identity, the fact remains that they pick up signals of differing expectations from the culture. The greatest point of demarcation has to do with emotions and relationships.

Psychologist Alvin Baraff writes in *Men Talk:*

> Girls are taught to honor and understand their emotions. Conversely, boys are encouraged, even forced, to hold in and suppress their emotions. There is hardly a man in America today who didn't grow up hearing such admonitions as "Big boys don't cry!" or "Be a man!" These commands form the young boy's reality.

What Baraff describes is buttressed in the passage of time. A boy learns not to reveal or express his feelings. He discovers that he is expected to operate from a position of strength and superiority, even if it is a pretense. He is encouraged to find his identity through competition and winning. And, as a result, he slowly distinguishes himself from other males, maintaining friendship only when it is to his advantage. His becomes a world of exaggeration, bullying, tests of strength, and winning. Here is emerging man defined as hunter and fighter. The only alternative to these is a life of introversion, withdrawal into self.

Again, Alvin Baraff writes:

> The result is that a man in our society grows up feeling innately, internally alone. He has learned independence and self-reliance and considers them to reign supreme among his values. He wants to be in control. He cannot imagine ever needing to go for help and rarely considers it an option.

On my library shelf is a small book, *The Misunderstood Man,* the last written by a man I once considered a friend, the late Walter Trobisch. His wife, Ingrid, who finished the manuscript, wrote the foreword. The first sentence of her introduction to the book captures me:

> *"Man is suffering, but woman (sic) don't know it."* I once saw these words painted on a small bus in Accra, Ghana. Perhaps this is the essence of what Walter wants to say in this book (italics mine).

What Ingrid Trobisch calls to the reader's attention is thoughtful. Each gender has its own unique suffering. Women cry for the opportunity to reach their full potential without feeling the restrictions of what is perceived to be a male-dominated society. Men long to find their true selves and to rejoice in that self. But in the absence of that discovery men must often flail about, trying somehow to *obtain* manhood or to approximate in one way or another what they think it might be.

That's why it is tempting for males to become more interested in the *image* of manhood than the *substance*. The temptation can be overwhelming: pick someone who seems the epitome of masculinity and replicate him. The cowboy, the athlete, the motorcycle jockey, the soldier, the muscular iron pumper, the CEO, the lover, the wilderness man, the hero in the midst of a disaster. All these, and others, are included on the menu of false fronts any male might choose in his quest to join the company of the males.

One of the great adventure stories in all of literature is that of the Hebrew shepherd boy David. His story contains virtually all the elements designed to thrill a male in his search for authentic manhood.

It begins with the fact that he is the youngest and the most obscure of the family. There are hints all the way along that his older brothers hold him in disdain and his father perceives him as insignificant.

His brothers go off to war under the leadership of Saul, king of Israel. There on the battlefront they and their compatriots face a severe test of manhood, one they fail miserably.

The enemy, the Philistines, have a major player on their side. His name is Goliath. He is not only physically big (some say more than nine feet tall), but he has a big mouth. He manages to push virtually all the buttons that turn on the fighting instincts of any male.

In full armor and with heavy weapons, Goliath marches out into the no-man's-land between the two armies and shouts:

> Why do you come out and line up for battle? Am I not a Philistine, and are you not the servants of Saul? Choose a man and have him come down to me. If he is able to fight and kill me, we will become your subjects; but if I overcome him and kill him, you will become our subjects and serve us. . . . This day I defy the ranks of Israel! Give me a man and let us fight each other (1 Sam. 17:8–10).

This is Clint Eastwood saying, "Go ahead, make my day." But it's also a chance for the men of Israel to prove themselves and save their nation. Now is the time for all good men to come to the aid of their nation (to employ a phrase). But . . .

> on hearing the Philistine's words, Saul and all the Israelites were dismayed and terrified (1 Sam. 17:11).

This goes on for forty days. Morning and evening Goliath the giant challenges the men of Israel, and no one moves an inch.

Now young David comes on the scene with food and supplies from his father for his brothers. He arrives just in time to hear Goliath on his daily rampage. "When the Israelites saw the man," the ancient writer says, "they all ran from him in great fear" (1 Sam. 17:24). That leaves David wondering who he has come to cheer up. Not a good first impression.

> Now the Israelites had been saying, "Do you see how this man keeps coming out? He comes out to defy Israel. The king will give great wealth to the man who kills him. He will also give him his daughter in marriage and will exempt his father's family from taxes in Israel" (1 Sam. 17:25).

You can appreciate why a young man might be attracted to this set of motivations. Embedded in this set of rewards is everything he might want to authenticate who he is as a man. Win this one, and there's no limit to the rewards: wealth, the king's daughter, family privilege, and honor.

But David is a different kind of man. These rewards are not his primary motivation. Not that he would refuse the wealth, the woman, and the tax benefits, you understand. It is just that they are not the definers of his manhood or his reason for springing into action.

Rather, what drives David seems to have something to do with a different kind of manhood. Something in the heart, the soul, of David that longs for the pleasure of his Creator.

> Your servant has been keeping his father's sheep. When a lion or a bear came and carried off a sheep from the flock, I went after it, struck it and rescued the sheep from its mouth. When it turned on me, I seized it by its hair, struck it and killed it. Your servant has killed both the lion and the bear; this uncircumcised Philistine will be like one of them, because he has defied the armies of the living God. The LORD who delivered me from the paw of the lion and the paw of the bear will deliver me from the hand of this Philistine (1 Sam. 17:34–37).

Soon after, the writer tells us, David enters the no-man's-land, unarmored and unarmed except for a sling shot and five stones.

Out in the valley, Goliath talks trash: "Am I a dog, that you come at me with sticks? . . . Come here, . . . and I'll give your flesh to the birds of the air and the beasts of the field!" (1 Sam. 17:43–44). Apparently, they talked that way in those days.

David replies:

> You come against me with sword and spear and javelin, but I come against you in the name of the LORD Almighty, the God of the armies of Israel, whom you have defied. This day the LORD will hand you over to me, and I'll strike you down and cut off your head. Today I will give the carcasses of the Philistine army to the birds of the air and the beasts of the earth, and the whole world will know that there is a God in Israel. All those gathered here will know that it is not by sword or spear that the LORD saves; for the battle is the LORD's, and he will give all of you into our hands (1 Sam. 17:45–47).

Moments later Goliath is dead, and his countrymen sprint for home. When, as a boy, I saw this story laid out on the flannelgraph (a 1940s version of video), I thrilled to it. I knew then that David was the man I wanted to be.

But I was basically attracted to the *image* of manhood. I liked the strength, the courage, the skill, the applause, the favor of the king, the thanks of the father, and the vindication before small-thinking brothers. That was the way of a man.

An adult reading offers me something better for my private thoughts: the *substance* of manhood. David is a man not because of what he does or what he receives as direct and indirect rewards. He is a man before he ever enters the battle.

Somehow out in the fields as a boy, separated from his father and his brothers, left alone with sheep and vulnerable to wild animals, David develops a sense of manhood in his soul as he communes with his Creator. No one is there to impress with the images of hunter, lover, or fighter. Just doing the work; keeping the covenants; serving his father and his father's God. And it makes all the difference. The boy becomes a man out there. Later a writer of Psalm-songs would say,

> He chose David his servant
>   and took him from the sheep pens;
> from tending the sheep he brought him
>   to be the shepherd of his people Jacob,
>   of Israel his inheritance.
> And David shepherded them with integrity of heart;
>   with skillful hands he led them (Ps. 78:70–72).

The interesting point about David is that he is a successful hunter. And he gains the approval of women. And he is a powerful fighter. But these things do not make him a man, and they are not the things he chooses (in his best moments) to boast about as a man. His confidence is not external; it is internal. It is the state of his soul as he anchors his life in the God of Israel and His purposes.

There was a time when a man like me could be easily intimidated when my manhood was challenged. Not David! His identity is affirmed. It is as if God had opened the veins in His arm and welcomed him into a godly manhood. And this He has done for every male who would be a *real man.*

CHAPTER 2

THE MYSTERIES OF INTIMACY

In the files of a man's private thoughts, few topics take up more room than ones that build off a cluster of questions something like these: Whom do I really know? How well do I know them? Who knows the real me? And (now that I think about it) what is there about me that is worth knowing? And if anyone took the time to know me (I mean really, really know me), what's to say that the person would want me as a friend, as a husband, as a father?

These are merely sample questions. There are scores of others behind them. They're jagged, inconsistent. But they speak to a confusion that often whirls in the private thoughts. Why do I struggle to connect naturally with other people? There are some mysteries here. And the greatest mystery is what *intimacy* really means.

An ex-marine looks back to another time in life:

> I never thought I'd say this, but some of the best days of my life were in the Marines when we were in 'Nam. I ran with a bunch of guys who went through hell together. We saw men die, get shot to pieces, go crazy. And in the midst of it all we got closer as friends than I ever believed possible. There was nothing we couldn't say to each other, nothing we wouldn't do for one another. You've heard about the guy who throws himself on a grenade to save a friend's life? Any of us would have done that. . . . We talked about everything. We laughed; we cried; we hated; we dreamed; we screamed . . . even had some fist fights. Everything together. But one thing we knew more than almost anything else. *We loved each other in a way that I have never experienced since. I don't think*

I'll ever have friends like that again. . . . I miss that kind of closeness. The guys I know at church, at work? There's nothing like that with them. Even my wife will never know me like those guys did (italics mine).

The man describes a version, a powerful version, of *intimacy:* what happens when men begin to connect beneath the surface of events and circumstances somewhere near the level of the soul. Men and women can work together, engage in sexual relationship together, and share strong moments of emotional intensity together. But they may not necessarily ever *know* each other in this way.

We were built for intimacy, this linkage of souls, but most of us men rarely experience it. And its scarcity breeds *loneliness* (I don't really know anyone) and fuels *remoteness* (no one really knows me).

A man feels this loneliness when he analyzes the conversations that mark his day. Why, he wonders, is it a no-brainer to discuss ball scores, investments, bad general managers, and how the other political party is ruining the country? In contrast, why is it a struggle to explore matters of the soul with others: where I'm at (or not at) with God, why I admire you, what I wish I could change about my life, how sad or fearful I feel, and why I feel so ashamed?

Why, the wondering continues, do I have the impulse to cover up my weaknesses when I would really like to talk about them with a mind toward improving upon them? Why do I feel strange in moments when something like tenderness is called for? Is there a reason I feel as if I fall so far short of whatever it is that would satisfy my wife's desire for understanding?

Let me talk about a book that bothers me.

INTIMACY THROUGH FICTION?

In the early 1990s the novel *The Bridges of Madison County* appeared on the best-seller list. Bookstores struggled to keep enough copies in stock to satisfy the demands of the reading public. The explosive interest in *Bridges* came from women, and it was mainly the consequence of word-of-mouth advertising, a publisher's dream. One woman simply told another, "You've got to read this book."

The "serious" literary world insisted that the book was bad literature, and reviewers did their best to bury it with sarcasm and ridicule. But they failed. So what was there about this book that gripped the attention of millions of people?

Tom Clancy novels sell well to those who are looking for adventures in a world of modern military technology. John Grisham novels attract readers who love the mind games of lawyers. Novels by horror-story writer Stephen King appeal to people who are interested in the dark side of the spiritual world.

But *The Bridges of Madison County?* To whom did it appeal? And why? Its pages do not include war scenarios, courtroom confrontations, or tales of the occult. So who was the audience? Answer: the millions who have felt cheated by relationships in which they anticipated the possibility of soul-to-soul connection but were disappointed.

I doubt I would ever have read *Bridges* had it not been for a breakfast meeting with a friend one morning. In the course of conversation he mentioned the book, and I acknowledged that I'd seen some put-down comments about it in the *New York Times Book Review.*

"Have you read it?" my table guest asked.

"No," I answered. "I'm not into Gothic romances."

"You'd better not miss this one," he said with a hint of sarcasm. "My wife insisted that I read it. All of her friends have read it, and they're shoving it at their husbands. Since you do a lot of speaking to men, you had better ask why a lot of women want men to read this book."

"You know why?"

"Yeah, I think they're sending a message."

"Save me some time," I said. "What's the message?"

"I think the women are trying to tell us that we don't get it. That we're out of touch with what they hoped marriage would offer. They may be saying that they're disappointed, that they'd hoped for a man who . . . well, read the book. I'd rather not spoil it for you. Oh, and by the way. When you read it, you better be aware: there's some stuff that's not too Christian. So ask yourself why some people who call themselves Christians are reading it and recommending it."

I bought the book, and after a chapter or two, I thought I saw the reviewer's point. But I also began to see something else. For as I read *Bridges,* I began to hear the deep groan of a group of people (mostly women) in our modern population who seem to have everything (material convenience, access to almost every conceivable sensation, unlimited amounts of information), everything but *enduring and satisfying human intimacy.* Intimacy (again a working definition): the experience of human connection far beneath and beyond the level of the sexual and the intellectual—the connection of hearts.

The Bridges of Madison County focuses on a midwestern woman,

Francesca Johnson, who lives on an Iowa farm/ranch with her husband and two children. At first glance the scene seems idyllic. If there is distress or unhappiness in this marriage and family, it is well hidden. What we see is a good state-of-the-art husband, an admirable, hardworking wife, and well-raised, Beaver Cleaver-like children. All healthy, happy, secure. What more could one want?

But, you tell yourself, something's missing. You feel as if you've been in this seemingly vanilla home with people like this numberless times. People who appear to be doing all the right things, but somehow missing one another.

In *Bridges* the something-missing is not related to anything so obvious as money or suffering or a pending disaster. The bank isn't about to foreclose on the mortgage, and the children are not on drugs. The cattle aren't missing, and the crops aren't dying. So the something-missing must be below the surface, in someone's heart.

When the story gets rolling, Richard, Francesca's husband, and their children are leaving the farm for the Illinois State Fair where they intend to exhibit a "prize steer that received more attention than [Francesca] did" (see the hint there). They'll be away for a week; she will remain home.

Within hours of their departure, everything changes. A national magazine photographer, Robert Kincaid, drives into the farmyard. He is in the area, he says with a smile, to photograph the covered bridges of Iowa's Madison County, and he is temporarily lost. He needs directions.

But it doesn't take the proverbial rocket scientist to figure out rather quickly that he's going to get more than directions. No explanation is offered, but it is clear that two lonely people have found each other.

In the following pages the reader gets a slow-motion description of how a kind of "instant intimacy" (or supposed intimacy) begins. One hears how the eyes connect, how the voice penetrates to the heart, how a certain sensuality of body movement gains attention.

You sense where this is headed. Almost immediately something is happening that is usually described only by the poet or the romanticist. It has no technical explanation. Barriers begin to fall, as the author says. A spark jumps from the stranger to Francesca's heart. This a description of one middle-aged woman's feelings.

Not many pages pass before there is an intensity to this instant relationship. A conversation has led to a cool drink, to a second visit, to a casual dinner invitation, to longer conversations, to dancing, to . . . ! There are vivid descriptions of Kincaid's sensual and lyrical view of life, his ability to decipher the mind of a woman, to put into words what she feels, and to respond to her feelings. Their conversations descend to soul-level. Within a day she has found the way to his heart (and he to hers), something she'd found quite impossible to do with her husband. *Now* we know the something-missing. She is driven to comparisons between her marriage and this illicit relationship.

Why, she wonders, are these feelings missing in her marriage to Richard? What is it in their life together that has grown cold? What is it that her husband cannot seem to give her that she craves so powerfully, that this stranger finds so easy to offer?

Before *Bridges* ends (which is not a long time), there has been something we call an affair, a discreetly described sexual liaison or two, and a concluding moment of agonizing choice. Will she accept the invitation of this wildly poetic, romantic, highly sensitive photographer who asks her to leave what had seemed a solid marriage and family for a carefree, vagabond life? Will she run from the sterility of a life that offers security, stability, and predictability but no connection, little appreciation, and minuscule understanding? For the reader who thinks herself to be wildly romantic or bored, lonely, and misunderstood, Francesca's choice seems tough. As my friend says, this is not a Christian book, and it attempts to glamorize and vindicate the "choice" of infidelity.

So then what are women like the wife of my breakfast partner saying when they hand this book to their husbands and ask them to read it? Are they secretly wishing for their husbands to turn into a Robert Kincaid? Are they crying for help in the midst of a frozen marriage grown silent where two people pass like ships in the night? Or are they saying in the only way they know how, you do all the right things, but *you take no time to know me and you do not let me know you?*

If there is a word to describe the something-missing, it is *intimacy.* Use words like *connection, communication, bonding, caring,* and *closeness,* and you hover all about the meaning of the word.

THE NEED TO CONNECT

If food and water are essential to physical life, *intimacy* is essential to spiritual life. The word covers the exchanges of positive spiritual energy that occur between one person and another.

All of his life a man, in his deepest parts, wishes to give love and receive it. That he may express himself otherwise is a betrayal of his real self. A betrayal that happens near the surface of himself in the world of the rational where winning, achieving, accumulating, and overpowering become momentarily important. But descend through the trapdoor of all this sound and fury, and you will find in the deepest parts a desperate desire to be (as the Bible puts it) "one flesh" with other human beings.

Whether we use the word *intimacy* or the biblical term *one flesh,* the meaning is pretty much the same. Do not reduce the word to mere sexual intimations, or you will miss a large part of its implication.

The woman on the Iowa farm was not seeking sexual intimacy when she met Robert Kincaid. She was apparently quite happy with life as she knew it. Happy, that is, until Kincaid came and represented new levels of possibility that she either had never known or had chosen to ignore.

Her husband, the faithful farmer, knew how to provide for her, protect her, and maintain all the routines of life on her behalf. But he did not know how to *know* her. And he did not know how to *make himself known.* More than anything else *The Bridges of Madison County,* whether we approve of its story line or not, is a book about intimacy, becoming one flesh. It features a man who, according to the author's definition of intimacy, knew how to do that and another who did not.

The message is a simple one. As a rule men struggle to connect. Most of them, in our modern world, do not connect very well. *Connecting,* a substitute word for *intimacy,* describes the ability human beings are said to have that (let me use language from the computer world) enables hearts to handshake.

Why do men struggle so much in this area? Why do a significant percentage of the female population find such disappointment in the shallowness of connection that they ultimately feel with their husbands? Why do most children feel a lifelong distance from their fathers? And why do men confess that making and sustaining friendships is among the most difficult challenges of their lives?

Samuel Osherson writes well on this issue in his book *Wrestling with Love* and employs an interesting term: *attachment battles.*

An attachment battle is an inner conflict between our need to connect and our reluctance to connect. It occurs, often unseen and unnoticed, in relationships with women, children, parents, colleagues, and other men. I believe this is one of the most important issues facing men today. Often we fight with those we love, or become sullenly detached or abusive because we are unable to deal with the ambivalent yearnings that love creates for us as men.

For those of us who turn to the Hebrew/Christian Scriptures as the starting point for our view of reality, intimacy is best understood in its most positive form in the earliest pages of the Bible. The biblical writer describes the first man and woman in terms like these: the two are naked and feel no shame.

We often use the word *naked* to refer to the unclothed human body. My bet is that the biblical writer uses it in a much larger sense. Here nakedness has to do not only with an unclothed body but also with an unclothed soul. If the soul is understood to be the deepest depths of the human being, then nakedness suggests two people who are totally open to each other. No secrets!

There are reasons for such a relational status. First, all energies of each person are thoroughly attuned to engaging the other for the highest and best purposes. There is a common sense of mission in life. To honor and obey the Creator who has challenged them to manage creation (whatever that means, and it's a lot more sophisticated than this or any human mind can figure out).

Second, there seems to have been an appreciation of each other's beauty. Adam sings the first known love song as he gazes upon Eve:

> This is now bone of my bones
> And flesh of my flesh;
> She shall be called Woman,
> Because she was taken out of Man
> (Gen. 2:23 NKJV).

One picks up a sense of unvarnished delight in the prospect of being together. This is in contrast to the loneliness felt before Eve entered Adam's life.

Third, there is an absence of any shame or guilt. Neither has offended the other, nor have they offended God. So embarrassment, humiliation, and fear of being found out do not exist in this relationship. Each can present his or her soul to the other without fear that something is amiss.

Interrupting this narrative, the writer of the story looks to his own time and explains why men and women seek each other out: "Therefore a man shall leave his father and mother and be joined to his wife, and they shall become one flesh" (Gen. 2:24 NKJV).

Implied in this sentence are these things: a man has experienced intimacy of a kind with his father and mother. Now he seeks a *different* (I am not prepared to say a greater) intimacy with his wife. He is also, by implication, to find other kinds of intimacies with friends and, later, his children.

I believe that this magnificent biblical story is among the most important stories of a man's life. For it is our beginning point. It explains *what we were made to be and to experience.* It explains why there is a longing, a deep sense of loss in the soul of every man. It suggests how we were wired by the Creator, and points the way to why we feel bad when this spiritual circuitry does not work.

But something went terribly wrong in the story. In the long view of things, it went wrong when our ancestors, the first generation of men and women, made choices that severely restricted their ability to be intimate with each other. They found themselves hiding from God, ashamed of themselves, accusing and blaming each other, and running from self-exposure. They were trapped in a strange ambivalence. They had a desire to know each other intimately, but it was blocked by an even greater need to hide from each other.

Even though this instinct to experience intimacy—connection at soul-level—has been terribly wounded, we nevertheless feel the loss when we cannot experience it.

VERSIONS OF INTIMACY

All of our lives we pursue differing versions of intimacy. As I will point out in chapter 3, we experience our first sense of intimacy with our mothers and then, we hope, with our fathers. If we fail in these first two pursuits, we are likely to live with the loss for the remainder of our lives.

Soon there are those first intimacies with boyhood friends. We build forts together, start clubs, fool with secret passwords and codes and signals. We play on teams, explore the topic of sex (as much through humor as anything), complain about our parents, and fortify one another in our first attempts to figure out the world of girls. Some of us develop remarkably intense friendships with friends that will last a lifetime.

Then the time arrives for us to understand intimacy in a third category. We experiment with the meaning of connection with a woman. Can she be trusted? Will she find value in me? What do I have to offer?

In each of these phases—from parents to friends to women—there are all sorts of ways in which our experience can be inhibited.

We are most prone to engage in intimacy in places we think to be safe. Safe in the arms of a mother; safe in the presence of a father; safe with friends with whom we have built up trust. In such safe environments we experiment with opening up our deeper selves and in exploring the hidden parts of others. But if ever the trust is betrayed, we may spend a lifetime in the belief that no place is safe and that no person can be trusted. Therefore, little or no intimacy. Some examples may clarify this point.

The ability to engage at intimate levels is affected when, in moments of high trust, we are humiliated or betrayed.

In a discussion circle a man tells us his story:

When I was about five or six, I told my mother one evening about a girl who lived near us and who was in my first grade class at school. I thought I loved her, I said. Some day I would marry her, I predicted, and we would live down the street not far away so that I could come home and have dinner every evening. Kind of dumb, huh? But that's not the end of the story.

An evening or two later my mother entertained a group of women in our home. I was in bed trying to go to sleep when I began to hear peals of laughter from downstairs. Wondering what it was all about, I tiptoed to the top of the stairs and began to listen. They were talking about their children, exchanging stories about crazy things kids do and say. Suddenly, I heard my mother begin to tell the women what I'd confided to her a few days before. And what made it worse for me was the realization that the mother of the girl I'd talked about was there in the group.

I can't describe what it did to me to hear my mother telling my secret to those women, especially to that other mother. And the feeling was compounded when my mother made a joke of it and everyone joined in even greater laughter. It was as if I'd been stripped of everything. And I remember thinking that night, *I'll never tell my mother a secret ever again.* And I wonder if that was the night I decided I'd never tell any woman my secrets. For the only thing worse than my mother's voice was the pain of that laughter. I feel a coldness in myself whenever I hear women laugh at a table in a restaurant or in a corner at a cocktail party. I have this irrational feeling that they're cackling about something some man said or did.

Intimacy is affected when we are brainwashed into believing that we must go it alone and trust no one.

A group of men are telling father-stories. One of them recounts:

My dad was from the Old Country. He was tough and he worked harder than anyone I've ever seen. He ran a one-man coal business, and when I was old enough he had me down at the coal yard running errands, cleaning things, and finally even beginning to deal with customers. I bet I heard my father say the same thing in the same way ten thousand times: "You can't depend on anybody in this world. If you want something done, you do it yourself. Never get in a spot where you need anybody."

And if I felt sick or tired, he'd say, "Don't bleed on me. No one's interested in how you feel. Stand on your own two feet. Gut it through."

You hear that sort of thing enough times, and you begin to believe it. And that's the way I've learned to live life. I don't depend on nobody, and I don't bleed on nobody. Not my wife, not my kids. And I work too hard to have close friends. So I guess I've become what my father said I should.

The ability to be an intimate person can be affected when nothing in our present experience matches the past. A former athlete states,

I was an interior lineman, starting freshman. And I played every game for four years without a serious injury. There were three other guys on the line that played with me almost the entire time. I can't tell you how much we loved each other. We won; we lost; we helped each other through injuries, through good and bad romances, through studies. There wasn't anything we didn't do together. I could cry with those guys. I could sit up all night and drink with them. And there wasn't anything we couldn't say to each other. I mean there were some times when we got good and mad at one another. I guess that says it all.

And now I'm thirty-eight. I'm still grieving. When football was over and we said good-bye it was like a death.

Intimacy is affected when someone we love turns against us. We've come to a point where "nakedness" feels good and things held down in the heart are beginning to reach the surface where they can be appreciated and processed. And then . . .

We'd been going together since high school. And after two years of college we decided that we couldn't wait any longer so we got married. It was a tough time. She had to quit school and work so that I could finish. But I did finish. Even did some graduate work. I thought we were really on our way. And I really loved her. We didn't have a lot of money, so we had to do a lot of cheap things like camping and hiking. Then the roof fell in.

One day she told me that there was someone else. She'd been fooling around for almost a year, and I'd never picked up a hint of it. How's that for being sensitive? So she left, and she's living with him. Now I think about all the times we were together. The things I felt free to tell her. And I thought all the time that we were getting closer. But she was moving away.

I think the thing that has really gotten to me is the feeling that I'll never be able to trust anyone again. You talk about opening your soul. Look where it got me.

When men open the files of their private thoughts and ponder the issue of intimacy, these kinds of stories may bubble to the surface. You can easily detect the hurt and disillusionment, and you're not surprised if one of the storytellers admits that he's had a difficult time trusting ever since. Many of us have stories that are thirty or forty years old, but the feeling of betrayal has lasted with an unexplained freshness. How we deal with these stories and how we decide to seek healing of wounds that have caused us to build walls around ourselves may be among the most important decisions we ever make.

CHAPTER 3

SEXUAL INTIMACY

When men think private thoughts, the sexual dimension of personal reality will occupy more than a few files of the mind. The following letter touches the tip of the iceberg:

Dear Gordon:

The announcement for the upcoming First Monday meeting says that you're going to talk about men and sex. I don't want to be offensive, but if you're going to raise the subject, and I'm glad you are, can I please suggest that the last thing we need to hear is one more talk on purity . . . what we aren't supposed to be and what we shouldn't be doing.

Most of the guys who show up at First Monday are there because purity is already a given for them. They don't need to be persuaded. They're all for it . . . if only they were sure what sexual purity really means and if, in fact, it's possible to live up to it. And most of us don't feel that we are. Not that we're a bunch of perverts, but you listen to guys talk, and you realize that they're terribly confused as to why they are the way they are. Especially when it comes to thought life. When it comes to dealing with temptations. And when it comes to being so stinking vulnerable when something in a guy's sex life isn't going right. Worst of all, we've all discovered that our wives can make us look like perfect fools in this area if they want to. We wish we knew why, but we don't.

Most of the time in life men are hearing one of two messages. The world out there is saying, "You're a free man; do whatever you want and have fun because everyone else is." Or more on the home front (and sometimes even in church) you're a bad guy because sex is all you think and talk about.

So what we need from you, Gordon, are some ideas on how to keep the mind under control, how to live in a society that seems obsessed with the subject of sex, and how to understand why we get so many confusing messages from women.

I could go on and on. *Why* does the mind seem to go wild at times with thoughts about this woman or that one? And *why* are we always sizing up women in terms of their looks and their physical proportions? *Why,* even when you love your wife as much as I do, is it difficult not to be curious about what's in some pornographic magazine? And *why* do we always feel like a jerk when we compare our attitudes towards sex with the attitudes of our wives'? Why is it all a problem for us and not for them?

Sometimes I want to curse myself for my seeming lack of control about sexual things. My wife, on the other hand, never seems to be tempted. She never seems curious about things like pornography. And she never seems to have any problem with control whatsoever. If she does, she isn't telling. Are we men just a bunch of immature jerks? See if you can help us understand ourselves as sexual men, will you? We'll be very thankful.

Lots of men could have written all or portions of that letter at one time or another. It expresses the confusion and the sense of mystery that many men feel as they wrestle with things sexual.

My strong suspicion is that most men will carry these confusions all the way to the grave. They begin in the earliest days of boyhood when we become mystified over the physiological differences between boys and girls and start asking questions that our parents struggle to answer.

The confusion grows, and its mysteries are generally later expressed in the crude humor and the imaginative stories boys begin to trade when no one else is around to hear. "I saw . . . ," and "I heard . . . ," and "Did you hear the one about the farmer's . . . ?"

Of course, these confusions are exacerbated with the early exposure to explicit sexual activity (in humorous and dramatic forms) that pops up every day and evening on television and in the movies.

Puberty comes, hormones rage, and the boy finds himself thinking about and occasionally acting out his sexual urges. He is desperately curious about the ways of his gender counterpart, and he spends inordinate amounts of hours thinking and talking about the possibilities. He feasts on rumors and stories about this girl and that one. Everything and nothing is believable.

If the surveys are to be believed, a significant percentage of boys are sexually active in one way or another before leaving high school. Despite the best intentions of all the youth-based organizations (church, school, etc.), the interpreters of the social scene suggest that there is relatively little difference in the sexual attitudes and activities of young men no matter what their religious and sociological backgrounds. If a significant parental figure does not satisfy the curiosities, answer the questions, and set forth a comprehensible picture about sexuality, everything the church, the school, and other social organizations do will fall far short. What is left is the peer group with its shared ignorance and generational autonomy.

It is a strange era in which we now live. Strange in that it departs so dramatically from the moral standard the men of my generation were taught in their younger days. We lived in a day when premarital sexual activity was certainly not unknown but was still hushed up and generally regarded as shameful and sneaky. Our day was one in which most couples did not live together before marriage. And fathering and mothering a child outside marriage was not considered a noble matter. The result was that most of us married at a relatively early age and assumed that we would remain married to the same woman for the rest of our lives.

Today, outside the Christ-following community, these standards of the past are often treated as strange and outmoded. Perhaps the contemporary position is best expressed by the young woman on the television program *Coach* when she says to a boyfriend whose bed she shared the night before, "Just because two people sleep together does not mean that they have to fall in love."

The letter at the beginning of this chapter reflects the comments and perplexity of many men. Not just in my generation but also in those of the younger set. In discussion groups after a First Monday session, a young man is embarrassed as he discloses his private thoughts: "There are times when I seem to be obsessed with thoughts of sex. I can't keep my mind under control. And I don't want anyone recommending cold showers or hymn singing." A married man in his high thirties speaks of his marriage: "We've got a good thing going, my wife and me, but there is a woman at the place where I work. And I can't stop thinking about her." And the older guy, whose wife is gone, the one you would think has left sexual thoughts far behind, says with a tear, "I'm so lonely. You have no idea how I ache to hold someone in my arms, to make love again."

Is there something better to tell these men with their private thoughts than merely that they are bad or sinful? Is there any explanation for the dominance of the sexual in the minds of men?

My nomination for a starting point in the discussion is the simple, but then emergingly complex, question: What's behind the intense drama of relationship between a man and a woman?

INTIMACY OF THE WOMB

"I suggest we begin with the womb," I say to a crowd of men who've come to First Monday. Some of them look at me with an expression that insinuates, "Are you crazy?" They've come to hear about sex drives and tips toward a better love life. And I want to begin with the womb?

No, I think the womb just might be the right place to start if we're going to sort out private thoughts on this matter of male sexuality. Think about it! The womb of a mother offers the first experience of intimacy, and I'm just convinced enough about this to suggest that what happens there may set in motion an entire lifetime of urges toward or away from intimate connections between two human beings.

"Now, cut me a little slack in order to speculate, gentlemen," I say to the First Monday gang. "Because I want to propose to you that a mother's womb could be the most ideal living space any human being has ever known. Cramped, perhaps. But anyone who has ever lived in a New York apartment knows better than to worry about this. The womb: possibly better than Hawaii in winter; better than a mountain trout stream in the summer. Imagine its virtues.

"First, in the womb there's an ambient temperature that is apparently never too warm and never too cool. Then, there's this ambience of peace and tranquillity. Unless you're a twin (or more), you've got a private accommodation. There's a wonderful rhythmic beat of your mother's heart not far away, a kind of natural Muzak. Its steadiness says that this womb is a safe place. No need for anxiety here. When you travel on a business trip, you carry a white noise-maker with you to drown out the distracting sounds of slamming doors, ice makers, and elevators in the hotel. In the womb all that's taken care of with your mom's heartbeat.

"And food and drink? Hey, there seems to be an undiminished supply of life-giving nutrition available around the clock. And it has to be good stuff if it can help you more than quadruple your weight in a short period of time.

"Last but not least, you could say that there is a spiritual sense of connection or intimacy in the womb. You are as one with another human being as it is possible to be and still be your own autonomous self. Could it be that the intimacy of the womb is the most complete, the most satisfying experience a human being will ever know? That everything else from this point forward is merely an imitation of those moments? Almost downhill by contrast?"

By this time a lot of men are chortling. They can't believe I'm saying this. But I want them to realize that these experiences in the womb are among the very first impressions encoded on the innermost being of a person, male or female. I'm speculating that what is experienced in the womb *forms* some of the personal values and desires we will pursue and want to live with for the rest of our lives.

When the uneasy laughter is over, I remind the men at First Monday what I've just said: "Listen again to the list of amenities you might experience in the womb: comfort, peacefulness, nurture, oneness, pleasure, response. Ever ask yourself as a man what you're seeking in the arms of a woman? Isn't that a fairly similar list?"

Some men say, "Ummm." The brave guys nod their heads. Someone starts to clap.

Think of it: in the womb you are (to use the biblical term again) one flesh with another human being. Not for minutes or a short period of time. But day after day after day. Every heartbeat is felt; every joy; every anxiety. The two—mother and child—are as one organism. She feels him kick; he senses her stress. She will risk her life and give everything she has to sustain him; he responds by creating a love in her mind that completes her womanhood and leaves her never to be the same. This womb-experience between a mother and a child: it conveys everything we mean by the word *intimacy.*

Now here is the important question, and I ask the First Monday men, "Why would anyone want to leave this ideal environment in which one, humanly speaking, has everything?" This question is not meant to be funny even if some laugh. I go on: "If protection, nutrition, warmth, comfort, and connection are all there is to life, the womb beats any place I've ever heard of."

But leave the womb we must. And when the leaving comes, there has to be an inconsolable feeling of grief that is written upon the heart of the one who leaves. And not a little grief, perhaps, for the mother also who, in spite of her physical relief, says good-bye to this bundle of life and flesh she has carried within her. For the two of them, it has not been a spatial relationship; it has been a mystical, spiritual relationship. The child has been "bone of her bone, flesh of her flesh." Now he or she is taken out of woman, and the parting is as much like a death as it is a birth. Some things will never be the same again.

But our subject is men and their private thoughts about women in the sexual dimension, and I want to center in upon the birth of the boy-child in this moment. For it is my contention that when girls and boys are born, boys take the greater hit in the long run. Of the two, the boy suffers the greatest loss in the intimacy column. The nature of the loss becomes apparent when a boy becomes old enough to look at his mother and his father and conclude, *I'm more like him than I am like her. There's a journey ahead of me, the one that takes me from the arms of my mother to the hand of my father.*

INTIMACY OF THE MOTHER

When a boy-child is born, he is drawn from his mother's womb—this place we have called most ideal. Soon, if not immediately, he is placed on her stomach, and his mouth is directed to her breast. As I've said, these last hours have been an awful trauma for the newborn. In the womb he has known the pleasure of an essentially trouble-free existence. I repeat this for emphasis.

But here he is now at the breast, perhaps the best substitute there is for a womb. Here he may find echoes of that blissful existence within his mother's body. Warmth, closeness, the sound of the heart, nurture, and protection all seem to be here to the limited extent that it is now possible to find them. Perhaps, instantly etched upon his tiny mind is one of the first messages of the post-womb lifetime: *at the breast there is a modicum of peace and connection,* the components of intimacy. If I cannot remain in the womb, he wordlessly concludes, I will find what I need as often as possible in this new alternative place. And he does.

But there is not only the proximity of the breast; there is the taste of the milk drawn from it. This reassuring nutrition that fills a craving stomach and all the other parts of this boy-child's body that ache for energy with which to sustain an amazing growth rate. This is milk that gives strength, and its life-giving stream is among the most important things inscribed upon the boy-child's perception of reality.

Beyond the breast in these earliest of moments there is the voice of his mother. He has heard its sound many times while still in the womb. Its unique timbre has by now been burned upon his heart and has been differentiated from all other sounds. When that voice speaks, he knows that he is enveloped in safety.

The voice soothes; it casts a spell of well-being. The resonance of the quiet, female voice fills the ear just as the milk fills the stomach. Perhaps the mother sings as she strokes the child. Her words are decoded as kind, accepting. Oh, this voice! From the very beginning, he learns to trust it. Whatever it says is counted as reliable and true. It overcomes and neutralizes other harsh sounds: the sounds of technology, the sounds of a hostile environment, the deeper, base sounds of the male. The boy-child becomes quiet when the soothing voice of the mother prevails.

And the eyes. Cradled in his mother's arms, he looks up and into eyes that are only inches away. At that distance infant eyes are soon capable of focusing and discerning. And what does he see? An entranceway into his mother's soul, perhaps a sense of the former place where he'd been so close, so intimate, for nine months. He searches the eyes for signs that all is well. The mother's eyes look back upon the child. Most often they are soft, inviting, cherishing eyes. In the communion of the eyes, there is a sweetness of peace.

Then there is a mother's scent. Who knows how significant are the unique pheromones that highly sensitive infant nostrils absorb? All the newborn boy knows is that when he smells his mother, he is safe, and he is connected to the one who gave him life. It is pure pleasure, this mother-perfume, as an infant might define pleasure.

In her arms he is stroked and patted. All of his being is excited with the physical feeling, this reminder of being fully enclosed at an earlier time. The pleasure of being rubbed and caressed is one more reminder of the meaning of intimacy—this greatest of all human needs.

When you total up these experiences, you realize that each of the baby's five senses has been activated: tasting, hearing, seeing, smelling, and touching. All are in motion drawing from the mother the security and intimacy once experienced in the womb.

If there is any doubt about the significance of these experiences for the newborn boy, all one has to do is turn to the mountains of research that point to the essential and indispensable nature of these experiences. Without them, many children die. Those who do not are adversely affected emotionally and spiritually for a lifetime.

These tastes, sounds, sights, smells, and touches are a boy-child's first inner language. They assure him that the world beyond the womb can be pleasant. He eagerly waits for all their messages. He wants to "hear" them again and again.

In Ashley Montagu's book *Touching,* he records the memories of Kabongo, Kikuyu chief of East Africa:

> My early years are connected in my mind with my mother. At first she was always there: I can remember the comforting feel of her body as she carried me on her back and the smell of her skin in the hot sun. Everything came from her. When I was hungry or thirsty she would swing me round to where I could reach her full breasts; now when I shut my eyes I feel again with gratitude the sense of well-being that I had when I buried my head in their softness and drank the sweet milk that they have. At night when there was no sun to warm me, her arms, her body, took its place; and as I grew older and more interested in other things, from my safe place on her back I could watch without fear as I wanted and when sleep overcame me I had only to close my eyes.

Should it then be a surprise to any man or any woman that these aspects of a woman's being may indeed be the first things a man is instinctively drawn to when he looks upon any woman for the rest of his life?

When I ask this question at First Monday, the room becomes silent. Laughing has ceased. No one is moving. You get the feeling that some mystery is in the process of being revealed. A few good men are on the edge of understanding something about themselves they'd never before taken into account.

INTIMACY BEYOND THE MOTHER

Good things have a way of coming to an end, and there is a time when this intensity of connectedness between mother and son must be modified. The boy-child will leave the breast. Now his journey takes him even farther from the ideal of the womb. He is likely to find an alternative, but nevertheless temporary, place of pleasure upon his mother's lap when she holds him close. Here the former things will remain important: the softness of her body as she holds him close, the sound of her voice as she speaks to him in tender tones, tones that become word forms penetrating the left side of his brain, to the more rational process. And her eyes, always her eyes. What is the message of the eyes? Soft, inviting, offering a welcome back to her soul, a reminder of the original connection within.

More and more he will wander away from this point of pleasure. There is a world to discover, places to go. With each venture, he will move farther away and stay away for longer periods of time. But he will always return when he feels he has reached his limits, when he can no longer handle the anxiety, when he needs once again to connect and draw from that one trustworthy source the love that intimacy provides. He still needs to be one flesh with his mother. Once it was constant; now it can be sporadic.

Things are changing. The separations from his mother grow longer. Weaned, he no longer tastes her milk but accepts the more general tastes of strange foods and drinks to nourish his body.

And the voice? It continues in significance and dominance. Sometimes now the voice is different. It is not always the soothing voice of the beginning days. Soothing may now turn to scolding, tones he has never heard before. These new scolding tones cause fear and a sense of separation. They make him feel less than secure, less than whole, less than accepted. He will do almost anything to avoid the scolding voice . . . at first.

The eyes—while still important—are now farther away. Those eyes—once full of warmth and open invitation—can become cold with wrath and disapproval. The scent declines in significance, but the memory of its pleasure will always linger. In worst-case situations, the arms and hands that once held this boy-child so close may now spank and cause pain.

In certain moments, the boy will wish for the earlier experience so badly that he'll do anything to restore the pleasure. At other times, if he feels overpowered, he may run from it, defy it, or—the very opposite—capitulate to it and feel his own spirit sag in vulnerability. The perception is that this woman holds the key to life and to something like death. He is beholden, maybe even trapped, by her and something reminiscent of her breast and her voice and her eyes and her scent and her caresses.

Conclusion: A man is likely to live his entire life with these sensitivities and these issues emblazoned in the deepest recesses of his mind.

In his maturing years when he looks upon a woman, it will not be surprising if he is likely to notice the line of her breasts. More than likely it was that soft mound upon which he first found intimacy beyond the womb. And the more the woman seeks to accentuate its line or creatively (or seductively) reveal its form with the openness of her costume, the surer she can be that he is likely to notice. Perhaps more than notice. Accelerate his curiosity might be a better description. At the deepest levels of his being, he is responding to the primal realities of his life as a child. At the breast he spent some of the best moments in his life. He had intimacy, connection, there.

And the voice. The voice that once soothed the troubled child in the darkness of night, when he faced the anxieties of being in a strange world. That cooing, soothing voice. Does one dare to think that the sound of that voice has actually been forgotten? A lifetime is not long enough to forget its soothing power. And if the solitary voice of the mother has long ago been set aside, the feminine voice of any woman will approximate it.

Men have made fools of themselves over the female voice. They seek to trust it. They are drawn toward its soothing tones as surely as a moth is drawn to the candle. Something in the soul is excited, activated. And the words carried on the waves of the voice are capable of making some men do strange, awesome, or terrible things.

The Japanese knew—as all have known—that Allied soldiers fighting in the Pacific would much more likely listen to the intimate voice of Tokyo Rose than to the voice of a man. Even the makers of airline technology have decided that the synthesized warning in the cockpit of an airliner should be a woman's voice because it will catch the attention of a drowsy pilot faster than a man's voice.

A man will always be curious to explore a woman's eyes. He remembers the earlier connections. Watch men and women in a restaurant. You can almost always tell the pairs who are married and those who are not. Unfortunately, those who are married will more than likely keep their eyes averted, or when they talk with eye contact, their eyes will be reflective of more rational perspectives. The eyes will not dance with curiosity or excitement. The relative deadness of their eye contact will suggest that everything that can be seen or experienced has been seen, has been experienced. The mystery of the soul has disappeared. There is no curiosity any longer.

But watch a man and a woman where there remains mystery—which is the essence of romance. They will seek each other's eyes out, lock in long gazes. Each trying to look as deeply within as possible to plumb the riddles of how the other feels and thinks. This is a time when words may not be as important as the mysteries beneath the words.

In understanding these connections we come to better knowledge of the strange dynamics that pass between a man and a woman—dynamics that will never change no matter how we attempt to reengineer the politics of male and female relationships.

THE STRENGTH OF INTIMACY

Men and women have never seemed to face the enormous hold they have over each other. It has been easy for those in the feminist movement to speak of the forceful oppression to which men have subjected women. They consider it oppression built mainly on physical, brute strength. We are awash in news and speculation about the tragedies of sexual abuse and molestation, of wife abuse and beatings. We are all quite aware these days that it has been a man's world in terms of the exercise of privilege and power. This has been—for better or for worse—the sociopolitical alignment for, shall we say, fifty thousand or more years. It is a "politic" that is in the genes, packed in there after numberless generations. Now we are trying to change that politic recognizing its gross injustice. But even if our efforts are sincere, the changes will come slowly because we are not dealing with just changes of the law. Our misuses of strength must be wrung out of the bloodstream, and that will take more time than all of us will live.

What we have not looked at with a reasonable amount of candor is a second kind of oppression. For the generations have revealed not only a male who prevails through strength but also a female who counters with strengths of her own. Her strong grasp upon a man is not to be discounted. It, too, must be understood and dealt with in this time of sociopolitical change. She has what many men would die for: the key to his experience of intimacy, connection. It is written in his heart from the moment he began life in her womb.

If a man has learned to control through the force of his muscle, a woman has learned to control through the use of the very things she used to control the world of her newborn son.

Down through the ages, more than a few commentators on the life of a boy/man have noted the element of grief that marks his soul. A grief built upon a separation that begins the day the womb is left behind. From this point forward, it seems as if the boy is always *leaving* something he has come to cherish or depend on: the connectedness that was afforded at the breast, in the arms, eye to eye, hearing the soothing voice and smelling the familiar scent.

Something within the woman knows this, and when she chooses to use these secrets, she is often successful in neutralizing the strength (at least temporarily) of the man. She can draw a man through the exposure of her breast. Like it or not, she must realize that the contour of the breast is almost always going to catch his eye because it speaks to something that can only be called primal within him.

It is insufficient to regard all attraction in a man to the breasts of a woman as wicked or sleazy. In saying this I am not condoning the leering, jeering male who, in his uneasiness concerning his own manhood, demeans the female with catcalls and tasteless remarks. Nor am I in any way showing regard for the man who values a woman primarily on the basis of her physical anatomy.

But it is a one-sided matter if the woman is not sensitive to the allure of her breasts not merely as sexual objects but as symbols of those deepest memories and desires written upon the heart of almost every man.

A man will also always be drawn to her eyes. One cannot be so naive as to say that women do not know this at gene level when they spend the time and money they do on cosmetics that accentuate the eye and draw attention to it. Flirting is little more than the game men and women play to gain access to the eyes. When we flirt with a member of the opposite gender, it is as if we are knocking on the front door of a home. "Will you let me in?" is the question being asked.

Even if one or the other in this common little game is not interested in entering, it is nice to know, we think, that we could have entered into the soul of another if we had wanted to.

All a man knows is that these experiences have made their way into the center of his being. He will do foolish things or noble things to experience them again and again.

MISUSED INTIMACY

Among the most fascinating of all biblical characters is Samson. Endowed with remarkable physical strength, Samson was able to kill lions, bring armies to their knees, and lift city gates off their hinges. Samson was Israel's man, and as long as he maintained his strength, Israel felt secure.

But Samson offers a story for modern men. He lived in a day when brute physical strength was highly appreciated. Today, intellectual strength, deal-making strength, political strength, and persuasion strength might be just as valued. In fact, any kind of strength is coveted if it produces a power that can protect, overturn, or generate value.

Samson had a problem. He seemed to be incapable of resisting the seductive strength of beautiful women. Most of us are familiar with Delilah; few, on the other hand, are aware of the unnamed Philistine wife who preceded her.

Samson played strange games with his enemies. On one occasion he taunted the Philistines with a riddle, promising to pay them handsomely if they could answer. Of course they were stymied. Until they went to his wife, one of their own, and threatened her with death if she did not extract Samson's secret.

> Then Samson's wife threw herself on him, sobbing, "You hate me! You don't really love me. You've given my people a riddle, but you haven't told me the answer." "I haven't even explained it to my father or mother," he replied, "so why should I explain it to you?" She cried the whole seven days of the feast. So on the seventh day he finally told her, because she continued to press him. She in turn explained the riddle to her people (Judg. 14:16–17).

A fascinating and believable story! The biblical passage seems to depict Samson's wife in the act of using every persuasive gift she has. Her voice seems to lead the way, accentuated with tears, with accusations, with relentless demands. In the act of misused intimacy she coaxed, cajoled, threatened, bargained, and probably soothed. Samson caved in to it. His wife's people got the answer to the riddle, and Samson became the fool.

Samson did exactly what many men in search of intimacy do. They do it when they dial for phone sex. When they permit themselves to fall captive to a woman who speaks softly in soothing tones. And when they cower under the harsh, scolding voice that berates or threatens. Great strength is neutralized by a soothing or a scolding voice.

Let's agree that we can understand how a man might be tricked once by the voice of a woman who misused the pathway to intimacy. Let's give him a bit of grace. But twice! That's exactly what happened. Samson fell again . . . for the voice.

But it was the voice of Delilah, a prostitute!

> Some time later, [Samson] fell in love with a woman in the Valley of Sorek whose name was Delilah. The rulers of the Philistines went to her and said, "See if you can lure him into showing you the secret of his great strength and how we can overpower him so we may tie him up and subdue

him." . . . So Delilah said to Samson, "Tell me the secret of your great strength and how you can be tied up and subdued" (Judg. 16:4–6).

Several times, Samson refused to capitulate to her persuasive voice and continued to operate on the basis of his extraordinary physical strength to defeat the Philistines. But one gets the impression that even the greatest physical strength of a man is no match for the persistent soothing or seductive voice of a determined woman.

When Deliliah turned on her persuasive charm, what did Samson hear at the deepest levels of his soul? Perhaps phrases like, "Trust me. Believe in me. Put yourself in my hands." Maybe he'd heard similar messages in a positive and loving way when, as a boy, he'd known the affection of his mother and her intent to affirm and encourage him. But this was something different, quite different. Now the voice was that of another woman not intent on his best interest but rather committed to his destruction.

The soothing voice then turned to scolding, to nagging. This voice had once been powerful enough to draw the world's strongest man into love. Now from the same lips came words that cut, diminished the will to resist, made a man feel "tired to death."

Then Delilah said to him,

"How can you say, 'I love you,' when you won't confide in me? This is the third time you have made a fool of me and haven't told me the secret of your great strength." *With such nagging she prodded him day after day until he was tired to death.* So he told her everything (Judg. 16:15–17, italics mine).

And that was the day that Samson lost his great strength.

What happened? A man in search of intimacy never understood the power of his need and the ability of an enemy (male or female) to exploit that need and to cost him his integrity, his purpose for living, his life.

CHAPTER 4

THE CONFUSIONS OF SEXUALITY

You are watching professional football on television. In the final minute of a close game, one of the teams scores the winning touchdown. There is pandemonium in the stadium, and euphoric teammates dash toward the end zone to pile on the ball carrier. In their delirium they embrace, lift one another off the ground, and roll about on the grass. There are head butts, pats on the rear end, and even a few effusive kisses when the helmets come off. In any other setting we might think it not unlike a bacchanalian orgy. Where else would you see men show affection like this?

Well, you might see it on a battlefield. A dying soldier, for example, cradled in the arms of a buddy. We have all seen such pictures. The appearance is similar to a mother cuddling her child. So that's a second place where men might be observed showing strong affection toward one another.

A third place might be on a Latin American street corner where friends meet and exuberantly embrace each other with repeated slaps on the back.

A fourth: in those parts of Eastern Europe where men kiss each other on the lips. And don't miss the possibility that some good-natured wrestling among boys may be little more than affection in disguise.

Apparently, in the right place, at the right time, and in the proper cultural setting, men are not necessarily as undemonstrative, aloof, and dispassionate as we are led to think. With enough joy or sorrow or suffering or plain reverential love, you may have the ingredients for intimacy.

The Freedom to Be Affectionate

I was once asked to give some talks to several hundred men who had gathered for a spiritual retreat. At the beginning of one session I said, "Gentlemen, at the end of our meeting tonight, I'm going to challenge you with what Billy Graham calls an invitation. I'm going to invite anyone who hears God speaking to him on a personal basis about something significant in his life to come to the front of this auditorium and kneel for prayer. I'm also going to ask that, if any of the rest of you see a friend down here, you come and kneel with him and share the moment. Don't let anyone do something like this alone."

Then I started into my presentation and quickly realized that I was too tired to do a good job. Words weren't flowing; my recall of the outline was poor. I had the feeling that I wasn't really communicating well with the audience. As a result, I began to dread the upcoming moment of invitation because I felt sure no one would come to the front.

But I'd made a commitment, and I had to deliver. So when I finished my second-rate talk, I did as I'd promised. I invited men who sensed a need to respond to come forward. To my surprise, they did. Not just a few; but many. Before long, the front of the auditorium was carpeted with kneeling men, dozens and dozens of them. In keeping with what I'd asked, others came and knelt with friends. It was a remarkable sight, a witness to the fact that God doesn't need some eminent speaker to get His work done in the lives of men.

When it seemed as if no one else would come, I dismissed the rest of the crowd, asking them to leave in silence so that the auditorium could become a room of prayer. I slipped out a side door to get some fresh air and to be alone for a moment where I could apologize to God for my lack of faith. Twenty or thirty minutes later I returned. I have never forgotten what I saw upon entering that room.

My perception was that none of the men who had come forward had left. Rather, they were scattered throughout the room in groups of twos, threes, and fours. Two things immediately impressed me. First, the tears: many men were weeping openly. Second, the male intimacy: almost all of the men were touching, hugging, embracing—somehow, in a very quiet way, reminiscent of the winning team in the end zone and the wounded soldiers in combat. If they were praying, they prayed with arms about each other. I saw several men holding one another almost as a father might a child while one wept through some sense of spiritual brokenness or another.

I remember standing there in a state of total surprise. I'd never seen anything quite like it in a spiritual setting. I recall thinking, almost out loud, that there are two things men desperately need from one another that, generally speaking, they are not getting or giving: *permission to express their deepest feelings to one another and the freedom to be affectionate*. Apparently, most of us can experience them only when there is supreme joy, when there is intense suffering, or when something has touched the depths of our spirits.

It is the second of these two permissions that concerns me at this moment. For when men think private thoughts, they wonder about this strange mixture of instincts that draws them toward women but causes them to feel distant from other men. What is it that may have gone wrong?

A DIVISIVE ISSUE OF INTIMACY

I have this memory of a day somewhere in my ninth or tenth year when it came to me that I should no longer kiss or hug my father. I have no idea how he felt when I told him of my decision. It seems to me that he was the one who graciously suggested a substitute gesture—that we shake hands instead. For many years we did exactly that.

Why did I do this? It was a response to a pressure most (but not all) boys seem to feel. It is a pressure that says affection between men is not the male way. It signals a state of "sissiness," that one is not strong and cannot make his own way. If affection has something to do with a statement of needing each other, a boy who puts distance between himself and his father (as well as other friends) is saying, "I think I can go it alone because I hear the world around me telling me that I must go it alone. That seems the way of the man."

Then again, we live in a society that is deeply divided over the issue of homosexuality. Unfortunately, that division cuts right through the heart of the Christian community, each perspective represented by people whose minds seem closed either to examining the issues to see if there are higher and more helpful ideas or to accepting the notion of compassion and sensitivity toward those with whom they disagree. Because many people in the church today are so unyielding on this subject, more than a few families (I meet them quite regularly as a pastor) feel forced into silence when one of their children comes home and acknowledges a homosexual orientation. In most cases the moment introduces shame, a sense of isolation, and a feeling that something has gone terribly wrong.

As a result, the fear generated over the issue of homosexuality is constantly reinforced. We all remember the moment in the locker room when two naked bodies inadvertently touched in the shower, and someone yelled out, "What are you? Queer or something?" A boy needed to hear the derisive laughter only once. From that point forward he made sure he never touched anyone of his own gender.

Perhaps that's why some of us even recoil when asked to hold hands with another man in a prayer group. We're uncomfortable with most forms of male touching. The times and ignorance have done this to us.

THE LEAP TO THE FATHER

In the previous chapter we left the boy-child in the arms of his mother. He has made the journey from the womb, to the breast, to the lap, and perhaps, even beyond that, to a point where he is at least happy to return if only to wrap his arms around her leg. On each occasion there is a recurrence of intimacy, freely given and freely received.

But something new enters the picture. For the boy becomes increasingly aware, unlike a girl-child, that he is different from his mother. Psychologists have gone to lengths to describe this process, which they call *disidentification*. The boy must begin the search for his primary identity as a boy-become-man. And where must he go? We know that this is the time when he makes his first steps toward his father.

There is a single event in the life of Jesus that illustrates the process of disidentification. Jesus, Luke records, was twelve when He and His parents made a journey to Jerusalem to participate in the holy days. It came time to begin the long, northward trek back to Nazareth, and Mary and Joseph discovered, after a day's walk, that Jesus was nowhere to be seen. We can surmise that they had been traveling in a large group because His parents assumed that Jesus had spent the day walking with others. But it was a false assumption and required them to return to Jerusalem to find Him.

When they reached the city, they found Jesus in the temple courts in discussion with the rabbis and teachers, where, it is said, all were astonished at His maturity of thought and insight. While both parents were distraught, His mother, Mary, expressed the consternation: "Son, why have You done this to us? Look, Your father and I have sought You anxiously" (Luke 2:48 NKJV).

The peculiar response was, "Why did you seek Me? Did you not know that I must be about My Father's business?" Luke notes that they did not understand what He meant. The episode ended with the comment that He went along home "and was subject to them" (Luke 2:51 NKJV). But not before an important statement was made, a line drawn in the sand.

I suggest that this is one of the key moments in Jesus' process of disidentification with His mother *and* (in this case) His designated father, Joseph. It is the moment when He has declared His intention to identify with His true *heavenly* Father. This is the Father whose spirit He has within Him. This is the Father from whom He will draw energy for His mission. From this point forward the writers of the Gospels will frequently comment upon the bondedness, the intimacy of Jesus with His Father. At the temple, Jesus is making His first moves from one sort of connection to another.

We are seeing a perfect picture of a process that faces each boy on his way to manhood and the discovery of his genuine needs for intimacy.

A boy must begin to back away from the overpowering influence of his mother in the early years; nevertheless, his need for intimacy continues. He must connect. He must know a loving touch, the gracious words of assurance and approval, the sense that there are those who respond and who are drawn to what he is and what he does. If he does not connect, or if his attempts to reach out are rejected, it is likely that he will grapple for the rest of his life with the dynamics of intimacy and how it is best given and received. Things are happening in these first eight to ten years that will go a long way toward shaping his attitudes about sex, healthy relationships with women, and his sense of being accepted among the men as a man.

A crucial moment in this process arrives. For while he must begin to find strengths within himself, the boy must also begin to find connection with someone more like himself, someone who can offer him insight into what he must become. In most cases, that first someone, of course, is meant to be his father and, ultimately, the men (the friends) with whom his father associates. "I must be about my father's business . . . and my father's sense of personhood . . . and my father's energy."

If this transfer of intimacy does not happen, a number of alternative possibilities emerge. A boy may seek substitute forms of connection with his peers. Gangs are the most extreme example of this. If the boy has a predisposition to homosexual orientation (evidence grows of a predisposition similar to that toward alcoholism), an inclination in this direction may begin. Of course, we may discover that in the disappointment of not finding intimacy with his father, a boy goes running back to his mother . . . or to women in general.

A wise and perceptive mother encourages a boy's move in the direction of his father. It will be difficult, even strangely grievous, for her because the moments of intimacy with her son have brought a maternal fulfillment that is beyond words. In primitive societies, there are ceremonies that express this mother-grief. The tribal woman may even wail the laments of death as she acknowledges the inevitable separation that takes her son from her side to the company of his father and his friends.

A boy begins this journey as early as the third year of his life, as late as the fifth. Perhaps the journey is better understood as a leap toward the arms of his father. Be it a journey or a jump, the question that looms large is this: Will the father be there to receive his son? If so, he'll begin to develop another kind of intimacy: the connection of the men who offer one another what a mother has formerly offered—support, comfort, nurture and, now, wisdom.

But what if, when the journey or the jump commences, the father just isn't there? Perhaps—the worst-case scenario—he is absent in that he has abandoned both mother and son. Or, possibly, his absence is the result of other priorities such as preoccupation with career demands. Or still, another alternative, the father is there in body, but he is not there in spirit. He is bottled up within himself, unable to present himself emotionally or spiritually. The son sees his father on-site, but he sees a man who is hollow, aloof, and uncommunicative.

At the end of one First Monday a man got up and said to the crowd,

> There was a day when my father died as far as I was concerned. I'd had an incredibly good day at school and in athletics. Everything had gone right. And I was sure that when my dad heard what had happened to me, he'd be delighted. I think I was always trying to find a way to finally impress him, to get a reaction from him. Any kind of a reaction.
>
> I remember coming into the room and sitting down and telling him everything that had happened that day. The television was on, and he was watching the news or sports or something and kept looking beyond me, far more interested in what was on TV than what I was telling him. And when I got through, he mumbled a "that's great, son," and just went on watching the television. When the program was over, he just got up and left the room without another word. I felt like a fool. Everything I'd thought important just didn't count with him.
>
> I don't know what it was that I was looking for. He was not the kind

that would have hugged me, and I wasn't interested in that anyway. I guess I wanted him to stop everything like watching the TV and share my excitement. It would have been nice to know that what had happened that day was as important to him as it was to me.

I don't think I ever bothered to tell him anything important again. I wasn't going to take the risk again. So I stopped thinking of him as the man who would ever share my accomplishments and excitements.

What I think I hear being said is this: intimacy is something of a shared moment where we need someone who will validate us. The intimacy can be a caress, a kiss, the properly chosen words, a diverting of attention from other things to this important moment. You know it when you experience it! A bond between two people (in this case a father and a son) is strengthened, and both feel closer. But when someone misses the moment, the bond is loosened and the sought-after closeness becomes distance.

This boy who feels slighted by this father will have the same kind of feelings when, as a married man, he reaches out for the affection of his wife and she waves him off.

Here is another possibility. What if the father is there but fumbles or sabotages the relationship? He is harsh, critical, unaccepting, physically or, worst of all, sexually abusive. At the end of one men's conference, a man related this story to me:

> My father once told me of a moment in his life which marked him forever. When he was a boy, he was hospitalized and fell into a coma. No one was sure that he would recover. But some days later he did begin to respond to treatment. When he came out of the coma, *his* father was standing by his bedside. His first instinct was to reach out to his dad and ask if he would kiss him. But the father recoiled and stepped away from the bed saying, "You're not *that* sick!"

Call it a fumbled moment, probably soon forgotten by the father, but never by the son. In an instant, a perspective on intimacy is hammered into a boy's soul. This kind of connection—a simple kiss of joy—is not to be found with a father, with any man. Don't ever ask again. Don't expect. Don't assume.

This is a dramatic description of what many boys have experienced as they have made the journey toward their fathers. They are left with a skewed understanding of intimacy. Connection, they assume, can happen only when I am with a woman. I ought never to expect anything from other men.

The boy is left with difficult decisions when his father is not there to receive him. Does he turn back and try to reconnect with his mother? Does he separate from both of them and seek his own way? Does he assume that intimacy is a matter of relationship solely with a woman? It is my thought that it is this last conclusion to which the majority of boys come.

Samuel Osherson comments in *Wrestling with Love:*

> Women often don't understand the enormous power they have in men's lives. Having rarely found emotional support and help from other men, many of us come to look upon women as the sole repositories of safety, security, comfort, and support. Unable to obtain a friendly smile, soft touch, or gentle words of encouragement or kindness from men, a man may become an expert in finding such reassurance from women friends, or his wife. If he feels that the need for close touch and contact are not "manly," a man may turn to sex with women as the only available experience of touching and bodily comfort.

In another chapter we will talk more of the dynamics of the father-son connection. But the track of private thinking here, from which I do not want to turn aside, is what leads toward healthy intimacy between men and women. The fact is, it is unlikely that such intimacies will ever be sound if there has not been a different but nevertheless parallel kind of intimacy between a boy and the men in his world. In other words, *he must develop healthy relationships of male connection before he can return to the world of women and appreciate healthy intimacy with them.*

I would not like to get ahead of myself, but it might be timely to say that whenever I visit with a man who tells me that he wrestles with unhealthy perspectives regarding sex and sexual activity, I always want to question him about the quality of his friendships with men, including his father. Almost always he acknowledges that he has struggled with good male relationships throughout his adolescent and adult years. But more of that later.

HORMONAL AWAKENING

The coming to life of the sex glands—that time we call puberty— creates a whole new reality in the quest for intimacy. This hormonal awakening takes something that was once relatively simple, the relationship of male and female, and gives it a complexity not likely to cease until death. The desire to connect, as a boy once connected with his mother, and later with his father and friends, now becomes intertwined with the emergence of mysterious and intense sexual curiosities and desires.

These new hormones, at one moment seemingly dormant, at another moment raging beyond all control, have the effect of an inner tornado on a teenage boy. One summer he is turned off by the company of girls as he pursues his brands of male activity; the next summer he is obsessed with every female who crosses his path. He is interested in breasts, flirtations, sexual humor, and every opportunity he can find to be in the presence of girls.

He also struggles with the loss of control over his own body. Erections are beyond his control, for example. Is there a man alive who does not remember the anxiety caused by a penile noncooperation while sitting at a schoolroom desk? How about the fear that a teacher might ask you to stand and answer a question or the dread that the bell ending class might ring and you would have to walk out of class in such a condition? *And everyone would know!* It's not unlike the anxiety of some older men who fear that what once wouldn't cooperate will no longer function at all.

Not many men can remember the exact moment that new kind of awareness of connection between a boy and a girl began. I am one who does remember. It was the first day of school in the fall, sixth grade. I was sitting on a bench near the school's main entrance waiting for some friends to arrive. A girl named Barbara approached me. She was quiet for a moment, and then with one finger she pushed back the front edge of my very blond hair and said, "You have the most beautiful hair." I have never been the same since that moment.

I was without words. Her touch to the top of my head and her comment about my hair ignited something inside me. I lost all interest in waiting for my friends. Something magic had occurred. But if there was something profound that I should have said, I missed it, and soon the magic moment was gone and Barbara skipped off to other things.

From that day forward, my mother never had to speak to me again about my appearance as I left for school. Rather, she had to speak more about the amount of time I spent in the bathroom inspecting my face, my hair, all the things that might catch Barbara's, or any other girl's for that matter, attention. I suddenly knew who I wanted to please and how wonderful had been that touch on my hair and those simple words, "You have the most beautiful hair." I had experienced connection of a new kind, and all I knew was that I wanted more and more and more of it.

These are the times when all kinds of sexual storms are launched in the male experience. Issues and temptations that women do not seem to fully understand. Issues and temptations that may dog many men for the remainder of their lives. The desire for sexual stimulation and satisfaction becomes an inner storm of great magnitude brought under control only if it is supported by a sound belief system and a balanced set of healthy male and female relationships that provides various kinds of intimate connection.

But, again I ask, what happens when there isn't a sound belief system? When one suffers from a lack of healthy male and female relationships? When intimacy is confused? When loneliness and feelings of isolation are pronounced? Then there are likely to be sexual confusions of one kind or another. Sexual intimacy, meant to be satisfying and fortifying, becomes something else: a set of varying counterfeit experiences that can be destructive to every part of a man's life. For lack of a better term, I simply call them the great battles in male sexuality.

Five battles come to mind. Most men have fought in one or more of these battles. In all cases there is a reluctance to talk about one's battle experiences because of shame and guilt. But get a group of men in a place where they are willing to talk frankly, and almost all of them will admit that some of these battles have at one time or another been a real threat to their character and wholeness. Make a comment about such battles, and there will sometimes be a quiet but nervous laughter in the group, the kind that allows each person to admit without using words that he's gone through such a struggle at one time or another. Here they are.

FANTASY

The first battle is what we often call *fantasy*. The word is used to describe mental images and scenes that capture the mind. A sort of inner pornography. Most men and women know the experience of periods in their lives when they have found their minds abounding with endless minidramas that offer alternative scenarios to what they experience in reality. The fantasy world of a young teenage boy (or a man) is not to be underestimated. It is an amazing array of episodes, sometimes played and replayed to best suit the dreamer. In these fantasies he plays lover in one form or another to an endless list of women as he imagines all kinds of possibilities.

A lot of men live in such a fantasy world, and they lavish all the energies of their hearts upon these fictional or not-so-fictional characters who enter upon the inner stage. Those of us who were brought up in the church and constantly warned about the evils of *lust* (because that's the biblical word for this event) felt ashamed of our fantasy lives. We felt trapped by the teaching that most fantasies (if not all) were sinful and the fact that our minds, for the most part, simply wouldn't obey either our commands or the Bible's. The fantasies were there whether we liked them or not.

For a period of time, it seemed as if all of our faith depended on whether or not we could master our fantasy lives. My recollection is one of great desperation every time someone asked once again if we wanted to recommit (*rededication* was the word in vogue) our lives to God, to missionary service, to anything God might want us to do. How, we asked ourselves, could we be of use to God when our minds harbored such offenses?

Sometimes we boys heard that if we took cold showers, did a lot of singing, and made sure we were never alone, we could overcome the fantasy problem. But such remedies never really did much to solve the problem.

A college student leaves a note in my office box:

> I have a strong desire to be a man after God's heart. But I am a totally defeated person. I find that I cannot get my mind under control about sexual issues, and I get caught up in sexual thoughts at almost any time of the day. The worst is the realization that I can't even control my thoughts when I'm praying. I've asked God again and again to take these temptations away, but if anything, they get worse. Is this perversion? Is there anything you can tell me that would help?

There is one thing I can do to set his mind at ease in the beginning, and that is to assure him that he is not alone. As far back as sixteen hundred years ago, Jerome wrote,

> In the remotest part of a wild and stony desert burnt up with the heat of the scorching sun so that it frightens even the monks that inhabit it, I seemed myself to be in the midst of the delights and crowds of Rome. . . . Many times I imagined myself witnessing the dancing of the Roman

maidens as if I had been in the midst of them. . . . I tamed my flesh by fasting whole weeks. I am not ashamed to disclose my temptations.

Among the best-known missionaries of the twentieth century is Jim Elliot who, in January of 1956, was one of five who lost their lives when ambushed by the Auca Indians in Ecuador. Talk to anyone who knew this modern martyr of the faith, and you will get universal agreement that there was hardly a man in any generation who ever loved God, who wished to serve Him and obey Him, more than Jim Elliot.

That's why it brings comfort to any man to read the Elliot journal and discover that this man also struggled with sexual temptation. Credit him for remaining faithful to his commitments both to God and to his fiancée, Elisabeth. But remember that he also struggled in the loneliness of hours spent in the jungle where he served among the Indians. At a particularly lonely moment he wrote,

As I said, I want a woman—just one to hold and press against me, to feel and fondle with my lips and fingers. Disgustingly, it could be any woman, as I cannot seem to bring *her* [his fiancée, Elisabeth] fixedly to mind, and it is just the woman want [sic] that plagues me, the craving to feel one close to me.

On another occasion he wrote,

Yesterday walking back from Angu's house after injecting Augostine (who, praise God, is better after his near death struggle with pneumonia), I was alone in the cool, dark forest, and I knew then how vulnerable I am just now to attacks of fleshly temptations. Even then, I don't know how it would have been had I met an Indian woman alone in the trail. O God, what a ferocious thing is sexual desire, and how often it is on me now.

Two themes seem to dominate most fantasies. The first is *control*. In fantasies the dreamer is able to manipulate every circumstance to suit his own desires and expectations. It is an alternative to a real world in which he feels that he is never in control. That people he admires are not his to know. That circumstances in which he would like to be involved are not his to experience.

The second theme is *connection*. Fantasies are the first indication that a boy or a man feels lonely, cut off. The mind, in its great need for intimacy, will *create* connection in the fantasy dimension if it cannot experience it in real time settings.

The college boy who writes to me is involved in a campus lifestyle. Yet a conversation is likely to reveal that he feels close to no one. He has a need for conversation and human fellowship that he is not experiencing at levels satisfying to the soul. Thus his mind in partnership with his sexual drive employs sexual metaphors and word pictures to create an entire alternative life within. If connection cannot happen in real space and time, the mind is likely to create it in mental space.

In a wonderful book, *The Jesus I Never Knew*, Philip Yancey offers an observation made first by Francois Muriac, concerning the fantasy of older men (something many younger men will be amazed to know about since there is a suspicion that one grows out of difficulties with sexual fantasies): "Old age risks being a period of redoubled testing because the imagination in an old man is substituted in a horrible way for what nature refuses him." Or put in simple words, what nature denies, the imagination creates. I would like to enlarge the scope of Muriac's thought and propose that *what nature or custom or circumstance denies or forbids, the imagination is likely to create.* This is the source point for lust and fantasy, active imaginations that offer men (women also?) the opportunity to engage inwardly in activities that are not happening outwardly.

MASTURBATION

A second issue in the life of a growing male has to do with sexual self-stimulation or masturbation. One is probably not far wrong if he suggests that, sooner or later, almost every male has engaged in masturbatory experiences, and there have long been arguments about the significance of this act upon one's mental and spiritual health. Surely, we have put the concern of physical health (you'll go blind; your genitals are likely to fall off; you will lose your sexual ability) behind us by now. In the world of Christian sexual ethics, however, one will probably not find anyone who would encourage masturbation, although some psychologists and counselors have seemed to acknowledge the practice as a natural function. Their caution has been centered on the tendency for some to carry on an addictive pattern.

Like fantasy, masturbation is probably a signal, a statement about one's sense of loneliness and need for intimacy. The impulse to masturbate can be caused by the experiences of fantasy, exposure to sexually stimulating events (in movies and television programs), or one's feelings of social awkwardness and isolation. Unable to engage in satisfying relationships with others, a man finds it easier to retreat and create feelings of intimacy in his own private world.

The growing desire for intimacy—combined with the growing activity of sexual glands—makes masturbation almost a certainty in the lives of teenagers for a period of time. And it ought to be no surprise that more than a few adult married men, even sexually active in the healthiest fashion, respond to an occasional temptation to masturbate. In later years it will also be a strong indicator of a sense of isolation and loneliness.

PORNOGRAPHY

Pornography is a third response to an intimacy deficit. Most women find the use of pornography to be repulsive. Most men share this feeling. But men will nevertheless be a bit more understanding, for more than a few of them will go through a period in their lives when they find one form of pornography or another the object of such strong curiosity that they will finally surrender and indulge themselves.

Many of us were introduced to pornography when we were teenagers. If one grows up in a home where nakedness is seen as shameful, it is almost predictable that pornography is going to become a temptation. The magazines, the videos, and the pictures all seem to offer one thing: secrets. The secrets of women's bodies; the secrets of what people do together behind closed doors. And secrecy and intimacy parallel each other.

If the truest form of intimacy is what happens when people open their souls to each other, sexual intimacy becomes something of a substitute experience. In the marriage setting sexual intimacy is meant to reflect the drama of the other forms of intimacy. But when those are not available, a man is likely to be drawn toward what he can get. And that is what pornography *seems* to offer.

What is going on in the mind of the man who purchases a magazine, rents a video, or frequents an adult bookstore? He is seeking intimacy, although it may be of a kind that another person might not understand.

He is hungry to connect with another human being, and he is unable, for various reasons, to make it happen. He wants to know the secrets of a woman's heart, and her nakedness is symbolic of these secrets. Somehow the tricky mind begins to reason that to know something of a woman's nakedness, to be in a setting where she exposes herself in the most sexual or even the most perverse ways, is to bring her under his control, to know her in a satisfying way. To see her respond in intimate settings of sexual relationship will satisfy the curiosity. But for just a short time. Then the old curiosity will rise again.

Talk to any man who has become involved in pornography, and he will admit that the satisfaction from such an experience lasts but a very short time. Each journey into the magazine pages or the videotape carries with it such promise that the ultimate experience of satisfaction may be found. But it never is. It only creates the need for more.

SEXUAL PROMISCUITY OR SEX ADDICTION

A fourth route to unhealthy intimacy is that of sexual promiscuity. If the intimacy deficit is great enough, a man will begin his search for human connection by moving sexually from one woman to another, seeking what he believes to be the ultimate experience that will both satisfy the longing of the heart and prove that he is a man. He unconsciously concludes that the portal of human communion is sexual experiences and that in a multiple of lovers lies satisfaction for a lonely heart. Somewhere along the line when he is spiritually burned out, hardened in his cynicism, he discovers to his horror that what little ability to be intimate he originally had is now lost or impaired.

My belief is that we have a long way to go before we fully understand the mind of the man who is sexually promiscuous or (in the extreme sense) has a sex addiction. We do know that a pattern emerges in such lives that becomes very difficult to control.

A pastor visits with me:

> Among the very worst things I ever did was to bring the cable movie channels into my home. I found it easy to get back up after my wife and I had gone to bed and she was asleep. I'd watch some of the movie channels with movies where there was a lot of nudity and sexual play. All it did was rouse old feelings I thought I'd gotten rid of when I was married. Then I'd be sitting in my study one afternoon thinking about what I'd seen last night. That would get me thinking about that area of our city where they have a lot of adult bookstores. Before long I'd be driving through that area. The next day I'd go back, park the car, and walk the street. The third day I'd go back, park, walk, and poke my head into one or two places. The fourth day, I would be in one of them looking at magazines, watching videos in booths, and setting my mind on fire.
>
> Then I'd begin to feel very, very bad, and I'd have a moment in which I'd totally repudiate the whole thing. And I'd feel marvelously free. I'd

preach about sin the next Sunday and, more often than not, people would say I sounded like a powerful prophet. I'd think I'd finally beaten this temptation.

But a couple of months later, I'd find myself going back and repeating the same cycle. This has been going on for several years. Into this stuff, then out of it, then back into it again.

These are the words of a man who is probably struggling with an addictive pattern of sexuality. Unless he opens himself up to serious, ongoing conversation with a trained and compassionate person, he is not likely to beat the pattern.

Incidentally, I am not surprised that a pastor would tell this sort of story. Any man who is involved in work that concerns caring for people, motivating people, or helping people is likely to find himself tempted toward issues of sin pertaining to intimacy. As the politician is tempted to abuse power, and the businessperson is tempted to misuse money because of greed, and the intellectual is tempted to a kind of arrogance, so the "people-person" can be tempted toward sins that cluster about the issue of intimacy.

ABUSE

There is a fifth and (if these are to be compared) most tragic possibility in the life of a man who does not know how to enter into the relationship of intimacy. It is the foulsome events of molestation and physical abuse. We wonder in horror at the man who foists himself upon young girls (both in and beyond his own family) and forces them into sexual events that will play havoc with their minds and their sense of well-being for the remainder of their lives. We are shocked each time we hear of a man filled with rage who beats (or even kills) his wife or his girlfriend.

Until the last few years almost none of us had any comprehension of the number of women who reported that they had been sexually abused by their fathers or other men who, as family members or close friends of the family, took advantage of their position of power and influence. Our shock was exacerbated when we discovered that some of these men were professing Christians and leaders in their churches.

What should never surprise us is how deceived and twisted the mind can become through the power of evil as it rationalizes and justifies its way through events that have catastrophic consequences.

Various forms of abuse probably stem from early frustrations in the area of intimacy. Intimacy spurned, ridiculed, betrayed. Anger builds in the heart and mind of a man, and he begins to conclude that the only way he can relate to the opposite sex is by forcing himself upon girls and women who are in no position to defend themselves.

This book is not designed and its author is not trained to inquire into the causes of sexual abuse. But this is a moment to pause and plead with men who have struggled with their sexual desires and who have abused women who have loved and trusted them. This is the moment to tell them that help must be sought. It is an understatement to say that the life and well-being of a young girl, a wife, or a family may be in the balance.

The Need for Friendships with Other Men

These past pages have not been easy to write. Those who organize their lives around the Bible would be hard pressed to find any way to duck the realization that these sexual battles are identified with issues of sin. A man was not built by his Creator to live as a loser in any one of these battles.

It does no man any good if he takes a look at various forms of sexual deviance in his life and excuses himself as some sort of victim. The Scriptures call him to make a break with such behaviors (and I can hear some men say, "more easily spoken than done"). Nevertheless a man has to start somewhere if he wants to be a pleasure to his God and a healthy man in all of his relationships.

He begins with renouncing (or repenting of) his behaviors. No change is possible if there is not an inner agreement that something is morally and spiritually wrong. No excuses; no mitigating circumstances. Just renunciation.

And where does he go from there? Before I suggest a possible direction, let me recapitulate where we've been. These conclusions thus far:

- That men are in desperate need of intimacy (connection) throughout their lives.
- That intimacy involves connection of body, mind, and soul.
- That when soul and mind are closed off, sexual intimacy may be the only thing that appeals to men.
- That when men find themselves cut off from various forms of intimacy, they are likely to struggle with temptations toward fantasy, masturbation, pornography, promiscuity, and abuse.

Men are almost always surprised by my suggestion that one of the major keys to controlling sexual temptation is having close friendships with other men. In one sense, it's simple. If the need for connection is exclusively centered on the female gender, be ready for an onslaught of struggles with fantasy and lust at the very least.

You, my male friend, are a relational being; you must connect. God has made you to share life with a host of people, not just your wife. You are meant to share life with other men as you work with them, fight the battles of life with them, and discover the world with them. This is the meaning of friendship—walking through life with the brothers, encouraging one another, challenging one another, and assisting one another. When we retreat from this, cut ourselves off spiritually and emotionally from the other men of the village, we set ourselves up for sexual struggle.

Everyone who has ever evaluated the adulterous sin of David in the Old Testament has observed that his time of temptation came when he was alone in his palace rather than where he apparently belonged, with the men in his army who were engaged in conflict.

The Scripture is not explicit in saying this, but it seems reasonable to suggest that David did at least two things to himself. He created within himself an uneasy sense of manhood when he wasn't where the men were. Therefore, he had to prove himself in a different way, a way that proved to be sexual. Second, he was a pushover for the beauty (and it must have been beauty to David) of a naked woman.

I'm back to where this chapter got its start. Standing on a stage where men have come forward in response to my Billy Graham–like invitation. Scores of men are working through key issues in their spiritual journeys. Many of them are praying. There are lots of tears in this room—the kind that men don't often shed unless they have really gotten in touch with some deep feelings. There is lots of affection in this room— the kind you might see on an athletic field, a battlefield, or a place where two old friends are meeting.

I think about how we men have been so cheated by our culture, by our fear of the feminine in us. But let a man get down to doing business in his soul, and strange and wonderful things begin to emerge. One of them is a kind of intimacy that really does help a man become a man.

CHAPTER 5

FINDING A FATHER

Among the private thoughts of men, the topic of our fathers is likely to be raised with great frequency. It's hard to think of one person who is more apt to fill the thinking horizon than a man's father. Not always is it the case, but frequently enough to make this claim.

Some think privately about their fathers with sweeps of admiration and appreciation as did Matthew Arnold, who wrote of his father in one of my favorite poems, "Rugby Chapel":

> If, in the paths of this world,
> Stones might have wounded thy feet,
> Toil or dejected have tried
> Thy spirit, of that we saw
> Nothing—to us thou wast still
> Cheerful, and helpful, and firm!

Some will think their private thoughts in much bitterness. Such as Franz Kafka, who wrote in his *Letter to My Father:* "I was a mere nothing to you. . . . in front of you I lost my self-confidence and exchanged it for an infinite sense of guilt."

I have a friend who always seems to be telling Dad-stories. "My dad once said . . . ," he will recall, or "I remember the time my dad asked me to . . . ," or "You know, my dad always had a way of . . ." I love my friend's Dad-stories. They always convey some nugget of wisdom. But even more, they remind me of the connection that is supposed to exist between the generations, a connection marked with affection, understanding, stability, and direction. I guess there is hardly a man who wouldn't crave a bevy of positive Dad-stories as part of his heritage.

It's my observation that the men with positive Dad-stories tend to be in the minority. Frankly, the majority of Dad-stories I hear are mostly stories of regret and anger: "I never really knew my dad," or "My dad never seemed to be there at the right moment," or "My dad wasn't able to give me the slightest impression that he was glad to be my father, that he approved of anything I did."

I sit at lunch with a man I like who is battling depression. His state of melancholy mystifies me because everything in his life seems to be marked with so much success. In fact, I cannot find one event in his present life that might offer a key to his feelings. To the contrary, he has just completed a major project for his company that is going to make them and him more profitable than ever. I know something about his marriage; it's in great shape. I know his children; they're fine. And health is not a problem. So what's behind this despondency?

Somewhere in the conversation, I ask some questions about the past, and one of them is, "What was your father like?"

There is a grim smile, followed by a long pause in the conversation while he overstirs his coffee.

And then: "There's not much to talk about. He was unpleasable; that's it. No matter what you did, he wanted it done better the next time. Grades could always be better. The way you swept the basement floor could be done better. The way you played in a ball game could be done better."

I can tell that he isn't finished with this recollection.

"Have you ever watched the high jumper at a track meet?" he asks.

Being an ex-track and field man, I nod yes.

"Ever notice what they put the poor guy through? He leaps over the bar, and what's the first thing they do? The first thing?"

"They raise it," I say.

"Exactly. And they keep on raising it until he knocks it off. Until he fails! The sucker can't go into the locker room and call it quits until he fails." When my friend uses this phrase, he slaps his hand with anger on the table in time with each word: *until* (slap) *he* (slap) *fails* (slap). "That's what I remember most about my father. He was always raising the bar."

I see a connection. "Is that what's going through your head today?" I ask. "You've made a successful 'jump' in your work, and you have this inner feeling that someone, your boss maybe, is going to raise the bar again? So your mind relives the sadness of other days when your father kept pushing you?"

My friend replies, "Let me think on that one for a while."

SEEKING APPROVAL

These fathers of ours. Strange men sometimes. Strange and mystifying, too, are our relationships with them.

I walk through a crowd of men, and each of them seems faceless to me. I care little about who they are or what they think. Should they disapprove of me, it would have relatively little impact. But if one of the men were my father, his admiration or disapproval would have a profound effect on me. It would be the cause of joy or heartache in my private thoughts. If one of them were my father, I would give almost anything to hear that he was proud of me.

Winston Churchill's father, Randolph, is a study in bad Dad-stories. Among Sir Winston's biographers is William Manchester, who devotes many pages of *The Last Lion* to the relationship between him and his father. "Randolph actually disliked his son," Manchester comments at one point as he describes the many ways the father hurt the boy. Yet, strangely enough, the boy maintained a steady devotion toward his father, always wanting to believe that there would come a day when the two would find a connection. Looking back at his boyhood and his troubled relationship to his father, Churchill said,

> I would far rather have been apprenticed as a bricklayer's mate, or run errands as a messenger boy, or helped my father to dress the front windows of a grocer's shop. It would have been real; it would have been natural; it would have taught me more; and I should have got to know my father, which would have been a joy for me.

Later, looking back, Sir Winston's view of his father would change as he finally faced the fact that the two had never connected. Manchester notes a conversation with Frank Harris in which Churchill said "that whenever he tried to open serious conversations with his father, he was snubbed pitilessly." He recalled,

> [My father] wouldn't listen to me or consider anything I said. There was no companionship with him possible and I tried so hard and so often. He was so self-centered no one else existed for him. . . . He treated me

as if I had been a fool; barked at me whenever I questioned him. I owe everything to my mother; to my father, nothing.

In a strange twist of interpretation, Churchill would later write (Manchester records) that,

famous men are usually the product of an unhappy childhood. The stern compression of circumstances, the twinges of adversity, the spur of slights and taunts in early years, are needed to evoke that ruthless fixity of purpose and tenacious mother wit without which great actions are seldom accomplished.

What then is this mysterious bond, for good or for ill, that we seek to have with our fathers and, through them, the men of our worlds?

SEEKING LOVE

Back to this process of intimacy. There is a time in the first years of a boy-child's life (as I've already said, perhaps in the third or fourth year) when something—so mysterious that we cannot name it—in a deep interior place—so deep we cannot locate it—erupts with curiosity. It is a consciousness that there is another kind of intimacy he must find if his life is to be complete. To find that connection is to make something of a journey, a journey fraught with risk. It begins with putting a kind of distance between himself and his mother to find a balance between maternal and paternal love.

It is the father who will show the boy the way to manhood, what he must become. His mother is not equipped and shouldn't have to do this. When the boy awakens to this presence of the father and the bond they must develop, his journey toward manhood begins.

His mother's love has been protective, nurturing, and comforting: the things he needed to survive. But like a rich food, there comes a moment when too much of that love, unbalanced by another kind of love, becomes oppressive, and his appetite for its maternal intensity is considerably dulled. He must begin the trial-and-error journey away from her arms to seek not other female arms but the hand of his father and the hands of his father's friends. In other times and places, we might call his father's friends the men of the village.

The boy has previously known the love of the womb. But unbalanced *womb-love* (or womb-energy as Richard Rohr and others have called it) is suffocating. Alone, it cannot make a boy into a man. What is now needed is *phallic-love* (again, Rohr among others who speak of phallic energy). This is a generative, energy-giving kind of love that challenges him to move ahead, to explore, to change. It motivates him to take risks, endure hardships, resist adversaries. Its energy surges outward, thrusting, creating, innovating, acquiring. In its fullest sense, it is a seed-planting, generative kind of energy that is the trademark of the male nature. If womb-love nurtures life, phallic-love inseminates life. It initiates things. We, men and women alike, need both. And in the end, we (men and women alike) need to give both. Phallic-love is a complement to womb-love.

The phallic-love of the father and his friends invites a boy alongside to walk in a common direction.

Many boys and many men have insufficient exposure to phallic-love and phallic energy. They have little sense that such love can come only from other men and that this is the kind of connection that makes a man out of a male. Not understanding this, many males (now in a sexual fashion) will continually respond to the womb-love of the female hoping to find their manhood. A man I knew confided to me that he made a New Year's resolution during his college days that he would sleep with a different woman every night for a year. He claims that he kept to his resolution until April. I never figured out whether he was exaggerating or telling the truth. He would be an extreme illustration of my point.

Seek manhood from a woman's arms or from her voice, and you will be profoundly disappointed. Your search will go on and on until you are burned out. While there may be a modicum of pleasure and momentary solace, that inner sense of confident *manhood* will remain elusive.

Until we understand this, we will never fully appreciate why men make such utter fools of themselves as they respond to the seductions of the sort of woman who uses her womb-love attraction (the breast, the voice, the eyes, the scent) to spin an intriguing web to gain her "prize." We will never perceive that sometimes women and men—in search of false security—blindly use each other: the one to forge for herself the experience of being needed, the other to discover for himself a place of escape where intimacy of a sexual sort may be acted out but remains unsatisfying to the soul.

Before I am misunderstood, let me reiterate that we are speaking of two kinds of love that are equivalent in value and are necessary to the well-being of all people. But the need of one or the other may come at certain times and in certain places. Eventually, all children, both boys and girls, need phallic-love as badly as they need womb-love. But the lack of the former will tell first and most powerfully upon a boy.

I am not proposing that womb-love is the exclusive pattern of women and phallic-love the pattern of men. In a lifetime the mature human being will give and receive both kinds of love. Nevertheless, it is likely that we will see more womb-love in most women and more phallic-love in most men.

SEEKING BLESSING

If one looks back to the cultures of the Bible, there is an interesting contrast to be made with our time. It seems clear that there was an intimacy based upon phallic-love between a father and his firstborn son that was, quite likely, as important (if not in some cases even more important) as the intimacy between a husband and his wife. Our culture with its emphasis upon romance and the love of men and women does not understand this.

The ancient man believed that he carried within himself the spirit of his family. The sins and the righteous deeds of the past generations became his sins and his deeds, and he passed them all on to his son. Each generation carried the accumulated failures and achievements of the former generations. For the misdeeds from the past, he had to repent, and for the blessings showered upon the family, he had to give honor to God. To the extent that he looked forward to eternal life, he assumed that he would live on in the life of his son.

Thus, it was the father's delight to bless his son. Blessing has to be understood not only as a distinct act or ceremony but also as a process that endured throughout the relationship of father and son.

In the blessing—that great intergenerational exchange of favor—a father gave to his son several things as part of the larger birthright. First, he gave his son a name. And the name was tied to the father's name. Jeremiah son of Hilkiah; Nehemiah son of Hachaliah.

It was thought that the father also bequeathed to his son his quality of character. Like father, like son. Weaknesses and strengths of personality and spirit were passed on. That idea was a major impetus for a man to search his soul, to ensure that he did not pass on to his children the defects of his character.

In the first chapter of Job, we are told that Job would sacrifice a burnt offering for his children, "thinking, 'Perhaps my children have sinned and cursed God in their hearts'" (Job 1:5). That, the Scripture recounts, "was Job's regular custom" (Job 1:5). Why would he do that? Perhaps a hint pops up a chapter later when his wife said to him in the initial stages of his suffering, "Are you still holding on to your integrity? Curse God and die!" (Job 2:9).

A harsh statement, it seems. But perhaps Job's wife was speaking out of experience. Perhaps Job's wife knew that there was something of a family tendency to become angry and bitter, to quit in the face of adversity. Maybe Job's wife simply expected that of him, and if she did, she must have been surprised at his resilience. But the point of the story is that Job also feared that propensity in the lives of his children. That a character pattern prevalent in his family line had entered their lives as it had his. In his grief over the potential inheritance, he offered sacrifices on their behalf.

In the love of the father it was also assumed that he handed on to his sons a unique family capability. Carpentry, stonecutting, farming, pottery, hunting, to name a few possibilities. One of those skills was seen as part of the family heritage, and in most cases, a son did not dare depart from the activity of his father or his father's fathers.

But in a most significant sense, a father gave his son what can best be called the family spirit. One reaches for words to describe this spiritual reality, which is hard for Western, rationalistic man to appreciate or perceive. We must understand that in ancient times the family line was perceived as greater than any one member of the family. And each generation was the inheritor and the physical embodiment of the family spirit. This might also suggest why people normally accepted the passage of the power of a king to his son.

All of that was part of the rites and process of inheritance. Those things were probably much more significant than the passing on of the family wealth. And because all of it was so consequential, the father needed to train his son in not only the skills and character patterns, but also the deeper teachings: who was the family's God, and how He was to be served.

> In the future, when your son asks you, "What is the meaning of the stipulations, decrees and laws the LORD our God has commanded you?" tell him: "We were slaves of Pharaoh in Egypt, but the LORD brought us out of Egypt with a mighty hand. Before our eyes the LORD sent miraculous signs and wonders—great and terrible—upon Egypt and Pharaoh and his whole household. But he brought us out from there to bring us in and give us the land that he promised on oath to our forefathers. The LORD

commanded us to obey all these decrees and to fear the LORD our God, so that we might always prosper and be kept alive, as is the case today. And if we are careful to obey all this law before the LORD our God, as he has commanded us, that will be our righteousness" (Deut. 6:20–25).

Perhaps one can now imagine the horror of a man who found himself unable to father a child. That was the plight of Abraham whose wife, Sarah, was barren. Our understanding of this story is sadly restricted if we think that all that concerned Abraham was who might inherit his wealth. Of far greater significance to him was the question: Who will inherit and carry the family spirit? If Abraham were to die childless, would that mean he and his family line died as a result? Or that the spirit moved on—as Abraham feared—in the life of one of his servants, Eliezer of Damascus?

Phallic-love in that day and culture was seen in the progressive blessing of the son by the father. One cannot doubt for a moment that there is an intimacy of a kind in this relationship that is mysterious and beautiful. The generations are tied together.

Reaching back again into the biblical literature—this time from the New Testament—one can again appreciate the nature of intimacy between a father and a son if he takes note of comments made by Jesus regarding his relationship with His heavenly Father. Certain statements lifted from the Gospels tell the tale of their love relationship.

Remember from an earlier chapter? "I must be about My Father's business" (NKJV), Jesus, the twelve-year-old, tells His mother, Mary, when she speaks to Him out of womb-love. Her protective instincts seek to pull Him back from perceived danger or from a too-adult world. But Jesus will not give in to her maternal charm. He is on to the life of His Father, and He is not now as much in need of what she has offered so freely in the past. There is a hint in their exchange of the tidal clash between the two loves. Mary would like to keep Jesus in the environment her womb-love maintains. Jesus understands the progressive, risky leap into the world of His father and His friends. In this case it is not His father, Joseph, but His Father who is in heaven.

"I must work the works of Him who sent Me" (John 9:4 NKJV). This is an older Jesus fulfilling the dimensions of the family skills and vision. In His younger adult years He was faithful to the family skill of carpentry. But now that He is about His Father's business, the vocation is that of redemption. He has moved away from womb-love and is now fully in the gravitational force of the love of His heavenly Father. He is in accord with the family Spirit of heaven, the Holy Spirit.

"This is my Son, whom I love; with him I am well pleased" (Matt. 3:17). The well-known words are said to have come from a "voice from heaven" when Jesus emerged from the Jordan River having been baptized along with those renouncing their sins.

Often I have quoted these words to groups of men and asked, "Which of you would not cut off your arm to have heard your father say this about you?" There is always silence in the room, and if you look closely, you see a tear here and there, especially from men—and they are many—who never heard such a word from their fathers.

This is the supreme affirmation, it seems to me. It is the word of a man who is proud of his son, who loves him, who is wholly satisfied with what his son is and is doing.

"Anyone who has seen me has seen the Father" (John 14:9). Like Father, like Son. The words of the Lord are perfectly understandable to those who either accept or reject what He is saying. It was presumed that Father and Son were in such union together through phallic-love that to see one, to converse with one, to do business with one, was to have done the same with the other. We see in this statement the full extent of their intimacy, the male bond that is its own kind of one flesh.

Finally, "Why have you forsaken me?" (Mark 15:34), the words of the suffering Christ on the cross. These poignant words declare a moment that is the opposite of all the previous words. Union has been broken. The love of the Father seems to have ceased, and the two are estranged because the divine One bears the sins of the world.

Strangely enough, this is the cry of many sons who feel cut off from their fathers. A connection has been severed, or it was never made in the first place. And the cry of Jesus is the cry of many boys: "When I reached out for your hand as I leaped from the arms of my mother, you were not there. Why?"

Jake Lamar, writer for *Time* magazine, speaks of his feeling of being forsaken in his book *Bourgeois Blues:*

> Try as I might to suppress the past, memories of my father came rushing back like bad dreams. Usually, I'd tell myself I didn't give a [expletive deleted] about Dad or what he thought of me. Other times, I felt an almost desperate need for his approval, his sponsorship in the world. Then, I'd decide I didn't want his emotional support. Just an acknowledgment. I just wanted him to recognize me, to say, Yes, you are my son, you do exist.

This sense of forsakenness can take many forms. It can be emotional when the father has denied his son access to his heart. It can be spiritual when the father has not brought meaning to his son's life by telling him of his God. It can certainly be physical if no affection or playful touching has occurred. And it can be psychological when the father has never extended the signals of well-being, affirmation, or pride in what the boy is becoming.

One of the hidden beauties of the death of Christ comes in the final words of Jesus. In spite of the darkness of the perceived forsakenness, the Son on the cross dares to continue trusting in His Father. Thus, as He dies, He says, "Into your hands I commit my spirit" (Luke 23:45). It is as if He has said, "I received My spirit from You; I now give it back. And even if I have the perception that You have forsaken Me, something deeper in Me knows that You will raise Me up. Therefore, I give You My/Our spirit."

One more incident in the life of Jesus deserves a comment. The first resurrection appearance of record is that made to Mary Magdalene. She is distraught over the missing body of the Lord from the tomb. And when Jesus speaks to her, she is too overwhelmed to recognize Him. But when she does, it is clear that she seeks to embrace Him. It is the explosion of her womb-love, her desire to offer the best the woman has to give, her comfort and consolation, her desire to create the protected environment. But He does not permit it: "Do not hold on to me, for I have not yet returned to the Father. Go instead to my brothers and tell them, 'I am returning to my Father and your Father, to my God and your God'" (John 20:17).

The union of father and son is powerfully highlighted in these biblical passages. Both in the beauty of what one sees in the life of our Lord and in the tragedies of relationships that didn't happen and should have. In the Bible a handful of men of varying quality of character were dreadfully poor fathers: Eli the priest of Shiloh, Samuel the prophet of Israel and, as we have already noted, David, Israel's greatest king. These are stories of boys who grew up to betray everything their fathers stood for. In each case there is ample evidence that the father forsook the son, perhaps because he was interested in other priorities.

SEEKING MANHOOD

When the boy-child awakens to his need for male or phallic-love, he is probably seeking several things that, when received, will settle into the depths of his soul and begin the formation of his ability to function as a man in the world. His is a growing hunger for phallic-love. He cannot say in specifics what he wants, but more than likely, he instinctively knows he needs a handful of things. And—to a great extent—only his father and his father's friends can offer them.

I see in my mind the old film clip of John-John Kennedy rushing toward his father, the president, on the tarmac of the airfield. And it is a picture to me of almost every son who, sooner or later, rushes, arms outstretched, toward his father. And as he runs toward him day after day, *he seeks first a common identity (I and my father are one)*. It is not just that the two of them are physically similar, but there is something that the soul of a boy understands: my father is the man, his soul says, whose genes I carry. I am from him, and I must perpetuate his spirit.

This pursuit of male intimacy, in past times, may have been a relationship the father pursued more than the son did. Today, it often seems to be the other way around. The son pursues the father. He wants to know who his father is, what he does, how he feels. And more than anything else, the boy wants to know what must he do, what must he be, to experience his father's acceptance of him as a man.

> Oh, my father,
> Why didn't you open your real heart when I was looking?
> Why did you only show me strength
> When I needed to know it was OK to be weak?
> Why did you never tell me
> that you sometimes cried late at night,
> that you craved the intimacy of friendships,
> that you were afraid,
> that you sometimes raged with lust,
> that you occasionally doubted God,
> that you were worried about failing,
> that you didn't know all the answers.
> and that there were times when you wanted to break out
> of the "trap" of obligations and find the wild life?
>
> Oh, my father,
> Why didn't you open your real heart when I was looking?
> Why did you only show me perfection
> When I needed to know that it might be OK to be average?
> Why did you never tell me
> that you made a few stupid mistakes,

that you sometimes failed as a husband, and would liked
to have choked your wife,
that you often misjudged me as your son and probably
feared that I would amount to nothing,
that you may have betrayed a friend or two,
that you voted for the wrong president,
that you really would have liked to have had more money,
that you had dreams you never realized?

Oh, my father,
Why didn't you open your real heart when I was looking?
Why did you only speak to me of facts and opinions
When I needed to know that it was OK to feel?

Why, my father, did you never tell me
that you were sometimes so crushed that you wanted to
run away,
that you knew terrible disappointment when people let
you down,
that you may even have gotten mad at God once or
twice,
that you grieved because you didn't know your father
either,
that you tasted the anguish of loneliness and wished for a
friend . . . or two,
and that you may even have doubted your own manhood
now and then?

Why didn't you open your real heart when I was looking,
Oh my beloved dad?
Why did you only show me a caricature of a man that
probably doesn't exist? Not in you, anyway, and not
in me.
I needed some open heart, to know that it was OK to
stumble, to sometimes retrace my steps, to fail, and
to cry.
Why, my father, did you never tell me that being a man is
plain, pure, hard work?

This latter desire may be more than a father can give. Perhaps there
is a lingering division between them as they both harbor a need for the
mother's/wife's affections. More than a few students of human behavior
believe in this possibility. At levels of consciousness about which most
of us know nothing there may be competitive dramas that are played out

at a furious rate: the father wanting the space in the mother's arms that the son took for himself at birth; the son always jealously guarding his right and desire to return to his mother's arms whenever he wishes. Think about it.

For this reason there may be a bad habit arising from a tension within the relationship of father and son from the very beginning. It may be that a dark part of the father's soul never really wants his son to be a man in fear that he, the father, might be supplanted prematurely. And the son may try to prove from the outset that he is a man to gain his mother's further affections.

Second, *a son seeks from his father three assurances: that he, the son, belongs, that he is valued, and that he is competent.* Some have observed that these are the most important messages a father ever gives to his son.

The words that came to Jesus both at the banks of the Jordan and on the mountain in the mysterious scene called Transfiguration echo these three messages: "This is My Son" (belonging), "I am pleased with Him" (value), and "Listen to Him" (competence).

One is tempted to say that these messages are most frequently heard from mothers, less frequently from a lot of fathers. My thought is that a father must be more deliberate, more intentional about extending these assurances. And he must be careful to repeat his affirmations with frequency.

Third, *a son seeks a father who can help him calibrate his feelings, formulate his responses to situations, and control his appetites and passions.*

Feelings are the mysterious "gauges" given to us that monitor our deeper reactions to circumstances about us. For centuries, culture has required of men that they assume the warrior role in the village. And among the very first things that warriors have learned is the importance of disguising feelings, the feeling of pain, for example. From the physical feeling of pain to the emotional feelings of psychic pain, the warrior learns to hide it all lest the enemy gain an advantage.

Feelings need to be calibrated in our youth. And when they're not, they betray us for the rest of our lives. Anger is, of course, the most obvious of the feelings. A boy looks to his father to understand when anger should be expressed and in what quantities. If he never sees his father deal with anger, or on the other hand, he sees his father angry all the time, he is left guessing about the appropriateness of anger and ends up never knowing how to express it.

Side by side with his father, a boy learns when, how, and how much anger should be acknowledged. He learns the true meaning of sadness or joy, how to laugh, and when it may even be permissible to cry.

From his father, he learns a score of ways to operate in various situations where quick-wittedness is required. From one circumstance after another, he extracts principles that he can apply to experiences in his future.

You know that this principle is in motion when, in the midst of a troubleshooting conversation, someone tells a Dad-story: "I recall that my father was faced with similar information and he . . ."

A father also goes beyond this to demonstrate how a man controls his passions. He models that there is a time to fight, a time to retreat. A time to rest, a time to work. A time to be tender and forgiving, a time to discipline or seek justice. From the father, a boy learns how to treat the weak, how to protect the vulnerable, when to be generous, how to accept defeat, and how to be magnanimous in victory.

Fourth, when a son reaches out to partake of the phallic-love of his father, *he is asking for enlightenment when it comes to matters of belief.* What is his father's guiding star? What is the nature of his faith? From what sources does he draw his underlying principles for loving?

Rarely has a father ever had his son come to him and ask such a question. But the question is nevertheless being asked in a variety of ways. Sons are watching, always watching, always stuffing deep into the memory bank how their fathers react to one circumstance after another. And in each case the son extrapolates one more sense of understanding of what his father truly believes.

In *Beginning to Pray,* Anthony Bloom writes,

> I remember a certain number of [my father's] phrases. In fact there are two things he said which impressed me and have stayed with me all my life. One is about life. I remember he said to me after a holiday, "I worried about you" and I said, "Did you think I'd had an accident?" He said, "That would have meant nothing, even if you had been killed. I thought you had lost your integrity." Then on another occasion he said to me, "Always remember that whether you are alive or dead matters nothing. What matters is what you live for and what you are prepared to die for." These things were the background of my early education and show the sense of life I got from him.

A popular Norman Rockwell painting shows a mother, her son, and her daughter leaving the home for church services. Hidden, scrunched down in an easy chair is the father still in his bathrobe reading the morning paper. The mother's posture is stiff; her face signals strong disapproval of her husband's choice. The daughter follows the mother, her nose somewhat skyward. But the son is clearly torn. Trapped by his mother's womb-love, he must follow her to church. But all of his body language reveals where his heart is: it is with his father in that chair. If Dad doesn't have to go, why should I go? his face clearly shouts.

There is more to this picture than meets the eye. The boy has taken the measure of his father's view of faith. And unfortunately, he finds it more attractive than what his mother discloses to him. You know instinctively that there will not be many more Sundays before the son will be alongside his father reading the paper, watching the game on television, sleeping in.

A son seeks two other things from his father when he moves from the safety of womb-love to the risk of phallic-love.

He needs his father to introduce him to the "men of the village," his father's friends. These men will ultimately convey to the boy the full and unequivocating word: *you are one of us, you are a man.*

Among the hidden sadnesses of contemporary life is that many boys have little or no opportunity to connect with a multiple of male adults. And in the growing number of single-parent families, more than a few boys are left with no opportunity for connection with any men of any kind.

The men of the village have always been a diverse collection of every kind of man with every kind of weakness. Individually, few of them were impressive. Collectively, the men of the village offered a picture of manhood's great potential. As a boy lived and worked among the men of the village, he came to understand the possibilities of male strength and vitality.

I have memories of the last vestiges of this when I was a boy. There were the men who lived in the neighborhood and who lived there throughout my boyhood. One of them had a huge temper that exploded every time we boys ran across his lawn. But he could be warm and friendly on other occasions when his lawn wasn't being violated. Another neighbor had a huge motorcycle that he was always repairing. We boys stood in a sort of religious awe as he pulled it apart and put it back together again. And then we would step aside as he stomped down on the starter pedal. It always roared into life, and we were moved that he should be so smart as to make the motorcycle run.

Another neighbor loved to throw the ball with us and seemed to have more athletic skill in his little finger than all of the rest of us combined. It seemed that he would stand out in the vacant lot forever and pitch balls to us would-be home run hitters. And every ball came over the plate.

Another man was a storyteller; still another, a carpenter and brick layer. There were men who made us laugh, who knew how to do magic tricks, who knew how to wrestle with us, make tree houses, and take us on hikes. They were the men of the village. Collectively, we learned from them something of what a man was supposed to look like.

A father introduces his boy to the men of the village. He himself is one of them. And together they make it possible for little boys to acquire the instincts and perspectives that make them men.

Author Gordon Dalbey recalls the boyhood days when his father took him to the barbershop for haircuts. There came the day, he recounts, when his father and the barber decided that he no longer had to sit in the junior barber chair. There was a "coming out" of sorts in the symbolic moment. Gordon was on his way to manhood.

My memorable experience came later in life, at the age of twelve. My father and his friends planned a hunting trip to the eastern plains of Colorado in the middle of winter. In those days, the ranchers had a serious problem with an infestation of huge jackrabbits, and they welcomed hunters who would reduce the population. My father took me on the trip. I shall never forget how he placed a .22 caliber rifle in my hands and instructed me in its use. I spent the day with the men.

I do not think there has ever been a day in my life when I wished more for the sun not to set. My father had welcomed me to the company of the men, and like one of them, I carried my own rifle and hunted for my own game. As I look back on that day, I think it is safe to say that my life began to irrevocably change from that day. That morning I awoke perceiving myself to be a boy; that night I went to bed with the first feelings of manhood.

Finally, a father vindicates his son's decision to make the leap toward phallic-love when, having equipped him with all of the foregoing, *he releases him to his place in the larger world.*

This process of release is often jagged, fraught with turbulent feelings. Perhaps it happens smoothly for some, a mere instant in time. For other fathers and sons it may take a while. Maybe the truth is that a man has to have gone through it before he knows what it means to him.

My son, Mark, may see it differently, but for me the drama of this release event was clearly in evidence in our world the day the family began the long Massachusetts-to-Illinois drive so that he could begin his college experience.

For Mark this was a big moment. To use an old proverb: we had given him roots for eighteen years; now it was time for him to officially don his wings. He couldn't wait to get going. But his father? Deep down inside of myself (beneath all of the protests of joy and pride), I found this moment hard to accept. I felt as if I were losing my son, and it didn't feel good.

Years earlier I'd been invited to send Mark away to a fine prep school. At the time his mother and I had declined, and I had said, "Mark and I are too close to say good-bye now. We need one another, and I don't think I'm prepared to part with him until it's absolutely necessary." Now, a few years later, the "absolutely necessary" had arrived.

Because Mark and I had enjoyed such a smooth relationship all the way through his teen years, I was befuddled as to why we suddenly had trouble getting this trip to Illinois under way. He and I argued over how the car should be packed and when we should leave. Once the trip was under way, I found myself irritated at his driving habits. He was driving too fast, I said; then he was driving too slow. I told him he was making turns too sharply, that the trunk on the top of the car would fall off. It seemed as if no subject of conversation between us was without its disagreements. I was all over him. Bottom line: I found Mark hard to like for the hours of that interminable journey. He was leaving me, and I was angry at levels of my inner being that even I could not locate.

These were not the prevailing moods of a father who dearly loved his son, who had often stood on the sidelines cheering his every move in athletic contests, who had taught him to drive, who had spent countless hours in the kind of soul-level conversations that can only be called precious. Was this incessant carping coming from the same father who would battle to keep back the tears each time he would pass his son's empty bedroom back home?

What was happening? What had changed? The boy was passing out of my direct influence and beginning his passage into the larger world of other influences and choices. For him it was a beginning; for me it was an ending. There is nothing easy about that transformation. The words on a father's lips may acclaim the moment, but inside, his heart just may be broken. In the turbulence of my inner struggle, I was taking my feelings out on him. Maybe when I criticized his driving, I was trying to prove to him in small ways that he couldn't get along without me. And maybe when he found creative ways to defy me, he was trying to suggest that he was going to do it his way because he was capable and, well . . . he was going to do it his way anyway.

We quickly got over those horrid moments. Soon the adjustments to the relationship were in place. Today Mark is not just my son; he is my friend. I am not just his father; I am his friend. What we have today began on that awful trip. Only when Mark someday releases his son, Ryan, to the larger world, will he know what those moments cost me.

Having traced the steps of potential bondedness between a father and a son, I cannot go further without commenting upon one more aspect of that relationship. I'm thinking of the possibility that one day a son may have to become his father's "father."

In one of the most poignant stories I have ever read, novelist Philip Roth writes in *Patrimony* of the time when he had to help his father walk toward death through cancer. His feisty father had always been an independent, no-nonsense man. But he was growing weaker, and much against his lifelong instincts, he had to look to his son for strength and discernment.

Perhaps the peak moment of their story together came the night Philip Roth's father, in his illness, lost control of his bowels in the upstairs bathroom of their home. Excrement was everywhere, Roth writes.

> I smelled the [expletive deleted] halfway up the stairs to the second floor. When I got to his bathroom, the door was ajar, and on the floor of the corridor outside the bathroom were his dungarees and his undershorts. Standing inside the bathroom door was my father, completely naked, just out of the shower and dripping wet. The smell was overwhelming.
>
> At the sight of me he came close to bursting into tears. In a voice as forlorn as any I had ever heard, from him or anyone, he told me what it hadn't been difficult to surmise. "I beshat myself," he said.

It became Philip Roth's task to put his father to bed and to return to the bathroom to clean up the mess. ("It's okay," I said, "it's okay, everything is going to be okay.") And when he had finished his odious chore, he returned to check on his sleeping father.

> I felt awful about his heroic, hapless struggle to cleanse himself before I had got up to the bathroom and about the shame of it, the disgrace he felt himself to be, and yet now that it was over and he was so deep in sleep, I thought I couldn't have asked anything more for myself before he died—this, too, was right and as it should be. You clean up your father's [expletive deleted] because it has to be cleaned up, but in the

aftermath of cleaning it up, everything that's there to feel is felt as it never was before. It wasn't the first time that I'd understood this either: once you sidestep disgust and ignore nausea and plunge past those phobias that are fortified like taboos, there's an awful lot of life to cherish.

What of this moment? Many of us may never have the privilege of serving our fathers. Their passing from us may be sudden. Or perhaps we have fathers who are too proud to be served in their weakness. Or perhaps there is distance in the relationship to such an extent that the father would never permit his son to know that he was needed.

Returning to biblical times, we read of the intimacy between Jacob and his son, Joseph of Egypt. Separated for many years, they had been reunited through the effects of a terrible famine.

There came the day when the father grew ill. "Your father is ill," Joseph was told, and he took his two sons and rushed to his father's side (Gen. 48:1).

"When Jacob was told, 'Your son Joseph has come to you,' Israel [or Jacob] rallied his strength and sat up on the bed" (Gen. 48:2). Apparently, sons can have these effects upon their fathers in such a moment. There was a time of blessing as Jacob blessed both his son and then his grandsons.

> When Jacob had finished giving instructions to his sons, he drew his feet up into the bed, breathed his last and was gathered to his people (Gen. 49:33).

There was an explosion of grief.

> Joseph threw himself upon his father and wept over him and kissed him. Then Joseph directed the physicians in his service to embalm his father Israel. So the physicians embalmed him, taking a full forty days, for that was the time required for embalming. And the Egyptians mourned for him seventy days (Gen. 50:1–3).

Following the ceremonies, it was Joseph's task to bury his father, and he carried out the task in keeping with every detail of instruction his father had given him (Gen. 50:7–14).

Such is the privilege of a son who loves his father. The bond has been complete. He who has given life, who has walked his son through life, given him the energy to grow, introduced him to the men of the village, offered the way to the fullness of manhood, now receives his reward.

.His son walks with him into eternity. Blessed are both. And men wish for such a privilege in their private thoughts.

When I give talks to groups of men and speak of these things, two questions are always asked. Here are samples:

- I'm forty. My father and I have never shared the relationship you've described, and it's been a source of sadness all my life. Is there anything I can do to get my father to see what I wish existed between us?
- I have two sons, and I have this feeling that I'm not giving them the things you describe. What do I do?

These are big questions, and I always admire the fortitude of the man who stands up and asks one of them.

To the first, I find myself saying: a lot of us—perhaps the majority of us—have longed for a more intimate relationship with our fathers. But if you're forty (or whatever), you may have to accept the possibility that the relationship may never be the way you want it. We return to our fathers again and again, hoping that this will be the time when something special ignites between us. Frequently, we go away disappointed. Our fathers did not perform . . . on our terms.

Many of us have fathers who had to deal with their own "baggage" in life and came into adulthood unequipped to open their hearts to their sons in a way that would have been nurturing to both. They have not purposely hurt us, nor have they been totally aware of the effects of their actions.

Even if they never ask for it, our fathers need our forgiveness when they have failed to come close, when they have missed the opportunity to send the belonging-value-competence message. Concentrate on the effort to forgive, and you will discover that your own heart loses its capacity to be resentful or angry.

Then *keep on going back* even if there is another chapter of disappointment. *Keep going back!* Who knows what will happen?

To the second question, I often say: It's never too late to begin to build bridges to your sons. The longer you wait, however, the harder it becomes. Your sons are not as likely to respond to words as they are to actions. It is in the doing of things together that we create the proper ambience for conversation. It is in the mutuality of experiences that we suddenly find the moment in which an exchange of impressions is possible.

A boy wants to know how his father feels, where his father struggles, and what his father thinks is important. Most of all, a boy wants to know that he creates a healthy pride in his father's heart. Find a way to convey that sort of stuff to your son, and some barriers will fall . . . real quick.

"'Tis a mystery," the poet might say, this strange relationship between fathers and sons. And a mystery I believe it is. It is a wave of attachment that flows back and forth at levels within us that none of us can understand or define. If that mysterious attachment were not there, we would not long for it so greatly. We would not react with such feeling when it isn't. The man who is the most needy is the one who has stopped caring whether it is there or not.

So we go through life telling our Dad-stories. They dominate our private thoughts.

CHAPTER 6

THE AWKARDNESS OF FEELINGS

When men think private thoughts, they often deal with strange sensations that come from deep within. They are sensations of the heart. Samples are joy, sadness, anger, disappointment, fear, fondness, passion. But of all the things found in the archives of private thoughts, feelings may be the least understood, the least mentioned. Why? Perhaps because somewhere along the line, most of us have been told the sensations of the heart are not to be trusted, not to be acknowledged, not to be seen as part of masculine character.

A man writes,

> Two days before my fiftieth birthday I had a heart attack. It was a most surprising random act of kindness. I had lived the previous thirty years of my life as a powerful, successful, and amazingly productive man. I had also lived so cut off from my emotions that I couldn't even fathom what the whole fuss about feelings was all about. I had worn out the efforts of three good women, took pride in my unfeeling logic, denied that there was anything wrong or missing in my life, and was prepared to march stubbornly forward.
>
> Until I was felled and terrified by my own heart. That experience unlocked a lifetime of buried emotions. So, without knowing it, when the doctors revived me, they delivered me to a life full and more beautiful than I had ever imagined.

Among my boyhood memories are times when my father and a few of his men friends went to minor league hockey games and invited me along. To be included in the company of the men was a pleasure. But the pleasure sometimes was diminished by what happened once we were at the game.

At the ticket booth, the preference of the men was for seats behind whatever goal the visiting team would defend for two of the game's three periods. It became my perception (and I stress *perception*) that the seats were sought because they provided an opportunity to taunt the visiting goaltender, to see if he could be distracted from his game. And the baiting of the man in pads could be merciless.

My father and his friends never knew that I had no enthusiasm for the effort. It was not unusual for me to become somewhat emotionally involved and silently protective of the goaltender if I thought he was being treated inhospitably. And, as I said, that seemed to be what was happening. I visualized myself in the goalie's skates, hearing the hooting and gibes coming from the stands. If he allowed a goal, the crowd went berserk, and if possible, the derision worsened after that.

Sitting there I often felt sick inside, taking the ridicule personally, identifying with what seemed to me to be the total humiliation of a lonely man on the ice far from home. Although they embarrassed me, those boyhood feelings were real; I could not escape them. And I still recall them forty-five years later.

What fascinates me today as I relive those moments is how hard I had to work to conceal such feelings of sympathy. And why was it necessary? I suspect it had to do with the growing realization that boys and men were not supposed to deal in sentiment, to worry about how an opponent might feel. I think it had to do with my confusion over what was going on deep within me and how I was supposed to behave in public.

What the hometown crowd did behind the visitor's goal probably happened every night in every hockey arena. The catcalls of the crowd that strongly repelled me were part of the game, people said. But I wasn't persuaded. How often I yearned to stand up and shout, "Stop it! The man is doing his best. Get off his back! I'd like to see if you can do any better! Can't you see how bad he feels, how lonely he is?"

But I could not do it. Because boys and men didn't act that way, I assumed (and assumed wrongly). Furthermore, I couldn't surface my thoughts to my father because I was sure that he would be disappointed in me, that he would feel somehow that I was out of step with how real men thought about and did things. And, of course, such transparency might ensure that I would not be invited to the next game.

So I never told anyone that the mocking of the visiting goalie hurt me far more than it must have hurt him. Chances are that he heard far worse in other arenas night after night. For me, the only choice was to fake it, to conceal the perspective of my heart, to join in expressing a passion I really didn't feel. Perhaps a more courageous boy would have done differently.

AT HEART-LEVEL

Maybe you've also tried it, this disguising of real feelings. If so, you probably also know what it's like to curse the involuntary attitudes of sympathy wishing that you weren't saddled with such uncontrollable sensitivities. And you are likely aware as to how one feigns excitement when a hometown goal is scored, even though you're inwardly distressed and would almost prefer that you and your people lose rather than see a stranger feel so bad.

Today, the very sensitivity that caused me discomfort at an occasional hockey game—the aptitude to hone in on the struggles, the feelings, and the inner dramas of people—plays an important role in my life as a pastor. Not just to read the feelings of others, but to respond in kind on a feelings-level. A person insensitive to the feelings of others and unable to express his own feelings could not (and should not) do my job.

At issue here is the *heart,* a word I shall use in this chapter to describe the inner or personal world that each of us possesses and that is hidden, off limits, from the view of others until we choose to reveal it (sometimes, we discover, to our disadvantage). Much of what goes on in the heart is wordless. You can tell people what you're thinking at mind-level if you wish, but describing events at heart-level is another, far more personal story.

At heart-level we're dealing with emotions, feelings, fantasies, attitudes, and fears. And this short list is just the beginning. Much of it cannot be explained or defended. It is just us, a massive part of us, similar to the much larger but unseen underwater segment of an iceberg.

When the personal side of our world can get a message to us, it usually does so in the form of these feelings, moods, impulses, and passions. All these words are close to being synonymous. But each stands for a slightly differing experience as the world within each of us attempts to make itself known in the world beyond us. When the heart is permitted to speak, these are some of its languages.

It is my opinion that much of this personal world is initially shaped and heavily influenced by the womb-love that first marked our lives. A large part of what is in the heart can be called—as do many students of personality—our feminine side. Thus, the question of the moment for a man might be, How do I coexist with this personal world, the heart, if a large part of its activity is more representative of a feminine view of reality than a masculine view?

Answer: the strategy many men seem to have selected is to try *not* to coexist with it. What are some versions of this? A man refuses to respond to the signals of the heart, even to acknowledge the heart's existence. He locks much of this part of his personal world in the basements of life where no one can ever see it. And if he is good enough in doing this, even he may never have to see or deal with it.

Some men are very successful at this. They jam the signals of the heart with an overload of macho. Deny the pain; mock the feelings; squelch the impulses; reject the moods. Talk tough; swagger; deny softness; never cry! Language like this instantly suggests the stereotypical man on horseback, the rough rider of yesteryear. Nowadays these kinds are found in the marketplace, in bars, in traffic, and in church. They are illustrated best by the boxer who is walloped by a roundhouse punch to the jaw, who stands there dazed, in pain, out on his feet. But rather than drop to the canvas and acknowledge that he is beaten, he manages a smile and mutters, "Is that your best punch?"

In a feedback session at our First Monday events, a man reminisces,

> Do you remember those moments when you were just a kid and something happened that was terribly disappointing for you? Holding back the tears was virtually impossible. So you're standing there, you have your face as tight as you can make it so that no tears will show. But it isn't good enough, and you start crying. And your father shouts at you, "Stop crying. If you don't, I'll give you something to cry about. You're nothing but a crybaby!"
>
> I hear those words—"you're nothing but a crybaby!"—every time I feel any kind of emotion coming up from within.

In each of our cars is something we call a dashboard that includes a handful of gauges and "idiot lights" to inform us of the condition of the car under the hood and on the road. If we want our cars to be reliable, we learn to periodically check the temperature and oil gauges. If we want to make sure we'll reach our destination, we keep an eye on the fuel gauge. And if we want to comply with traffic laws, we consistently note the speedometer.

Based on this, let me engage in some foolish illustrations to make one point. Suppose someone challenges me to a race while we sit side by side at a red light. The speed limit is thirty, but I soon reach sixty. I've chosen to ignore the message of the speedometer because I want to prove that my car is superior to the one driven by the other driver.

Or suppose I am in a hurry to reach my destination and conclude that I do not have time to fill the car with fuel even though the needle on the fuel gauge hovers close to "E." I overlook the warning and press on. Depending on how far I have to go, I may or may not be in trouble.

Finally, pretend that I am driving through the night and the temperature light comes on, informing me that the engine is heating up. I am irritated by its glow, so I reach behind the dashboard and pull out the wire that connects the light to the engine. It goes out; I am no longer upset, and I drive on blissfully. For just a few more miles.

In these silly imaginations, I have tried to observe what happens when the boy/man who lives in a public world shaped by the expectations of the men of the village decides that he will ignore or reject the signals that come from the personal world within. Feelings, moods, impulses, and passions are something like gauges and idiot lights. Each is meant to be an indicator of a good or bad condition within us that defies easy definition.

I am convinced that 95 percent (a sheer guess) of what we are within is unknown to us. There are the realities that lie deep beneath the trapdoor of our minds. These realities have a life of their own, and they send up signals from time to time.

We feel anxious, but we do not know why. We are overtaken with a sense of sadness, but we have no idea of the mood's source. We have an awareness of well-being, of happiness. Why?

To be sure, signals from heart-level can prove to be unreliable, misleading, false. On other occasions they can come upon us, have no explainable origin. But the better and more frequent possibility is that the heart discerns things the mind cannot yet fathom. Like a mysterious control center, the heart calls to us as it processes reality in a far deeper way than we can ever imagine. Perhaps it speaks under the convictions planted there by God in creation, from stories heard and principles learned that have been filed away for this very moment.

Perhaps the heart conveys to us the voices of our father and our father's fathers: their pain, their dreams, their accumulated insights. The heart remembers many things we seem to have otherwise forgotten. Strangest of all, it is possible that the heart monitors the signals of other hearts, which could explain why we're drawn to some people and repelled by others without fully knowing why. The heart warns, encourages, cajoles, provokes.

KINDS OF FEELINGS

When you start listing the various feelings, moods, impulses, and passions any human being may have from the heart and other interior sources, you have a challenge on your hands. A sweep of all the possible feelings we can have from any source might include the following.

There are physical feelings: some that come to mind are various forms of pain (ache, sharp pain, burn, and dull throb), pleasurable sexual feelings, fatigue, and hunger. Each of them calls for a response. Not to have each of these feelings suggests a numbness or state of anesthesia, which is not always the healthiest thing.

We are accustomed not only to responding to these feelings but also to resisting them at times. Years ago Korean War negotiators told of long, long hours of discussion with their North Korean adversaries in which neither side dared to interrupt the meeting to withdraw to the bathroom. I'm not sure who defined the rules, but leaving the table to respond to this thoroughly natural impulse or feeling would have been interpreted as a sign of weakness. Recalling the experience, negotiators said that sometimes the pain of resisting that normal urge was close to unbearable. We've all known similar experiences, I suppose. On teenage dates, during a long sermon, in a traffic jam.

In sports we understand what is meant by the phrase "playing hurt." It means an athlete wants to win so badly that he is willing to ignore the pain that tells him a bone is cracked, a ligament has been torn, or a joint has been hyperextended. Or we speak of crashing through the pain ceiling to levels of performance that break world records.

There are moods or emotions: rage or anger, sadness, ecstasy, and fear.

My memory stores the picture of the face of an Ethiopian father as he watched his children dying of starvation and knew that he was helpless to do anything on their behalf. I was there; I saw despondency conveyed through the eyes in a way that needed no spoken language. He was not trying to hide a thing in his private agony. But then in contrast, there is the impassive face of a movie star when he learns that a rival has won the Oscar. He sits in his seat with a smile on his face, clapping appropriately. But inside there are feelings—disappointment? rage?—that are being stuffed, denied, and not revealed.

There are psychospiritual feelings: loneliness, emptiness, guilt, restlessness, a sense of helplessness, or contentment (it doesn't get any better than this, we say). A strange malaise overtakes the mind. Things that once were challenging, fun, or confidence building suddenly lose their positive impact; there is a growing desire simply to walk away from everything.

Or sometimes we speak of the "spark" that seems to be missing. It may be that one is quietly sensing the emergent competition of a new, younger (maybe smarter?) generation. Or the constant demands of cultural change become overwhelming. All we know is that it becomes harder to get out of bed in the morning, to develop the appropriate excitement over new opportunities, to join in the anticipation when someone in the organization lays down the challenge of a new goal.

There are also passions that reflect the state of our connection or relationship with another person: romantic feelings, hostility, pity and sympathy, admiration, disgust, jealousy, protectiveness, rapture.

What causes strong reaction and response within us when we learn of the family with a child who has leukemia? Suddenly, we find ourselves driven to make a contribution, pray, offer ourselves for a bone-marrow experiment. Or, and this is the opposite, we find ourselves living in the city and quite able to filter out all the sights of homeless people who stand on almost every corner with cups. We've quenched our sense of compassion with the rationale that they'll spend it on drugs or booze, that we're just encouraging indigence, and that we can't give to everyone. And our feelings of compassion are stilled. It's strange how it can work both ways.

How about impulses that reflect our social attitudes? A patriotic feeling of belonging when the national anthem is played, agitation, a strong urge to make great sacrifices when something or someone is in danger. The enthusiasm felt at a game when your team is winning a close one (and no one is riding the visiting goaltender).

I still remember my emotional euphoria when Whitney Houston sang the national anthem at the Orange Bowl game a few years ago. Her enthusiasm and vibrancy put an old, familiar—not especially good music—song across and captured the emotions of millions of people, including me.

Admiration and rapture characterize the words of a young father who opens his heart to a group of men at First Monday:

Last week I stood by my wife as she gave birth to our little boy. I've never felt the way I did that night. Watching her go through all that pain, all that pushing. All I could do was keep encouraging her, but I kept thinking that if it were me in that bed, I'd have given up. [He pauses, then starts to shake. Tears appear.] And . . . then . . . there was one final push, and the doctor said, "He's here!" And suddenly . . . we were . . . looking . . . at our son. [Now the tears run, unrestrained, down his cheeks.] I'm sorry to be crying, but that's got to be the greatest moment in my life.

Everybody claps.

As I review these indicators of the heart, I realize each time how fluid are the words, and how easy it would be to reshuffle many of them into other differing lists. That's because the words themselves are so inexact. And the inexactness should not be surprising because, as I've already said, it reflects realities going on deep inside us that are not always measured in rational terms.

One cannot measure or weigh, for example, what fear really is. One only knows when the feeling of fear announces its presence that something at soul-level senses danger, rightly or wrongly, and it counsels caution or prevention.

I have slowly and deliberately proceeded along this line of thinking to make this central point. That this entire range of responses and reactions is as important to healthy living as gauges and idiot lights are to the proper maintenance of an automobile.

But to a considerable extent, we men have trained ourselves (and expected of each other) that we will live as if these indicators make no difference whatsoever. We will not let them control us because many of them echo the messages we heard from our mothers: the messages of caution, of protectiveness, of minimizing risk. They are the messages of womb-love, and they do not belong in a world dominated by phallic-love or phallic energy. At least that is what a boy hears from most of the men of the village.

If a man finds himself dealing with the messages of the heart, he will most likely admit it to no one else. He may not even admit it or "discuss" it with himself. And if he does this long enough, most (if not all) of his inner message-centers will shut down, refuse to operate. And then he has trouble.

Again, the athlete on the football field is a case in point. He seeks to win, to be a reliable member of his team. He likely cannot do this if he succumbs to inner messages that counsel preservation and safety, things he first learned in the embrace of womb-love. No, if he is to enter into conflict of the sort that football demands, he must make a calculation. How much risk of bodily injury can I manage, he asks himself, before I have created intolerable odds against myself? And having made that calculation, he will go onto the field with a determination to throw himself into every play, taking on players whose size and ability may be superior to his. This is the masculine side in operation.

Most of his original feelings will weigh in on the side of preservation and safety. Thus, if he has decided to take the risks, he does at least one of three things with his feelings. He ignores them. Or he "psychologizes" himself against them. We might call this "turning my feelings off." Or he encourages other emotions that will speak louder and overcome the messages of the former gauges (sometimes athletes speak of getting pumped up). Thus, he may generate enthusiasm in concert with his teammates at a pep rally. He may engage in head butts and shoving matches (something like a tribal dance where warriors show their teeth and grunt a lot) with other players to get the adrenaline running so that he is freed of nervousness and fear. In the end he's likely to do all three.

We are not strangers to the news that a star athlete is playing hurt. Injuries have been taped up; there have been shots of cortisone or even painkillers. Protective devices shield an injury. Men admire other men who play hurt, who do not complain or whine about their pain. And there's a certain nobility to the idea. But not if it makes a total mockery out of this most important human function: the messages of our hearts.

In modern society this tradition of being willing to play hurt is celebrated. Boys are encouraged not to cry when they bloody a knee, take a blow to the groin, lose a tooth. They are told to "be a man about it." Fight till you drop! Phrases like these and correlates of them quickly take root in a boy's mind. He concludes that feelings betray manhood; thus to be accepted as a man requires a stoic approach to life. Never reveal that you're hurt, that you're tired, that you fear failure, that you can't handle the job. And this message is usually fully delivered before a boy is five years of age. And the counter message (less heard today than in other times), that it is all right for girls to cry, reinforces it.

IMPLICATIONS OF IMPAIRED FEELINGS

Let's think through the implications of this. Our daughter, Kristen, was born with an impaired sense of smell. She was five or six years old before we put the facts together and realized this. It explained why, at the age of two and a half, she had picked up a bowl of whitened turpentine, thinking it to be milk, and began to drink. Only quick medical response saved her life or spared her from damage to the brain or the kidneys. On a few other occasions she made strange choices that didn't make sense to us until our discovery that she was walking through life without ever smelling anything.

Today as a wife and mother, Kristy must be extra cautious in her home. She could not smell smoke if something began to burn. We are all amused (and not a little envious) that she cannot smell her daughter's diaper when it is full. But then she cannot smell a rose or a barbecue or the freshness of the air after a cool rain, either.

My point: Kristy is making it through life quite well. But she lacks an important navigating instrument that most of us take for granted. That she does so well means that she has learned to compensate through the use of other senses that might not otherwise be so important to her.

In an even more significant sense, the full panoply of feelings, when inoperative, leaves a man seriously impaired to live healthfully and effectively. Even as I write this I think of a conversation I had in the last few days with a woman whose husband holds an extremely high-profile position in the world of business. His name would be known to much of the public if I mentioned it.

She speaks of the pressure he is under at his work. Every symptom of his behavior suggests fear that he is not making the grade, exhaustion because of inhuman demands, and rage because he is not in control of his life. But he cannot bring himself to deal with these realities. Like someone who is irritated by the message of the gauges and the idiot lights on the dashboard and pulls out the wires that connected them with the engine, he has turned off all of his feelings. He refuses to acknowledge their veracity. And now only one emotion is left: rage. His anger can erupt over the silliest issues while he can remain impassive over the most significant matters. And he doesn't understand, nor does he want to understand, what is going on in his inner world.

His emotional tachometer suggests that he is, as we say, "redlined." Engines burn out when the needle stays too long over the red line. So do human beings. And so will he.

We think that if we ignore or stuff down our feelings long enough, they will go away. Interestingly enough, it seems to happen. The anger, the anxiety, or the melancholy does indeed go away. But not into thin air. The feelings sink to the bottom of the inner life. There they get the same treatment a compactor gives to trash. They get pressed down with other feelings. They just lie there, sometimes for years.

And then they reemerge, often with a furor that is many times more powerful than was known originally. Many men have this experience at midlife. Someone has observed, "At midlife we begin to pay off our emotional debts," meaning that suppressed, compacted feelings have a way of making their message heard at a time in life when we no longer have the immense amount of energy we once had to keep things hidden and under control.

The anger once ignored now reappears in new situations. The fears once unresolved reappear as new and different adult fears. The resentments once unresolved rear back up and pick targets in a new generation of relationships. *Feelings do not go away; they must be dealt with, never suppressed or disregarded.*

When we have refused to face the message of our feelings, they exert themselves in other less-guarded situations. We find ourselves angry, for example, at other drivers in traffic who, unknowingly, have inconvenienced us. Why is our rage out of proportion with the event? Perhaps because we are venting rage at a stranger that we would not have permitted ourselves to show to a spouse, a friend, a boss.

Or sometimes our feelings insist on working out their energy through our physical systems. Ulcers, heart disease, and headaches are pet ways that neglected feelings wreak vengeance upon us. It is the spiritual part of us saying, "I will not be ignored. The energy of the feeling has to go somewhere."

A third way in which neglected feelings express themselves is by shutting down one's personal life system. Call it depression. As I look about me, I think I see a large percentage of men who are living in mild depression. They are numb to much of what is going on in life. They have surrendered the initiative, and they merely respond to the overtures of people about them. They give up trying new things. Things they'd once dreamed about doing are no longer worth the effort. They lose interest in growth or self-improvement.

Robert Kipness speaks in *Knights Without Armor* of this kind of numbness and quotes a friend: "When I came home from work I didn't even want to talk to my family anymore. I headed for the icebox for a beer and the den for the tube . . . I love my wife and adore my little girl. What the [expletive deleted] happened to me that turned me into a dynamo at work and a zombie at home?"

Kipness, writing about men and their feelings, also observes that men who renounce listening to their feelings often end up responding to the feelings of others as a result. They may take their cues from their spouses, if married, and act in whatever way is appropriate based on the emotional structure of the other person. She is down; he is down. At work, they may take on the feelings and emotional structure of a boss or a colleague.

Let's go back to dashboard gauges. While driving in my younger days, I may have had a habit of reaching slightly excessive speeds on occasion. My wife, Gail, would eye the speedometer (one of those gauges), and she would comment on my lawlessness. Since it hasn't happened for a long time, I will now reveal that occasionally I would slip my hand to the switch that darkened the dashboard. She was unable to see what the speedometer indicated, and the darkness of the dashboard might take her mind off such a concern.

But often she would catch on, and with a firm voice she would say, "Turn the light on. Let's both see what speed you're driving at."

Now there's a thought for men who have struggled all of their lives with the matter of feelings. Turn the lights on! See where you're headed, at what speed, and how things are going under the hood.

DEALING WITH FEELINGS

That means, first of all, that you make the monitoring of your feelings a priority in the development of your inner life. *What are the feelings stored in the archives of your life?*

Each of us has an archive deep within us. On its shelves and in its drawers are the stories of a million past experiences. In the archives of many men are vast numbers of stories whose end has yet to be told. Each story lies like an open, discarded book. And the archive is a mess of uncataloged feelings and experiences as a result.

This is not an empty or meaningless metaphor for me. For the first twenty-five years of my life, I more or less determined that my feelings were unimportant. It was far more important to inquire of the feelings of others and take my cues from them. The good news is that I rarely offended anyone. I didn't disagree with anyone; I avoided harsh truths when they should have been spoken. I would go out of my way to assure someone else's happiness on just about anything, even if doing it made me unhappy. I built an ideology behind that behavior. I told myself that it was the Christian way, the way of love.

Well, it wasn't. And it wasn't until my wife, Gail, entered my life and challenged me to "down the periscope" that I found out what kinds of emotions were swirling that I'd refused to recognize. Each time the periscope went down, it found evidence of anger, disappointment, and maybe even some grief that had never been dealt with.

With the periscope down, I began to remember old stories that never seemed to have endings because I never gave myself the chance to resolve the events in the story and my part in them. And so I've learned to examine the stories of my life and bring each one to a proper resolution: to forgive where necessary; to give thanks where appropriate; to let some unresolved issues become buried in peace.

When we refuse to acknowledge our anger, it may ultimately rise up and betray us, laying the spiritual groundwork for bad choices, rebellious attitudes, patterns of resentment that neutralize us.

Second, *you learn to give names to your feelings*. In that story I was . . . ! And in this moment I am . . . ! Half the battle in dealing with your feelings is not being afraid to name what the message is.

I was taught from a score of sources that a Christian never became angry. So the rule by which I lived was to never show or admit to anger. What I did not know was that the anger was, nevertheless, there. It was deep in the archives, festering, seething, whether or not I chose to acknowledge it and name it.

Since the anger could not express itself in expected ways—sharp words, a raised voice, intense activity—it found other ways to get out. I discovered to my embarrassment that I'd acquired a withering glare. My facial expression said as much as words could ever had said. Sometimes in anger, I withdrew into silence and punished the other person by leaving her without a clue about what was wrong. I showed irritation at safe objects: the dog, an errant driver in traffic, a person on television—someone who would never know or never fight back.

What I and others have had to learn is how to say, "I am very angry about this. And here is why!"

You are not unwise to stop with reasonable frequency and ask yourself, What is the dominant feeling within me at this moment? Why is the enthusiasm I had this morning gone this afternoon? What troubles me about this decision? This person? What's at the root of my excitement, my impatience, my sense of being drawn to this or that person? What's behind the tightness in my stomach?

In the earliest paragraphs of Genesis, there is a frank conversation between Jehovah and Cain, the son of Adam. Cain is seething over the fact that God *appears* to favor his brother Abel's sacrifice over his own. And Jehovah asks: "Why are you angry? Why is your face downcast?" (Gen. 4:6).

The gauges on Cain's soul are working overtime. You could say that idiot lights are not only turning on; they are flashing strobelike. But Cain isn't interested. He chooses to defy his feelings by ignoring them and thus opening the door to destructive choices and behavior.

A third dimension may be that of learning to listen to the feelings of others. Too often the man who has stuffed his feelings for a lifetime makes the false assumption that no one else has feelings. It doesn't occur to him that people about him may be deeply disappointed, exorbitantly hopeful and full of anticipation, lonely and in need of a sensitive ear. But when he learns to ask the right questions, he may be surprised at how often he gets into the intimate settings of the lives of others. Settings he may not have known existed.

Some of us remember the wintry day when Senator Edmund Muskie stood on the steps of a newspaper building in Manchester, New Hampshire and protested the media's slanderous treatment of his wife. He was so intense in his remarks that he began to weep. Political pundits agreed that his tears cost him the nomination for the presidency of the United States. His expression of deep and genuine feelings became his downfall. And that was wrong. Where does a person speak out of his passion unless he is invited to do so?

Fourth, *men must learn to deal with their feelings appropriately.*

People who have organized their lives around the Bible feel that Jesus is the outstanding example of how this is done. They think they see a large array of feelings in the narratives of Jesus' life.

Jesus expressed tenderness as He engaged children, humiliated and beaten people, men who had embarrassed themselves in failure. He showed this to Thomas, the doubter, who simply couldn't go along with the rest of the group when word of the Resurrection had come to them. When Jesus appeared to Thomas, there was no berating him because of his reluctance. Thomas had said that he'd have to see nail marks in the hands of Jesus before he'd believe. And that was exactly what Jesus did. He played to the feelings and disposition of the man.

Jesus knew anger when He engaged self-righteous men who hid behind the banners of organized religion. His words were sharp and biting. They were designed to puncture hard-nosed men. And they did.

Jesus felt compassion. Seeing an enormous crowd that really represented an intrusion upon His privacy, He "was moved with compassion for them, because they were weary and scattered, like sheep having no shepherd" (Matt. 9:36 NKJV). The Lord is pictured by Matthew and Mark as well connected with the destitute nature of the crowd. Out of compassion He performed one of His most exquisite miracles, the multiplication of a single lunch into dinner for a crowd of five thousand.

Jesus was well versed with feelings of despair and anguish. Standing at the edge of the city of Jerusalem, He was sensitized to the evil gripping the city. His feelings rose to the surface and caused Him to cry out, "O Jerusalem, O Jerusalem . . ." The passion was a signal that the heart was in great disturbance. The feeling had to be expressed; it had to be vented.

And Jesus knew feelings of affection. I think we see that kind of feeling at the shoreline one morning when the Lord found His disciples exhausted after a night's fishing. He showed affection as a man of feeling would: He made them breakfast over a fire designed to both feed them and warm them.

I have known many men who have expressed strong feelings in a challenging moment. Healthy expressions of feeling? Not-so-healthy? Your call!

I have known, for example, a professional football player who played the game with such quality that he made the all-pro teams for several years in a row. I shall not forget the intensity with which he concentrated upon his preparation and with which he played. He knew how to take all the power of feelings and make them serve him.

I have known the feelings of an African-American man who expressed anger over the struggle of the black male in the urban community. One day, as he described the horror of watching one young black man after another die by bullets in the street, he buried his face in my shoulder and began to weep. Then he cried out, "My people are perishing; my people are perishing." I held him as he shook with the wrenching sobs that signaled the depth of his feelings.

I have memories of the grief of two brothers, farmers, who just an hour before had watched their aged father sink to the kitchen floor, instantly in the presence of God. As we sat together, the body of their dad lying covered on the couch in the living room, there was no need for tears. Sorrow of the deepest sort was quite apparent in the room. And it was being powerfully expressed. Then one said, "Dad died knowing that we loved him dearly. There were no unspoken things between us; no regrets. We can let him go." There was deep, deep feeling among men in that room.

I have known male passion for things righteous. A young evangelist sits across the table from me in a restaurant. He is exhausted from much traveling and putting his person and reputation on the line day after day on college campuses. He faces hecklers every day and takes them on. "What makes you do it?" I ask. His answer comes with a force, a power that is very emotional. "I hate sin; I hate it; I hate it," he says.

STILL OUT OF TOUCH?

Some years ago the auto manufacturers in America began to replace the gauges on the dashboard with what came to be called idiot lights. Oil pressure low? A red light came on. Temperature too high? Another red light. Red lights for serious problems; yellow ones for caution; and blue for things like high headlight beams. For a moment in time, the buying public thought the change was wonderful. The absence of old-fashioned gauges seemed to be another sign of modernity and technological progress.

But then people noticed that the sports cars had more gauges than ever. And so did the cockpits of airplanes. And space vehicles. And a lot of us began to feel left out. Gauges were a sign that we were in touch with the vehicle. Real men who drove sports cars and piloted planes had gauges. And before long, some started paying a premium price for cars with lots of gauges that gave more information about a car's performance than was really necessary.

We like the gauges because we feel we're part of a breed of people who want to be in maximum touch with the systems that make their cars go. Now if we could learn that same lesson about the feeling "systems" that the Creator gave to us. . . .

CHAPTER 7

THE SEARCH FOR FRIENDSHIPS

Intimacy includes the subject of friendships. In the storehouse of private thoughts that men think, you'll find a large area reserved for those times when a man asks: *Who are my friends?*

Questions like this begin to erupt when life becomes too heavy to be lived in perpetual aloneness. Who do I really know? What man in my world would take the time to hear me out if I had to talk about some heavy stuff? Who would come running to my side if I was in real trouble? Are there other men who see me as having something to offer or to give?

You ask these kinds of questions when you see a beer commercial on television that features a bunch of men camping, canoeing, or playing touch football together. When was the last time I laughed with a bunch of guys like that? Why don't I ever take the time anymore to just horse around? How did I ever get so isolated? (You also wonder about the sincerity of friendship when, in quest of a brew, a guy says, "I love you, man.")

Apparently enough men are having these kinds of thoughts that one Atlanta businessman thought he could make some money out of it. In a front-page story the *Wall Street Journal* notes:

> Atlanta: Mike Correll, a 54 year old entrepreneur, has built a healthy business here on a peculiar, if pragmatic, belief: Successful men have little time for making friends—but enough money to buy them.
>
> That's right; for a fee that runs as high as $1,200, Mr. Correll will go out and buy you a buddy. Not just any buddy; not *for* just any buddy. Rather, Mr. Correll specializes in the corner office: matching harried and

isolated male executives who claim they can't find the time to make close friends.

"It's tough to admit," says John Heagy, a local real-estate executive who hired Mr. Correll, "but men have a very difficult time establishing relationships with other men, other than for business reasons." He pauses and sighs, "It's not like the days at the fraternity."

TIES IN THE PAST

Most of us have recollections of splendid ties in the past. Experiences that welded two or more guys together, creating indelible memories. Moments of youthful craziness when we dared each other into "courageous" efforts. Remember boyhood exchanges similar to these?

Okay: when I set the bag of dog dirt on fire, you ring the doorbell; then, we run into those bushes. Old man Johnson comes out on the porch, sees the fire, and stomps on the bag.

Come on: just pick up the phone and call her; get it over with; you know she's going to say yes. What's the worst thing that can happen?

I was talking to my cousin, and he's going to leave school for a semester and backpack Europe. He's looking for a couple of guys to go with him, and I thought we . . .

I had great friendships as a boy. I can name at least a dozen best friends. And when I look at school pictures, for example, from the fifth and sixth grades, I am impressed with how many names I remember. Together as friends, we built forts, played baseball and football in the streets, and collected wire coat hangers so that we could resell them to the cleaners (five for a penny). We went off to camp together, conspired against parents, and exchanged scattered (and wildly inaccurate) pieces of intelligence about sex.

I also had many friends as a teenager. Together we hiked the Colorado Rockies, learned how to shoot rifles, and worked as grocery sackers in the supermarkets. We continued the summer camp routine; we kept conspiring against parents; we intensified our curiosity about sexual issues. A growing preoccupation with the world of girls altered the nature of our male friendships, of course, but they nevertheless remained strong.

There were also good friends during the college days (and probably would have been in the military if I'd enlisted). Together we went camping, played intercollegiate and intramural sports and, when not otherwise engaged, found work together on the truck docks in order to pay college expenses. Sexuality remained a major (no, dominating) topic of discussion as did the meaning of marriage, career, politics, and the uncertainties of a future that might end up in being drafted and shipped off to Vietnam. The friendships were powerful and supportive.

I took all this time and space to reminisce about my friendships as a boy, as a teenager, and as a young man because I wanted to say that something changed drastically when I married. Suddenly, it seemed as if male friendships (as I'd once known them) came to a screeching halt. Acquaintances? Men in the orbit of work, church, the neighborhood? Sure, many of those! But friendships as I'd once known them? No. Those seemed to end.

What I had never understood is something that could be called the doctrine of friendship: *friendships do not just happen. They are sought; they are developed; and they are maintained.* Friendships are not accidental; they are not self-perpetuating. They must be cultivated much as a plant is carefully developed from seed to blossom.

So what happened to many of my friendships? Looking back to my earliest married days, I realize that I was too busy developing a new kind of relationship with my wife, Gail: seeking to become the "perfect" (my tongue is in my cheek) husband. We would do everything together, we said, and in the midst of a busy life where time was scarce, priority choices were made to establish a good marriage. Whatever social time was left was invested in relationships that contributed to my work. Two children joined this marriage, and it was time to become the "perfect" (the tongue in check again) father. And like many men, I worked hard at that.

I was on the sidelines of each game in which our son or daughter played. I was there for recitals, dramas, and concerts. I made it to the parent-teacher conferences. I was home for dinner most nights. We worked hard at family time: recreational, spiritual, educational. I mean no arrogance when I say that I was there for our kids, and looking back, I have no regrets. But there was a cost, at least the way I was going about it. And the cost was the loss of good male friendships. In that department, I and a lot of guys just drifted apart.

It never occurred to me until much later in life that I may have made a serious error in judgment. That I could have been a better husband, a better father, a better man if I'd kept the old friendships alive. Or at least pursued new and fresh ones.

Carl Jung once wrote an essay, "The Noon of Life," in which he suggested that human personality reveals what he called masculine traits and feminine traits. The masculine traits, he noted, tend toward the functional—what we do. And almost all aspects of a man's life push him toward the strong expression of those traits. A man's sense of value, his identity, and his major choices all aim at accomplishing something.

But the feminine traits are relational, Jung further observed. Now we're talking about connection and nurture, sharing and supporting. One wonders how Jung would react to the new world in which we live. Would he be impressed with the fact that many women have begun to opt for the masculine side of human personality—accomplishments and function—at the expense of the feminine?

In his essay Jung went on to suggest that somewhere near the age of forty, what he called the "noon of life," a shift of perspective may begin to take place. The man who has worked hard to fulfill his masculine orientation (that is, *achievement*) becomes slowly aware of what might be called his missing feminine side *(relationship)*, and he begins to regret its absence in his life. The best word to describe this regret is *loneliness*.

Loneliness is expressed in the question, Who do I really know?

Pastor Mac, your talk last Monday on men and their friendships was a wake-up call. I've been married for eleven years, and I can't remember the last time I did anything with a friend. My best friends were on the swim team at A— College. For four years we worked out together almost every day of the week. We traveled to meets. We won and lost together, and that meant lots of excitement and lots of despair. We were there for each other when there were injuries, and we helped each other through difficult classes. There just wasn't anything we wouldn't have done for a teammate. Then one day it all ended. We graduated. It was kind of like a mass death. And aside from being in each other's weddings in the next few years, we hardly ever saw each other again. Like everyone else, I got married, started working, raising children. And just as you said, I never found another man (or men) where there could be a relationship like the ones at A——.

For all these years I've been disappointed in virtually every guy I met. It would be hard to guess how many times I found myself dreaming of getting in my car and going back to the campus with the hope that all the guys could meet and relive old times. Every time there's been an alumni weekend I've wanted to go. I think I was reaching backwards to the old days of great friendships. And now I realize that what I've been doing is comparing everyone to the kind of thing I had back at school.

Similar words could have been written by men who have looked back to a military experience or to any other period of life where men were forced by circumstance to work and live together. When ended, it is almost impossible to replicate at another stage of life. Unless we are determined to make it happen.

Friendship is a version of intimacy, but speak of it in such a context, and most of us immediately think of the male-female relationship. And we shouldn't. What we have failed to understand as men is that there is more than one kind of intimacy, that a cultural system has encouraged a breakdown of a key set of relationships that every man desperately needs. He needs friendships (deep and personal) with other men.

MALE FRIENDSHIPS ARE A REAL CHALLENGE!

Let me offer the speculation that our modern system of living has turned men into competitors. Because our sense of manhood has not been established through the traditional rites of initiation, we may somehow be tempted to establish our identity by proving that we are better than someone else. Subconsciously, we may see other men as the adversary.

This can lead to the logic that one does not share his private thoughts with anyone who might be able to use such data to his advantage. If, for example, I admit to fear, exhaustion, or ignorance, I offer a "competitor" a chance to get ahead. Something in my brain tells me to keep such information to myself.

As I've already commented, in my generation friendships became difficult to maintain because we saw marriage as a supreme and exclusive relationship. This may have been particularly true in the Christian community where interpretations of the Scripture often center on a nuclear family arrangement. Naively, many men, as they say, put all their eggs in one basket: the relationship with a woman. Without appreciating the implications, we saw our wives as the source of all the relational energy we would need. "My wife is my best friend," a man would say. And it sounded nice and proper.

But in making a wife into a best friend, we may have done both genders in a marriage a disservice. Perhaps it needs to be said that a woman cannot offer a man some things in a relationship. Just as a man cannot offer a woman everything she needs. Today, my wife, Gail, and I have no significant secrets from each other. But that does not mean she fully understands the way I think as a man. Nor does it mean that I fully appreciate how she feels about certain things as a woman.

Our marriage is not diminished by the fact that some male friends understand my male perspective better than she does. And I am not threatened by the fact that a few women appreciate Gail's female orientation better than I understand them.

When the Bible speaks of the family, it envisions something far different from what we know today. It sees the family more like a clan, a minitribe, made up of uncles and aunts, grandparents, cousins. Biblical families live in close proximity: the men and the women working, conversing, supporting one another. The marriage may be a centerpiece in the relationships of this extended family, but it is not *the* exclusive relationship that we have tended to make it into in our modern world.

Friendships among men become more difficult in an age when time is so scarce. Economic conditions seem to dictate that, in most families, both spouses must produce income. Men work longer hours, live with increased job pressures, feel the anxiety that their professional position is in constant jeopardy. The available hours for any kind of connection quickly diminish, and the choices of where to spend time become increasingly complex. Tell a man that he ought to take time for friendships under conditions like these, and he'll think that you're some kind of a nut.

So the point is fairly obvious: men do not have time to make the investment that friendships demand.

Ask men how they think they're doing in the pursuit of good friendships, and you'll hear comments like the following:

> Friendships? You can't be serious! I'm on the 7 A.M. American flight to Chicago every Monday morning. Home on Thursday night. Soccer leagues every Saturday morning. My wife expects some sort of time for the two of us Saturday night. You expect me to be in church on Sunday morning. And I spend Sunday evening getting ready for Monday morning. Tell me where friends fit in.

> I think friendships are essential. But have you ever tried making one? Call five guys—get four answering machines. Suggest a weekend in the White Mountains. You'll hear that no one can get away. Even try for a lunch, and you'll have to plan it three months in advance. I'm too tired for friendships. I'm working an average of two hours more every day (and earning less in buying power, by the way). It's not unusual to have to go in on Saturdays. Just getting a Monday evening when I can make it through

the football game before I fall asleep is a great luxury. I'd love to have some friends . . . maybe next year.

Perhaps friendships become a problem for a man if in his fast-track life, he begins to lose touch with his soul and his feelings. For the kind of relationship we're talking about calls for men to connect with each other at soul-level. Doing things may be a prelude to lasting friendships. But it is not enough. In the sharing of common meaning, the ability to speak of common goals and dreams, and the pursuit of a common spirituality, friendship begins to grow and become fruitful. In his autobiography, Albert Speer, Hitler's architect, wrote of the kind of relationship he and others had with the German dictator:

> I suppose if Adolf Hitler ever had a friend, I would have been that friend. Hitler could fascinate. He wallowed in his own charisma, but he could not respond to friendship. Instinctively, he repelled it. The normal sympathies that normal men and women enjoy were just not in him. At the core of the place where his heart should be, Hitler was a hollow man. He was empty. We, who were close to him, or thought we were, all came to sense this, however slowly. You couldn't even enjoy eating cherries with him. We were all of us simply projections of his gigantic ego.

I'm impressed with Speer's words; in an extreme situation they reveal something I think I've seen too often in the lives of ultra-busy, super-important men. There is no room for friendship when people choose to live this way.

But what if we discover that the most important reason many men struggle with the issue of friendship has something to do with the fact that we've never really thought through what genuine friendship looks like? In the turbulence of competition, in the grip of busyness and fatigue and in the pressure to concentrate solely on the building of a marriage and a family, what if we have simply *forgotten* what friendship is?

If I needed a reminder, it was offered to me the day I read the following on my computer screen as it flowed out of an Internet conference:

> Friday evening . . . my 8 year old son came to me and asked what cancer was. At this point my *Encyclopedia Britannica* paid for itself 10 times over. I sat him down, read and explained, and asked several times why he wanted to know. He would not tell me. Finally, I closed the book and told him I would not go on until he told me why.
> He then informed me that the friend in his class who had been out for

several weeks came back to school, and that he has cancer. He also told me that all the kids made fun of him because he had no hair. He said that he and one of the other boys were trying to be nice to this boy because he was their friend, and that they had decided to do something that would make the other kids stop teasing him.

When I asked him what they wanted to do, he informed me that they wanted to have their heads shaved so that they looked just like their friend with cancer. I was so touched by my son's show of empathy for a friend. I immediately got on the phone to the other boy's mother. She had just gone through the same conversation with her son.

Saturday morning we met at the barbershop and had both children's heads shaved. This morning we both got phone calls from the school commending our children for showing such unselfish and caring feelings toward another child, and they were both going to be rewarded for their heroism at the school's last day ceremonies.

From a compact disk. André Previn introduces his jazz group, which includes Ray Brown and Mundell Lowe, to a SummerFest La Jolla concert audience:

> There will be practically no talking at all during this which I know you'll be pleased about. Introducing these two people is the most unnecessary task of the year. But there we are anyway: Ray Brown and Mundell Lowe. . . .
>
> In this particular kind of festival . . . everybody seems to be quite relaxed and everything is extremely well-rehearsed. . . . We spend a great many hours rehearsing [things] down to a fine point. However, this cannot be said of tonight. You saw me come out with this [list]. This has on it the names of tunes we might play and the keys in which they might occur. It also says "Take the 10th Street exit off Interstate 5." And that's the extent of the rehearsal. *However, we are all old friends.*

And Previn has said it all. Three experienced men who have worked together for endless hours. Each knows the others' heads and hearts. Each enjoys a common history in the pursuit of remarkable jazz music. And each longs to make a masterpiece of a simple melody by supporting and highlighting one another. No competition here; no pursuit of praise that outdistances the other. Just three old friends who know enough about one another and trust one another that the only rehearsal they need is instructions on how to get to the concert hall.

Or to put it in one other way. Here's Jesus on genuine friendship:

"Greater love has no one than this, than to lay down one's life for his friends" (John 15:13 NKJV).

FRIENDSHIPS DISSECTED

During the last few years, Gail and I have made it a point to take a few midwinter days away from our work and to journey to Colorado where we have skied the slopes of Aspen. Good friends who live there have welcomed us to their home on each occasion, and we have found our time in the Rockies to be restful and restorative.

Our ski trip this year coincided with the writing of this chapter, and I had many quiet moments while ascending the mountain on the ski lift to think about the nature of friendship. As the days passed, a feeling began to grow within me that I was experiencing something around me that presented a helpful picture of what we mean by the word *friend*. It was the very last skiing day when the bits and pieces of my thoughts came together.

I realized that all week long, my skiing experience had been guided by four kinds of people that I'd encountered on the slopes. Let me describe them for you.

AMBASSADORS

I met the first of the four kinds the second day of my ski week. I had just sat down on the high-speed quad with three strangers. Almost immediately the man to my right introduced himself: "Hi, my name is M——. How's the skiing?" I was a bit surprised because most banter on the ski lift is rather mindless and usually amounts to "Where you from?" or "Terrific day, isn't it?" or "You ever see such powder?" Respectively you answer these questions: "Boston," "Yup," and "Nope." But this guy didn't seem to know the rules. He actually wanted to introduce himself and talk.

Somewhat reluctantly (I was too busy thinking about *friendship*), I turned to reciprocate the introduction only to see the word *Ambassador* on the front of his parka. So after I'd offered my name, I asked, "What's an ambassador?"

"We're volunteers from around here, and we're here to enjoy the skiing with guests like you. We want to make sure you're having a great time and all your questions are answered. We want to hear anything you might want to tell us that would help us improve the skiing. But mainly we're here just to ski the hill with you."

I was impressed. And later I thought that this man, the ambassador, represented a kind of friendship. There is a place in a man's life for a friend who is there just to ski the hill with you or, more aptly put, to walk through life with you. Nothing heavy. Just a guy or two who, as they say, help you smell the daisies.

A friend like the ambassador is there to join you in discovering life and all it has to offer. He shares laughs, helps make good memories, doesn't mind if you say something stupid. You feel comfortable with an ambassador friend. He doesn't compete with you, doesn't make you feel that you have to perform, doesn't take more from the relationship than he gives. You need (we all need) an ambassador or two in your life; they're there to help you enjoy the ride. And, lest we forget, there's a lot of enjoying to do.

Over the past eight years I have worked hard to develop some friendships that might fit into the ambassador pattern. I say that I've had to work hard because making a friend is not an easy task as one gets older. And because the development of friendships takes time that many of us tell ourselves we do not have. If you wait until you have free time or until your work is ended, it's probably never going to happen. Friendships have to make their way into the planning calendar, sometimes weeks in advance.

I have telephone friends—a man or two with whom I keep in regular phone contact. Naturally, these relationships have limitations, but there is something very helpful about such occasional thirty-minute conversations. One thing I've noticed is that the talk tends to be substantial. Phone time is expensive. So when you know the meter is running, you make sure that the subject matter is mutually beneficial.

I have two or three friends who live at a distance. We have to schedule meeting times in their city or mine or someplace in the country where our schedules take us. We agree to spend the better part of a day together, usually sitting in a restaurant or walking in some park or country place. We talk about what we have read, the issues we're facing, the questions we're asking. We catch up on our marriages, our view of life, our hopes for the future. We speak of feelings and fears, dreams and disappointments.

We do reality checks on one another. When I told one of my friends that I wished someone would occasionally ask me what Jesus was saying to me, I began to get occasional phone calls in which, when I'd lifted up the phone, the first words were, "So what's Jesus saying to you today?"

Reality checks include these questions: What's the state of your soul? What is your calendar looking like, and are you taking the time you need to restore yourself? Does your wife still like you? Are you taking care of your health?

I have some terrific ambassador-type friends who are around me almost on a daily basis. We work together, pray together, often eat together, laugh, weep, complain, and reminisce together. We have worked hard to develop a freedom to be truthful.

It's a very comforting thought for a man to know that there are friends who will go all the way with him, no matter what. Somewhere in the annals of the monastic tradition, this story can be found:

> Two monks have woven a number of baskets, and now they are carrying them to town to sell on the market day. As they reach the edge of town, one says to the other, "You sell your baskets at that end of the market, and I will sell mine at this end." This being a wise strategy, they part and go about their business. Later, having sold all of his baskets, one returns to the meeting place and waits. And waits. And waits. Only after a night has passed does the second monk make his appearance. And when he does, his face signals intense sorrow. "I cannot return to the monastery with you," he says to the waiting friend. "I have done a terrible thing. Yesterday, I was greatly tempted, and I succumbed to temptation. I committed fornication last night, and having broken my vows to my brothers and to God, I cannot go back." The first monk listens to this confession and then says, "Come, my friend. We will go back to the monastery and repent together."

What is the story's strange message? Several possibilities. First, the first monk is saying, "Your sin is my sin. We will make the repentance in such a way that no one will ever know which of us did this deed. *I will bear your shame with you.*" Or perhaps he is saying a second thing: "I identify with your sin because under the appropriate circumstances, I might have capitulated to the same temptation. *I understand your vulnerability.*" Or perhaps he is saying, "If I had stayed at your side rather than left you alone, I could have helped you avoid this temptation. *I bear mutual responsibility for your sin.*" Whatever you think the appropriate interpretation to be, the conclusion is the same: genuine friends—the ambassador type—bear one another's burdens in good times and bad times as they ski the hill of life together.

LIFT ATTENDANTS

I saw a second person on the slopes (or should I say persons?) who gave me insight into the nature of friendships. They were the *lift attendants*. They were all young men and women whose job it was to stand at the bottom and at the top of ski lifts and make sure that you, the skier, got on and off safely. They were also there to make sure that your equipment was secure, that you had all the information you needed, that you got going up the hill in as short a time as possible. I enjoyed the young people: every one of them was cheery and eager to serve. And that's the operative word about these friends: they *serve*.

We're talking about a friend who looks deeply into a brother's life and spots need. He doesn't have to be told that something is wrong or inadequate. That a guy needs encouragement, a prayer, a helping hand. He makes it his business to know his friend well enough so that words are not needed. He just knows! And knowing, he sets out to make sure that his friend receives whatever is needed. And when he finishes the serving (whatever it is) and you say thanks, he replies, "It's no big deal."

These friendships are not cheap relationships. What keeps them going are frequent expressions of appreciation, encouragement, and personal inquiry. One of my closest friends entered my office a few weeks ago. He knew that I was going through a very difficult period in my work. He was aware that I wasn't sleeping well, that I was living with more anxiety in me than was proper. He sat down and was silent for a moment. Then he looked at me and said, "I need to ask you a question."

"Go ahead," I said.

"You're my friend, and I want to know: Is everything all right in your personal life? I mean are you okay, or is there anything we need to talk about?"

I loved him for asking that question. He was looking at my eyes that were tired, and he was hearing some conversation (perhaps a bit of whining?) that was out of character. He may have seen some reactions or responses that didn't fit. And it all triggered the question that every man needs a friend to ask.

This aspect of friendship has to go in both directions. It's a poor friendship indeed if all the serving goes one way. But find two or more men who are carefully monitoring the needs of the others and doing what's necessary to make sure everyone gets up the hills of life, and you're seeing a friendship in motion.

Just a week or two before this writing, one of my close friends and I spent time with a leader in our country who lives with heavy responsibility. The three of us had met in his office and talked about prayer, the struggle for integrity, the reality of evil and its effort to derail our best intentions. As my friend talked, I found myself praying for him and the one we'd gone to visit. Praying that his words would be wise, memorable, motivating. And when it was my turn to speak, I noticed that my friend looked right at me, nodding his head, seeming to say with all his body language, "Keep on going, Gordon, I'm right with you."

And when we left that office having given our very best to our host, we looked at each other and laughed. We—men in our fifties that we are—exchanged high fives and said, "It doesn't get any better than this."

SKI INSTRUCTORS

The third group of people who made my skiing experience complete were the *ski instructors*. Now I am not a bad skier. Not among the best, you understand. But I have been seen on the so-called black diamonds, the expert slopes. My form may not be pretty (not Olympian), but I don't fall much. My friend Greg, who is among the best on the hill, taught me something very important. "Always take a lesson . . . every year," he said. "No one ever gets so good that he doesn't need the analysis and advice of an expert. He'll spot your bad habits, and he'll show you something each time that will make your skiing experience all the better." And Greg practices his own preaching.

So I began to take a lesson from a ski instructor each year. Greg was right, and I came to appreciate what a good teacher can do. I've watched the instructor at work with other skiers. He glides down the mountain making graceful balletlike turns, and the students follow along in his tracks. The instructor suddenly stops and watches. "Weight on the inside edge," he cries. "Shoulders facing down hill!" "Arms up!" And so the instructions are barked out. Then, "Terrific!" "Super, super, super!" "Now you're getting it!" "Yesssss!" Always teaching, always challenging the student to a better, more efficient performance.

I need friends like the ski instructor. Friends who have something to teach me because they're better at, more knowledgeable about, something than I am. Away with jealousy, competition, intimidation. What is more valuable than knowing a friend who can teach you something? So I ask, whom can I follow down the hill of life and learn by emulation? Where is the friend who is not afraid to show me my need for improvement and how to make it happen?

Herein lies a barrier to many friendships. Some men do not want to get close to anyone who appears superior to them. This reticence has to be beaten if we are to grow. In my world, I decided that if there were men who'd open their lives to me, I'd be ready, notebook open (if necessary), ready to profit from all they had to offer. Today, I delight in friends who have achieved more, who are smarter, whose lives seem to have far greater character than my own. These friends are treasures.

Some call this kind of friend a mentor. In Greek mythology, Mentor was the man charged with the responsibility of raising Telemachus while his father, Ulysses, went off to the Trojan Wars. From his effort, it is said, came recognition of one of the greatest human transactions: the process in which one person sets about to help form the character, the knowledge, the direction in the life of another. The Jewish theologian Abraham Joshua Heschel was thinking of the mentoring relationship when he said, "We have to have more than textbooks, we need text-people."

A good mentor is never forgotten. Lee Iacocca wrote of the man who changed his life:

> Charlie Beachem could be a tough boss when he thought the situation called for it. At a dinner celebrating my election to the Presidency of Ford in 1970 I finally got up the nerve to tell Charlie publicly what I thought of him. "There will never be another Charlie Beachem," I said. "He has a special niche in my heart—and sometimes I think he was carving it out by hand. He was not only a mentor, he was more than that. He was my tormentor, but I love him."

One of my heroes, David Elton Trueblood, once wrote of his intellectual mentor:

> Always, as I write, I try to keep in mind the arduous standard which my teacher, Professor Arthur O. Lovejoy, demonstrated and expected. After his death, one of his former students said, "With his eyes upon you, you would weigh your words twice before uttering them. His presence discouraged laxity of thought, intellectual bravado, and facile talking."

I enjoyed this sort of genuine ski instructor friendship with several mentors: a track coach, a Presbyterian pastor (and his wife), an older single man with whom I shared an apartment, and a seminary president. There were others. But in these four cases, I can recall story after story in which they opened up new worlds of thought and possibility to me. Like the instructors on Aspen Mountain, they were unafraid to rebuke me; delighted to affirm my growth; quick to elevate my sights as I thought of the future. Most of all, they offered me an understanding of the Christian life by the way they lived it.

When we talk mentoring, we're talking about an unusual kind of devotion: the older to teach, the younger (the novice) to learn. And that devotion is in scarce supply today. Young men (and there are many) regularly cry for mentors from the older generation. But all too frequently they hear from would-be ski instructors that there isn't enough time, or, as one said, "I'm not into that stuff."

Conversely, more than one instructor has said about an abortive mentoring friendship, "I was really prepared to pour myself into that kid, but he doesn't really care to hear the hard stuff and stick in there for the long haul."

It is said that a visitor to an Eastern monastery asked the abbot how many monks lived within the walls. Ten thousand was the answer. Then the follow-up question: How many disciples? And the response from the abbot: only four or five.

The ski instructor friendship may be one of the most crucial relationships among all men in today's world. With the paucity of good father relationships on which to pattern the male life, a whole generation of young men seeks direction, correction, and support. It's a great day for any older man who wants to pour himself into the young.

Mentoring is a highly specialized form of friendship. Unlike the ambassador kind of friendship, it is a relationship that is meant to have a point of termination. If its purpose is to build in the life of a young man, there comes a moment when that young man becomes mature enough to launch off on his own.

Jesus was speaking to the termination point when He told His disciples, "No longer do I call you My servants, but you are My friends." He was preparing them for His leaving, for the fact that He'd given them all they needed and that it was time for them to move ahead on their own as they were guided by His Holy Spirit. Think about it: it's both a frightening and an exhilarating moment when your mentor says it's time to head out on your own.

In one of the great memories of my life, my father played the literal role of ski instructor when I was about nine or ten. The day made such a strong impression upon me that I've written about it many times. It was my first time on skis, and we were at the top of the hill. My dad set me and my small skis between his legs. "Just lean against me," he said, "and you feel everything I do with my weight." And down the hill we went pressed tightly together as I slowly began to imitate all of his moves. We made several runs like that, and each time he would push me farther from himself so that I could increase in my independence. And then the moment came when he simply pushed me out ahead and said, "Go ahead, son, you're on your own."

In *The Seasons of a Man's Life,* Daniel Levinson of Yale calls a moment like that BOOM (Becoming One's Own Man). It's the moment your mentor says, in effect, I've given you everything I've got to give for now. Go for it.

But BOOM can be painful, and Levinson, having identified the moment of BOOM, acknowledged that there can be more than a little pain as the mentor and his disciple move apart: the younger attempting to assert his independence, the older attempting to demonstrate that the time for the parting has not yet come. Nowhere is this more apparent than the common struggle fathers and sons have as a boy comes near to the time of leaving home. I wrote about my own experience of BOOM in an earlier chapter.

Moses had a ski instructor relationship with Joshua. They spent years together, and then it came to an end. God spoke to Moses and said, "Commission Joshua, and encourage and strengthen him, for he will lead this people across [the river] and will cause them to inherit the land that you will see" (Deut. 3:28). And that was the moment when the mentor pushed his protégé out in front and, in effect, said: "Go ahead; you're on your own." His investment in Joshua paid off handsomely. It was quite a friendship.

SKI PATROL MEMBERS

On the mountain you meet a fourth kind of person dedicated to maximizing your skiing experience. These are members of the *ski patrol.* They wear red parkas. They're all slim, tanned, and tough. One morning I rode up on the lift with a ski patrol guy, and I asked, "What's a typical day look like for you?"

"Oh, we get to the hill at about 6:30 A.M.," he answered. "If there's been new snow overnight, we head up to the top and throw bombs."

"Throw what?"

"Bombs. Light explosives wherever there are possibilities of avalanches. We don't want any skiers hurt or buried if the snow becomes unstable."

Now that's interesting, I thought. *There's a kind of friend for you.* The buddy who's concerned enough that he looks out for your best interests.

And if he sees you headed for some trouble, he'll throw a bomb out ahead to make sure you're not in danger of getting hurt. He cares enough to take some risks on behalf of your welfare. Where do you find friends like that?

Ski patrol members check the slopes for spots that are icy, bare, or rocky. Of course you never see this in Aspen, but if it ever happened, they'd jam tall stakes into the ground to warn you. Without the stakes, you'd hit the dirt, and your skis would stop while you, now a nonskier, would head for an unhappy landing. Ski patrol folks try to help you avoid this airborne experience.

And that's not all the ski patrol people do. They hold skiers accountable to stay on the trails. They can get pretty touchy when they see someone outside the boundary markers. Members and friends of the British royal family tried defying the rules of the ski patrol a few years ago in Switzerland, and the result was a loss of life. Bottom line: you are (or you better be) very careful to listen up when the ski patrol tells you that there's trouble to the right or left. And they're there to make sure that you keep the rules, or you're history real quick.

Without ski patrol people, the slopes would be life-threatening. You'd soon be dodging skiers on drugs, on booze, on ego trips as some nuts try to set a world downhill record. Everyone needs a friend who represents the attitude of the ski patrol. He's the guy who holds you accountable to living inside the rightful boundary lines. Who warns you of the danger spots. Who throws "bombs" into the dangerous places, if necessary. He does it all with the purpose of keeping you out of trouble. Do you know any friends like this?

But there's even something else that the ski patrol folks do. They come after you when there's a disaster. If you hurt yourself in a skiing accident, for example, all you have to do is plant two skis upright in the snow and cross them. This X pattern is like a visual siren; it draws the patrol in a matter of a minute or two. They come careening down the slope with rescue sleds and medical supplies. They can diagnose an injury and estimate its severity almost instantly. They can stabilize a broken limb or treat frostbite. And if necessary, they can call out the snowmobiles or a helicopter to speed you off the hill and out of danger.

A man needs a friend like those in the patrol. For more than a few of us, there comes the inevitable day when we find ourselves down, out, or severely injured because of bad choices or circumstances in life. In moments like these, some people will ski right on by. They may even cluck their tongues and mutter that anyone stupid enough to fall and hurt himself doesn't belong on the hill again. And so they cross you off, move on, assuming that you're someone else's responsibility.

But the ski patrol members think differently. If you're down, they take you on as their responsibility. They don't *talk* compassion; they *walk* it. They can be counted on to be there. And what's more, they think it's just terrific when they can get you put back together so that you can get back up on the slopes once again. I've known a few ski patrol friends in life, and I dearly love them.

There you have it: four kinds of friends. The one who simply wants to enjoy the ride with you. The one who wants to maximize your experience by helping and serving. The one who's there to make sure you're growing and learning. The one who holds you accountable to keep your commitments and your purposes but who's also there when you're helpless and broken. Are there four people like that on your horizon? Then you're a most fortunate man.

There comes a moment when I say good-bye to my friends, when I go home to my wife to resume the intimate life of a man and a woman living in covenant together. I suspect that when I get there, she usually finds me confident in my manliness, refreshed in my determination that I will be a good and resourceful husband. And she knows that I've been with my friends. And we friends have been with Christ.

CHAPTER 8

LIFE'S REGRETS

Not long ago I was in the midst of a rather disorganized crowd waiting for a train (two hours past scheduled departure) headed south. There were Florida-bound vacationers, mothers with seemingly endless numbers of children, older people, and others like me, headed for North Carolina, who were impatient (a mild description) to get going. I confess that I took every opportunity to edge forward in the hope that when it came time to board, I would be able to get a good seat.

Finally, we heard the boarding announcement. The crowd quickly arranged itself, picking up infants and bags, getting tickets ready for collection. Then this: "Families with small children will go first." That instantly set back my strategy for getting the seat I wanted. Then, a moment later: "Travelers headed for Florida will be next."

The sorting of the crowd provoked me. I know that Christian grace should have caused me to be more patient, gladly standing to one side while everyone in America trooped past me to fill every seat in the train before I got there. But Christian grace seemed in short supply, especially when the next announcement came: "Senior citizens will board next." Someday this privilege will be meaningful to me, but not yet. So I began to imagine myself standing all the way to North Carolina. Worse yet, I visualized being bumped from the train.

As my anxiety grew (and I am not proud of this), I realized that it was not difficult to be innocently "pushed" ahead by the crowd of mothers, Floridians, and seniors. And before long, there I was at the gate handing my ticket to the gate agent. When he saw that I had no children, wasn't headed for Florida, and had no resemblance whatsoever to a senior citizen (a good man!), he started to motion me back into the waiting area. But people were pushing ahead, and he was smart enough to see that I'd cause more trouble trying to go backward than going with the flow. So he said with a wave of the hand, "Just go on ahead!" And I did! Secretly proud of myself, glad in the knowledge that I would in fact get the seat I wanted. And feeling reasonably (but not perfectly) "pure."

I charged down the platform. Walking faster and faster. Past some of the families with small children. Past the people headed for Florida. Past the senior citizens. What good fortune! I would be among the very first to board the train.

When I reached a coach that looked best suited to my interests, I saw a conductor at the door, flashed my ticket past his eyes, and said, "Can I get on here?"

"Yup!" he answered. "Go right up." I did what I was told.

Seconds later I was in my seat, the good seat I'd wanted so badly for more than two hours. I'd beaten the system, and within four hours I'd be in North Carolina hugging my grandchildren. Almost immediately the train began to move.

Wait a moment, I thought. *This train shouldn't be moving. The Floridians, the mommies and their babies, and the senior citizens can't have boarded yet. Besides, we aren't supposed to leave for another thirty minutes. What's wrong with this picture?*

I turned to the woman across the aisle who was at work with her laptop computer. "Excuse me, could you tell me where you're going?"

"New York," she said, never looking up from the screen, "and you?"

I looked at the man behind her. "You're going to . . . ?"

"Philly!" He anticipated my question.

New York is north. Philly is north. And trains headed for North Carolina out of Washington, D.C., do not pass through those cities.

"Oh, boy! Oh, boy! Do I feel like a jerk," I said out loud. "I think I'm on the wrong train." I said this as the train was still pulling away from the platform. Out the window I could see a sign that said TRACK 25. And I remembered that the train headed for North Carolina and points south was supposed to be on Track 26. Furthering my sense of stupidity, I could see all those families with children, those people headed for Florida, and those senior citizens calmly and happily boarding and probably all headed for *my seat.*

HAUNTING THOUGHTS

The feelings and thoughts surging within me as the train pulled beyond the Washington, D.C., train station are descriptive of regret. The mind fires into motion. What have I gone and done? How could I have been so dumb? How did this happen? Whose fault is it (certainly, not mine!)? Is God punishing me for my impatience when I maneuvered my way to the front of the line? Is He telling me that He likes families with children, people headed for Florida, and senior citizens more than me and that this is what I get for trying to get ahead of them? The mind is trying to bring a sense of meaning to the unexpected, the untoward. It probably won't help matters, but the mind likes to do this sort of thing.

Regrets can account for many of the private thoughts men think. And the regret-driven thoughts can increase with age as the consequences of many life-choices mount up. And if not properly processed, regrets can do a lot of damage.

My mistake cost me almost twelve hours of traveling time and almost an entire night's sleep. But most of us know of mistakes in the archives of our private thoughts that have changed the course of our entire lives, and we sing with Frank Sinatra, "Regrets! I've had a few."

Somewhere in his voluminous writings, William Barclay tells the story of an older man lying on his deathbed. What are your thoughts? he was asked.

As I recall the answer, it went something like this: "I keep on thinking of a time in my boyhood when some friends of mine and I decided to reverse some signs at a crossroads. And I can't stop wondering how many people were sent in wrong directions as a result and how it must have completely changed their lives."

This is the nature of a regret. It is a looking back, a brooding upon an event that we now wish would not have happened, taking rueful stock of its results.

I have heard the following regrets when men have shared their private thoughts with me:

> All my life I have known that God wanted me to be in some form of ministry. But I chose to marry a woman who would have nothing to do with Christian service. So for thirty years I've assumed that I was living apart from the call of God.

> When I was in school, I started having too much fun. Before long I was kicked out. Now I'm fifty, and not getting that degree has haunted me ever since.

I can remember my father warning me that our family was full of alcoholics, but I was convinced that I had my drinking under control. I would give up my legs and arms to roll life back to the day I made the decision to have that first drink.

I kept telling myself that I was working hard so that we'd have the kind of income we needed to give my wife and the children a comfortable life. Then one day my son was headed off to college, and I realized that I hardly knew him.

I knew that money wasn't mine. But I kept telling myself that I wasn't really stealing it; I was just borrowing money from one account and putting it temporarily into another. It would help get me through a tight spot. Then the market went "south" and I had no way to recover. Now they're calling me a crook.

I guess I felt a bit bored with our marriage, and she was everything I wished my wife was. So I . . .

You know, if I'd not been so frustrated and tired, I might not have . . .

If I'd only have told him how sorry I was.

I was too bull-headed . . . too angry . . . too drunk . . . too proud . . . and so I . . .

POTENTIAL EFFECTS

Regrets can paralyze us. Having gotten on "wrong trains" in the past, we become fearful to board new ones. We convince ourselves that nothing ever turns out right. So why try? It would be better to take fewer risks and stay on the safe and predictable side. We lose our confidence.

Then again, regrets can distract us from doing what we should be doing. We slip into playing the game of If-Only. If only I'd married a different woman. If only I'd stood up more to my father, gotten a better education, not quit that job. We're left in a perpetual state of discontent. Nothing is ever good enough.

Or regrets can make us bitter and resentful. We play the blame game and focus our thoughts on all the people who contributed in one way or another to the events about which we now feel sorry. We grow envious and resentful toward those who did not experience the same results. They didn't spend their money as we did. They chose to change jobs; we didn't, and now it's clear that we made the wrong decision.

Regrets can be the cause of overcompensation. "I have never gotten over a broken engagement that hurt me beyond words," a single man says. His regrets and unresolved woundedness are so great that he cannot now enter into any relationship with a woman and feel free to trust her. He looks over his shoulder at the past bad moment and assumes that it will happen again in the present situation. Result: his inability to dissolve a regret is likely to assure that he will never be able to give himself to a woman in a way that would foster a healthy relationship, which might lead to marriage.

A man has a bad experience in church leadership. He promises himself that he will never again get involved in a church.

NUMEROUS CAUSES

Every man who is at all reflective looks back upon the track of his life and sees the places where he boarded wrong trains.

Some regrets are the product of bad choices. I can't help wondering about a Vancouver man who, with his wife, concluded one day that life in the big city was too stressful. He wanted to get away to a quieter place. He quit his job, sold his home, and moved his family to the Falkland Islands—arriving there just three weeks before the war between Argentina and England began in earnest.

In the book *Den of Thieves*, which tells the story of the great Wall Street scandals, is the account of the development of the relationship between Martin Siegel and Ivan Boesky, which eventuated in the prosecution conviction of both men for insider trading.

Author James Stewart describes Martin Siegel's mood at the time when the opportunity to cross the line into illegality presented itself. Not only was he feeling financial pressure (a $500,000 annual salary was not adequate to meet his needs), but

> he was feeling the pressure of his work. The intense, high-stakes combat of a hostile takeover pumped him up with adrenaline, he'd be putting in hundred-hour weeks, then it would end. Suddenly he'd feel despondent and lethargic. He'd go to bed by 9 or 10 P.M. He suffered from mild allergies, and began taking Nyquil cold medicine in steadily increasing doses. Some nights, he downed 7 to 10 ounces of the remedy. At the end of every deal, he grew more nervous, wondering if it was the last.

Under such personal conditions, Siegel began to listen to the proposals of Boesky that the two collude when it came to passing pieces of information back and forth. Though plainly illegal, the effort would nevertheless be profitable for both.

"If you put me in situations with plenty of lead time, I'd pay for that," Boesky told Siegel.

On a certain level, Siegel could think of this as an innocent suggestion. He could identify likely takeover targets based on his experience and expertise at what qualities made companies vulnerable. On the other hand, there could be no doubt that they were crossing a line. Plainly Boesky was asking for inside information.

Then Siegel did make the choice; he crossed the line. "I'd, like, negotiate a bonus at the end of the year," he told Boesky. Boesky nodded.

Not long after that conversation, the collusion began. And at the end of the first year a briefcase from Ivan Boesky was put into Siegel's hand containing a $150,000 "bonus."

Siegel went straight to his apartment on East 72nd Street. He closed the door, put down the briefcase and quickly undid the clasps. There, in neat stacks of $100 bills tied with Caesar's Palace casino ribbons, was the money.

Siegel stared at it. Everything had gone without a hitch. It was his money now; he'd earned it. He ought to feel great! Instead, he felt ill. He sat down and put his head in his hands, waiting for the nausea to pass.

It was a moment that cost Siegel his reputation and credibility as a businessman. Just a simple choice, rationalized in a mind convinced that there was a need for more money, a feeling that one was unappreciated by his boss, and a belief that everybody was doing it. Why not Siegel? Regrets? He had a few.

Sometimes regrets emerge from the feeling that a wonderful opportunity was missed. Some time ago I had the privilege to be invited to a breakfast at the White House, which was hosted by the president and the vice president. Fifteen of us were to be seated at the table, and there was to be ample time for discussion of issues facing our country.

In a conversation the night before with one of the president's aides I learned that the invitations for the breakfast had gone out, first, by telephone about two weeks before. The phone calls were followed up by engraved invitations (meant, I suppose, as souvenirs) that arrived at the offices or homes of most of the invitees the same day as the breakfast.

When telephoned, one of the people on the guest list refused to believe that the call was actually from the White House. It was a joke, he assumed. And nothing would persuade him differently.

The presidential aide said to me, "Can you imagine how he feels this morning as he opens up his invitation with the official seal of the president and realizes the opportunity he missed? I wonder what he'll tell his grandchildren?"

Life is full of opportunities a man passes by. We think of things we should have said, places we should have visited, relationships we should have cultivated, jobs we should have taken. Or the opposite! Opportunities we had to take a courageous stand; the occasion when we could have helped someone avoid a personal catastrophe; the chance to have provided leadership that would have caused people to move in a different direction.

And the pall of a regret hangs upon us for years afterward.

Regrets occur when we have quit something prematurely. I enjoyed a brief "career" as an athlete on the track during my prep school and early college days. My days as a high school runner had been good ones, my competitive times just good enough to earn me the attention of the coach of the University of Colorado track team. A scholarship was provided, and I entered university life with a free ride if I would live up to my potential as an athlete.

I didn't! The coach watched me run, took me aside, and informed me that he could make me into an Olympic contender if I was prepared to pay the price. The price meant pain, he said. It meant working harder than anyone else on the team. Being on the track seven days a week throughout the year. Being willing to say no to lots of things in life for the next few years that were attractive and pleasurable. Was I prepared? I said yes . . . for a few weeks. After the first year, I quit.

I have regrets about that decision to quit. Two of my former teammates went on to compete in the Olympics, one of them winning a gold medal. They paid the price; I did not. For the rest of my life I will quietly wonder what would have been different about my life if I had responded to the challenge of the coach and embraced the pain and the disciplined life required of a top athlete.

But I quit. I have looked back at other times in my life when I quit. Quit in the higher pursuit of excellence and quality. Quit in the face of opposition. Quit because of fatigue. And in each case there is the feeling of regret. This is the story of many men who look back and wonder,

What could I have accomplished? Where would I be? What would I have? And there is no answer. There never is if one quits. All of us share those moments.

We can regret botched relationships. A relationship with a woman where we said or did the wrong thing and refused to make it right. A friendship we have betrayed. A loved one we have hurt too much for there ever to be healing.

For some there are the regrets of a first cigarette that kicked off a seemingly irreversible habit. The first drink. The initial dabblings with cocaine, pornography, or gambling. Why was it so easy to get involved with that sort of thing? Why, a man asks, didn't I heed the warnings of those who said that a significant percentage of boys or men who are attracted to these things will never find release from them? *If only I had listened.*

Sometimes the regrets center on poor judgments. A seemingly wrong marriage decision. A career choice in which one was lured by a quick buck, an attractive part of the country in which to live, somebody's promise of an opportunity for quick advancement.

They were laying off people in my department right and left. And I knew that it was just a matter of time. So when I heard that there was the chance of a transfer to N——, I scooped it up. We sold our house, moved to N——, and I thought I'd really beaten the system. But within six months things started to sour. I was working for a boss much younger than me, and I could quickly see that she didn't like me. In fact she didn't seem to like anyone from my part of the country. A year later I was out of a job due to a "restructure." Here we were in a strange city, almost no friends, in an economic environment where there was no hiring. We went through our savings within months. One day I found myself with a family to support and not a dime to pay the rent. It brought on marital stress. I totally lost my self-confidence. How do you get into situations like that so fast? One bad decision, and life seems changed forever.

There are bad investment decisions.

My wife and I spent twenty years saving and putting together a more-than-adequate pension program so that we could retire early. Then one day a guy I know came along with an investment scheme that looked fabulous. He was easy to trust, and I gave him access to virtually everything we'd put away. I did it because he promised me we'd double (maybe even triple) our holdings within a few years. Why in the world I wasn't content with what we had, I'll never know. Now we're in our late fifties. Nothing!

As a college student, I purchased a used sporty car because I thought it just might impress a girl whose affections I wanted to attract. There was nothing (and I mean nothing) wise about the purchase of the car. It should have been clear that my income would support either the monthly payment or the monthly food bill. But not both! I was purchasing it for all the wrong reasons. And to make matters worse, a spiritual mentor asked, "Gordon, have you even prayed once about whether or not making a choice like this is pleasing to God?"

No, I hadn't prayed. And, no, I didn't intend to pray. I wished he hadn't asked because I had a fairly strong suspicion about what heaven might say. I couldn't imagine God applauding such a decision. So why ask?

The day came to get the car. And true to my plans, a week later I was driving in the Rocky Mountains with the very girl the car was purchased to impress. As I anticipated, she was impressed. Then things went sour as we made a turn on an icy road. The car began to slide to one side, and before it stopped, we plowed into the rear of a pickup whose tailgate was down. When I got out of the car, I noted that the side of my once-lovely sports car had a four-foot strip neatly peeled similar to the opening of a sardine can. Repairs, I later learned, would be in the hundreds and hundreds of dollars. I was not insured. Regrets, I've had a few.

I stood there that day and shook my fist in the direction of heaven. "God," I said, "I know You didn't want me to have this car. But I'm going to keep it anyway!"

It wasn't many months later that a mechanic was telling me I needed a complete engine overhaul. Oh, and by the way, the girl didn't hang around, either.

The worst of all regrets from a Christian perspective is the one that involves defiance of God's laws. We call it sin. Regrets of this kind? I've had my share.

In the Bible, Jonah regrets a disobedient act in which he heads west when God wants him to go east. Peter regrets not standing with Jesus in a critical moment. You can't trace the journey of any person for long that you don't see places where something very dark within the human heart has caused a divergence from God's purposes. And the longer the event goes unclaimed or unaccounted for, the more the consequences of regret pile up.

A single professional man writes a six-page letter to describe a relationship with a married woman with whom he has been working. "We were just good friends," he writes. "But as we worked together, often late into the night and on weekends, we found ourselves getting into conversations that ranged far beyond the work. She began to tell me about her husband who often mistreated her and made her life miserable. I began to imagine how much better off she would be if she wasn't married to him and was instead married to me."

It isn't long before the conversations lead to walks in the park, lunches in quiet places, and late evenings in cocktail lounges. From hugs to sexual activity. And his conscience is terribly scarred with the realization that he has crossed a line, and there is no way to get back to what once was. He loves her and cannot stop the feelings. He has sinned with her and cannot live with the guilt. He has created a set of circumstances in which everyone is going to lose and in which there seems no painless remedy. Regrets! He has a few.

There are the regrets of not pursuing a deeper, more vigorous spiritual life. "If you've spent the first forty years of your life ignoring the ordering of your private world," a man writes,

> it's rather difficult to start at mid-life. Living out of the soul takes time and practice, and the fifth decade of life is kind of late for a start. Now I look back and remember all the times my mentors tried to get me to hunker down to a life of spiritual discipline. But I was too busy and too preoccupied. Now it is a terrible struggle to want to pray, to know how to pray, to really feel that praying is a good use of time. Somehow the circuitry just doesn't seem to be there. Talk about a regret.

Accumulate fifty or more years of life, and you will have more than a few regrets. And the list could indeed grow:

- Why didn't I seek out the wise voice of older and wiser mentors?
- Why didn't I take the advice of my teachers and study harder?
- Why didn't I push myself to learn more?
- Why wasn't I a better father, spending more time with my children?
- Why wasn't I a more attentive, more serving husband?
- Why did I hurt so many friends?
- Why didn't I take the time to know my father better?
- Why didn't I give myself to a deeper walk with God?

- Why wasn't I more thorough in my preparation to preach the Bible?
- Why have I tried so hard to please everyone?
- Why did I allow grudges and resentments to cloud my thinking about certain people?

MANAGING REGRETS

Over the past few years automobile drivers have become familiar with something called Jersey barriers, the low concrete walls found on road construction sites. They protect the workers, and they guide the movement of traffic around the work. Unresolved regrets become like Jersey barriers. They channel the thinking and perception of a man and often squeeze him into opinions of himself and others from which he cannot escape.

So what do we do with all of these things we call regrets? Do we permit them to fly about as private thoughts and do their damage? Paralysis? Distractions? Bitterness? Overcompensation? Or can we manage our regrets and choose to turn them into leverage points for life-change?

I wonder if anyone in the Bible lived with regrets more than St. Paul? For the first thirty-four years of his life, he focused on being the most righteous Jew of his generation. His way of thought led him to a dangerous zeal, which eventuated in his being the point man for the persecution of Christians. He said,

> I . . . was convinced that I ought to do all that was possible to oppose the name of Jesus of Nazareth. And that is just what I did in Jerusalem. On the authority of the chief priests I put many of the saints in prison, and when they were put to death, I cast my vote against them. Many a time I went from one synagogue to another to have them punished, and I tried to force them to blaspheme. In my obsession against them, I even went to foreign cities to persecute them (Acts 26:9–11).

In one sense Paul never seemed to have gotten over his gruesome past. One gets the feeling that his private thoughts often reverted to those days: the memories of the screams of the persecuted being separated from their families, beaten, even killed. Perhaps he recalled his arrogance and self-righteousness as he did his best to stamp out the very cause to which he became totally committed.

"Although I was formerly a blasphemer, a persecutor, and an insolent man . . . I obtained mercy," Paul wrote toward the end of his life, "because I did it ignorantly in unbelief. And the grace of our Lord was exceedingly abundant, with faith and love which are in Christ Jesus" (1 Tim. 1:13–14 NKJV).

It's clear that Paul brought his regrets under personal management. And he was able to do so because he had two strong perspectives on personal reality.

The first: Paul understood and accepted himself as *a sinner.* That's not easy for a lot of men to do. And it must not have been easy for Paul. He spent a large part of his earlier life trying to convince everyone that there was no sin in him, and he ended his life trying to convince everyone that he was the "worst" of sinners. What happened? Somewhere along the way as he confronted the majesty and holiness of Jesus Christ, he came to see his real inner self.

His conclusion: given half a chance, there was enough evil within him to be destructive beyond words. In fact—it could be said—only the grace of God prevented him (and prevents us) from being any more destructive than he was. It wasn't that Paul was trying to excuse himself ("The devil made me do it!"), but that he came to appreciate the darkness of the human heart and its capability to engineer one regrettable event after another. So with the perspective that faith brought to him, Paul was able to gain a new perspective on his behavior: "When I want to do good, evil is right there with me. . . . I see another law at work in the members of my body, waging war against the law of my mind and making me a prisoner of the law of sin at work within my members. What a wretched man I am!" (Rom. 7:21–24).

The second perspective Paul gained in his later years was that of *grace.* In that one word is the promise that all regrettable acts are to be forgiven the one who comes to God in repentance. A word that, in simple terms, means to name what you have done, take responsibility for it, renounce the event, and exchange your behavior for something better. In other words, go in another direction.

All sorts of implications flow out of that. A man of grace looks back on his regrettable moments and permits them to generate genuine humility within him. He becomes quieter, less accusing of others, more forgiving when someone acts offensively against him.

He looks squarely at regrets and asks if any of them need to be covered in restitution. Are there accounts to be settled, things to be made right? And what are the lessons to be learned that can reprogram his character? What actions can be taken to make sure that the events and attitudes behind regrets will never be repeated?

Then grace also means that a man accepts the mercy and forgiveness of God and chooses to live as a "mercied" man.

On the other hand, the so-called male pride will never permit the dynamics that enable a man to manage regret. Male pride says, Don't admit failure or weakness. Don't give the upper hand to your adversary by admitting fault. Rather than name the regrets, deny them; try and forget them (you won't!); run from them. But grace says, Turn the light of God's love on them.

And that's what Paul did. He spent the rest of his life "making" Christians rather than persecuting them.

GETTING BACK ON TRACK

The train pulls out of the station, going the wrong direction. *What an absolute fool I am!* I tell myself. *Better to be standing on the other train while it goes in the right direction than sitting comfortably on this one while it takes me farther and farther from my destination. What to do?*

I see the conductor coming. Shall I try to get his attention in a quiet corner where no one else can hear my admission that I have made a stupid blunder? No point in doing that. The folks around me already know what I've done.

So he comes to my seat. And I say, "Sir, have you ever had someone get on one of your trains and discover that he's on the wrong train?"

"It happens all the time," he says. "That your problem?"

"You've got it."

He studies his timetable for a moment.

"Here's what you do. We're stopping about ten minutes up the line. Get off, go into the station, and tell them what you've done. They'll give you a ticket back to D.C., and you'll be able to get on the 8:30 P.M. train. It's going to cost you a few hours, but you'll get where you want to go."

And that's what I did.

"It's going to cost you a few hours," the conductor said. And that's exactly what it did cost me: a few hours, some lost sleep, a late arrival in North Carolina so that I didn't get to hug my grandchildren until the next morning.

But sometimes regretful events cost a lot more than a few hours. An entire life is irrevocably changed by consequences that can never be reversed. Someone is hurt in a way that can never be fully forgotten. An opportunity is lost that will never be retrieved. A man does something so bad that there are those who will never forgive him, never let him forget, never let him off the hook. There seems to be nothing that can secure their pardon. Result: a man's private thoughts become tainted with the realization that his resume of life will carry a permanent blemish and that it will go with him to his grave.

A significant number of men can identify a regret in their lives that fits this category. And what does one say to them? First, that if no one else is willing to forgive, God is. Second, that if the entire world would choose bitterness rather than grace, there is no ample reason to reciprocate the attitude of one's critics and judges. An embittered heart is a shriveling heart, and a man with regrets cannot afford to sink into this experience. He must set out to live in the mercy God has given even if the world around him has none for him.

Third, a man with an indelible regret may have to face a tough question: What can he do to undo or mitigate some of the deeds for which he has been responsible? And there is a key word: *responsible*. We must not misunderstand the concept of Christian grace as a license to walk away from the responsibility of misdeeds, to claim God's forgiveness and pretend as if no one has suffered because of what has been done. There is a place for restitution, repayment, actions that seek to compensate for an offense. And some regrets will never be softened until the matter of returning to the scene of the sin has occurred, sincere apologies rendered, and attempts made to restore what has been disrupted or destroyed.

Regrets can be cause for turning one's life in a new direction that stands in defiance of the earlier events. I'm thinking of the old slave trader, John Newton, who awakened one day with horror to the fact that he had sunk so deeply into an evil way of life that no human atonement would suffice to free him. But if no one else saw the brokenness of his heart and his expression of regret, God did. Through faith his life was changed. And he went on to live a life of defiance against the evil that had been his captor for so many years. In recognition of his liberty through faith in Jesus, he wrote words the whole world now regularly sings:

> Amazing grace, how sweet the sound,
> That saved a wretch like me.
> I once was lost but now am found,
> Was blind but now I see.

I don't think for one moment that John Newton didn't often look back at the slave-ship days and recall the screams of sick, dying, and tortured Africans whom he transported across the ocean. I know of no record that speaks of his dreams, his private thoughts about the past, any anguish he carried concerning the people whose lives he destroyed. But I feel confident that he must have struggled terribly at times. I also feel confident that when such thoughts rose to the surface of his private thinking, he took them straight to the Cross and reaffirmed his hold on the mercy of God. He could not reverse the consequences of things done; but he was never cavalier about his past. He could only live in humility and faithful service with the hope that his changed life bore testimony to his renunciation of the old ways.

Each day has its regrets. And each day has its mercies. The private thoughts of a man assuredly contain the first. With God's grace, they can also contain the second—those blessed mercies.

CHAPTER 9

WHAT
A WIFE
REALLY WANTS

It's First Monday at Grace Chapel, and the advertising for the event says, "An evening with Gordon followed by football and food." Newly arrived men are just outside the meeting hall drinking coffee. Inside, our homegrown jazz combo is on a roll. It's clear that there's an unusually large crowd of men assembling for the evening. The reason has something to do either with the topic—"What Men Need to Know About Women"—or the fact that the Monday night football matchup between Dallas and San Francisco will be shown in the gym after the talk. I'm not sure which it is.

A man I've not met before comes over to where I'm standing. He hands me something that looks like a gift. "A woman at the door gave it to me as I was coming in," he says. "She told me 'to give it to Pastor Mac before the evening begins.'"

I tear away the wrapping paper. Inside is a book. Its title: *Everything Men Know About Women*. I open it and discover that the book contains exactly one hundred blank pages. Not a word. Nada!

When everyone is in the hall and we've sung a few rowdy songs like the Notre Dame fight song, "Off We Go into the Wild Blue Yonder" (we're a high-tech air force community), and "I Want a Girl Just Like the Girl That . . . ," I am introduced.

I wait for the clapping and hooting (we're a tough group) to cease and then begin: "Gentlemen [said with a mental smirk], you all know the topic tonight. Here's what one woman thinks about the importance of it." I tell them how I got the book, note the title, and then flip through the pages so that they can see the "nothing" inside.

Some men laugh. Others decide the message is not funny. Is the woman's "gift" a practical joke or a serious message? None of us know. But it does concentrate the male mind.

TWO SIDES OF MARRIAGE

Somewhere in his voluminous writings, Leo Tolstoy said, "The vocation of every man and woman is to serve other people." Terrific!

This is a noble aspiration, and it suggests that the author Tolstoy possessed a remarkably high view of humanity's purpose. A woman, having heard that, might think to herself that this is the kind of man with whom she'd like to spend her life.

Not so fast! Something doesn't connect. Before you judge a man by his words, listen to his wife and get her perspective. Here's Mrs. Tolstoy on her memories of living with Leo:

> There was so little genuine warmth about him; his kindness does not come from the heart, but merely from his principles. His biographers will tell of how he helped the laborers carry buckets of water, but no one will ever know that he never gave his wife a rest and never—in all these thirty-two years—gave his child a drink of water or spent five minutes by his bedside to give me a chance to rest a little from all my labors.

So before we listen to a man's appraisal of his marriage (or any other relationships), better make room for a second opinion. Perhaps his wife's? Watch what a man's wife becomes over the years as a result of marrying him. Has she been challenged to keep herself fresh-spirited? Is she motivated to radiate a love for life and people? Is her mind a fountain of ideas, and is any gathering of people improved because of her presence? Is she a woman of deep soul, more pleasing to God, because of the man she married? Heavy, huh?

Or does she appear in public with a lifeless face? Is her conversation devoid of conviction or confidence, her self-assurance at zero? Does she retreat to a corner when a group interacts? Is her faith without joy . . . because of the man she married? Even heavier!

Think with me about one of those inevitable moments in a marriage when everything dear between a husband and a wife has collapsed. An issue has sparked a conflict, and something has been done or said that has escalated feelings of anger and recrimination to a point where resolution is momentarily impossible.

These two people lie in their bed where just the night before they made love in a tender, invigorating fashion that made them exclaim at the end just how unique was their life together and that probably no one else quite understood and cared for the other as much as they did.

But that was twenty-four hours ago, and a lot can happen in twenty-four hours. If there was blending then, there is distance, great distance, now. She lies but twelve inches away, but the distance feels more like a mile. Both are careful not to toss about in the bed in such a way that a leg or an arm would touch. That might mean an acknowledgment that the other person is really there. It might demand that something be said. And no one wants to say anything that could be construed as capitulation, surrender, acknowledgment of wrong.

In this bedroom drama both are awake, although they pretend to be asleep. Both churn with feelings that their point of view is the correct one and that if only the other would see it his (or her) way. And both also know that the impasse could probably be broken with a simple statement spoken out into the darkness of the bedroom: "I'm sorry." But for reasons too deep to express, the words will not pass from the soul to the throat.

He lies there in his private thoughts. He remembers the days when they first met. Perhaps he recalls the pilgrimage of their relationship, how it moved from a casual acquaintanceship to one in which they realized a commonality of purpose and commitment. There was a passion in those days: those wonderful moments when two people lost themselves in their hunger to share affection and thrilled at those moments when they discovered new mutual excitements about life. There were the heady days of engagement, the planning, the saving, the worrying. And there were the early days of the marriage with its hard work to keep ahead of the bill collector, to finish education, and to begin reaping the dreams. What changed? Where was it lost? What happened to the passion?

In this moment, it all seems so distant, a history that is almost fictional. Even the recollection of last night's intimacies, verbal and otherwise, now seems hollow and foolish. In his anger he is tempted to think that last night's endearing words were a joke. What is the more truthful statement about their marriage? The tenderness of last night or the hostilities of the last hour? And he wonders for the umpteenth time, *What does she really want? What does it take to make her satisfied?* And he concludes, *What was once so easy now seems so hard, so unattainable, so disappointing.* In this bitter moment all the promises that spoke of a growing relationship that would fulfill two people seem a lie.

THE MAN SHE MARRIED

When men begin to surface their private thoughts, you might hear something like the following comments:

> I'd really like to be a good husband. But there are times when I just don't know what it is that makes her happy. I know I'm not perfect. But if I knew what it was that she wanted, what would satisfy her, I'd at least take a hard shot at it.

> I started out this marriage with every intention of being the consummate husband. I was wildly in love with my wife. But something's changed. I get the feeling that she's constantly disappointed in me. Nothing I do seems good enough, and all my failures seem to be amplified.

> I liked my marriage better when we were struggling in the first years. Now with a house, kids, and enough money, we've settled into some routines that leave me cold.

> Making out in the back seat of a car was more enjoyable than the kind of love-making we do at home these days. We just take each other for granted; it's kind of like living with your sister. She's not the woman I married, and *I know I'm not the man she married*. I'm just plain disappointed.

What's being said in these comments? That there's more than a little confusion about what a relationship is supposed to be and what's expected of a man if he wants to be a good husband.

And these are the sorts of things that course through the mind of our man as he lies in bed, fresh from harsh words with his wife who lies inches away pretending that she's asleep. Each tries to feign disinterest and detachment. Yet inside where the private thoughts rage, each thinks frantically, *How do we break this impasse and rekindle what we both desperately need: love, connection, affection, encouragement, oneness?*

Back to First Monday. I put the wordless book entitled *Everything Men Know About Women* down and start into the talk I came to give: "Let me offer you ten ideas about things your wife might want and need out of your marriage." And here are the ten I proposed.

1. SHE WANTS TO GIVE HERSELF TO HER MAN, BUT SHE NEEDS DEVOTION FIRST!

Devotion is a spiritual word. It refers to the intentions of the heart. The ancient Hebrews understood devotion as one of the highest of all human interactions. An overused English word that is analogous to devotion is *commitment*. But sometimes a word like *commitment* wears out its welcome and its ability to provoke fire in the belly. So try the word *devotion* in its place.

Devotion is a habit of the heart. It is something that happens when we decide to invest the energy of our souls into the life of another person.

In the earliest days of my courtship and marriage, devoting myself to the Gail I first came to know was not difficult. Each presented the best side to the other in those first weeks and months. The subject matter of conversations was chosen to invite closeness and to avoid conflict. Every discovery of the other's likes and dislikes brought an immediate, positive response, a desire to please. The name of the game was Agree-Impress-Respond. It was a game that worked well—for a while. And it was very exciting.

In playing that game, it is entirely human for any of us to minimize (even disguise) the facets of ourselves that might seem offensive to the one we're out to impress. We are careful to bathe and douse ourselves with Old Spice. ("I'd kiss a dog that wore Old Spice," I heard a lovely young woman say when I was a teenager, and I set out to corner the market on shaving lotion.) The instincts for manners and politeness reach an all-time high. We are attentive to everything. It is a devotion of sorts. But, in the context of a longer life, a kind of immature devotion.

This sort of enthusiastic expression of commitment cannot last forever. Eventually, there is reality: leaving dirty socks on the floor, having an unshaven face, burping, forgetting promises, taking things for granted, not being thankful, being insensitive, being irritable, and a thousand other versions of reality. And that is when devotion undergoes its first major road test. Sooner or later, a man must decide whether he is prepared to be devoted to another person who is also something of a sinner.

You can't move in close to a person—as marriage requires—without discovering the so-called for-better-or-for-worse clause in the marriage vows, that we all drip with a myriad of imperfections. Faults and flaws emerge in the routine of life, and the majority of them never go away. So the inevitable questions arise, Can I devote myself to a person who is far from perfect but who wants to share a common life with me? Will I choose to love a person because she is perfect or because she is, through and through, who she is? Real devotion begins the day I accept my wife as a wonderful, lovable sinner.

I sense that the marriage Gail and I share today has passed through four stages of devotion. The first, described in the last few paragraphs, is what I call the devotion of romance. It is not difficult to devote to a person in whom there seems no wrong.

There was a second stage of our relationship that I call the stage of companionship. We both settled down to exploring the real person we'd married. It wasn't always an easy time, although we survived it and survived it quite well, it seems to me. Occasional tough moments, sure. We knew a few of those twelve-inches/one-mile nights in the bed (and that in a time when queen- or king-size beds were available only to the rich). We found each other's dark sides and learned how to describe them to each other with pinpoint accuracy. Fatigue, pressure, and relative immaturity fueled the difficult moments, but they were part of the necessary politic to learning how to cut through the gloss and remain devoted in spite of our imperfections. We were not going to let each other go.

We discovered a third stage on the devotional trail that I call the serving stage. It began in that moment when I discovered that my wife had great growth potential, and that her growth could be accelerated as I got behind her and helped. Today, people often ask my wife to speak at their conferences, consult with their organizations, and counsel them in their difficult moments. I take immense pride in her efforts because at a critical time in her life and mine, I began to see her potential and decided to do everything I could to get behind her development. There are many areas of life where I feel that she is far ahead of me in maturity and insight and capacity. Devotion means that I not only got behind her and pushed, but that I delighted when she jumped way ahead in some things.

I remember an important moment when a mentor-friend said to me regarding my wife, "Gordon, she's a thoroughbred of a woman. Don't squelch her gifts. Encourage them." Recalling that comment, Gail said to me one day with a smirk, "Think of it. What woman wouldn't give everything to be known as a thoroughbred." But she and I both knew the intent of the observation.

Perhaps I would have figured this out for myself. But I'm not sure. Because I have seen a bundle of men who have never reached the serving stage in the marriage. Rather, they have resisted helping their wives grow, for fear that they themselves would fall behind. Or they have been jealous. Or competitive. And everyone has lost as a result.

Today, I think we're in the fourth stage of devotion. I call it solidarity.

And I don't know if there are any more stages of devotion ahead. Solidarity includes romance, companionship, and serving, but it is light-years ahead of the others. It means that I have come to accept Gail not as Superwoman but as she really is: God's daughter, a remarkable human being, a person who carries the joys and sadnesses, the successes and failures, the strengths and weaknesses of a woman of more than fifty years. She has paid most of her dues in life and deserves devotion. I have no reason to demand that she change, that she be perfect, that she fit all the nooks and crannies of my needs or demands. I love her and delight in her exactly as she is. Of course, if she ever asks for some suggestions, I could conjure up a small list.

Solidarity—it wasn't always that way. In a past time, even though I perceived happiness in our marriage, I lived in anticipation that Gail would finally convert to being everything *I* wanted her to be. In that great gettin'-up-mornin' she would like to do everything I liked, want everything I wanted, respond to everything I initiated. She would indeed be the perfect person, and I was sure that day would come when she would see the light and make that happen.

But she didn't. And I stopped expecting that. Because I was wrong. And in some very tough moments I came to see that devotion meant loving my wife in her realness, her brokenness, her possibilities, in God's unique purposes for her life. And when I did that, a new and powerful love flooded my soul for her.

I knew I'd achieved that level of devotion when I awoke from a vivid dream one morning. In the dream we had been together in a life-threatening situation. There was a chance to save myself, but Gail was doomed. She shouted, "Get out while you have the chance!" And as the dream ended, I shouted back, "No, if this is the time to go, we go together!" When I awoke, I knew that my deepest parts were saying, your devotion is now real. You are *solid!*

The man in the bed who feels a mile away from his wife lies there in the darkness and in his private thoughts asks what she wants. One answer is this: she asks for his devotion.

2. SHE NEEDS TO BE CHERISHED; SHE WANTS MY AFFECTION.

I define cherishing as the acting-out of devotion. *Cherish* is an old word. Just old enough that it might also be ready for a return to the vocabulary as a fresh new insight.

What does cherishing mean? A man finds this out when he asks his wife how she wants to be loved. This is a significantly different matter from loving my wife in ways I want to love her. It is rather convenient to include my wife in my whims and desires. It is another matter to enter her life and discover what she finds important.

Cherishing begins with the symbols of a relationship. What gestures of affection are important? The touching, the holding, the kissing. The tender marks of love, not always sexual, but communicative of caring. The gestures that say one is dear, more dear than anything or anyone else. Manners and politeness—easy things to forget as the years wear on and we begin to take each other for granted.

Cherishing means that I take seriously the landmarks of our devotion, and cherishing happens on birthdays, anniversaries, and special events that punctuate our life together. She needs to hear in the form of cards and notes that I remember, that I am thankful, that I care. I write these words not in a cavalier way but with a certain amount of regret, for I recall the occasions when I failed to take notice of a memory or a tradition to which my wife ascribed significance and I walked past it in the busyness of my life. And in my neglect I not only failed to cherish, but I diminished the claims of my devotion.

Cherishing happens when I make the effort to search out and respond to her feelings and concerns. When I listen to her opinions and judgments about life in and beyond the marriage. When I begin to recognize that there are more than a few occasions when her ideas may be far superior to mine, that she has much to teach me, that she has perspectives on life from which I could greatly profit.

And cherishing is on the rise when I am prepared to enter into aspects of life that are important to her as a woman: learning, growing, watching a favorite TV show, simply talking. I'm eavesdropping on two men who are in the airline club waiting to board a flight. I hear one say:

> So she said, "Now that the kids are in high school, I want to go back and finish my degree." I had no idea that anything like that was on her mind, and I asked her how long she'd been thinking about it. "Ever since I dropped out to put you through," she said. Either she concealed that idea real well, or I haven't been listening. Anyway, she's back in, taken three courses, got A's in all of them. So now when we all go to a movie, I'm the only guy in the family that doesn't get a student discount. Crazy, huh? But I'm sure proud of her.

3. LIKE ME, SHE HAS FEARS AND WEAKNESSES; SHE WANTS MY PROTECTION.

It was much clearer in the olden days. Men were warriors, and women were the maintainers of the fire in the village. Protection meant going out to fight off the intruders and bringing home the bacon. It's different now!

Today, protection in a marriage has a lot more to do with the emotional and relational vulnerabilities of the person. In declaring our devotion we come to each other bringing all the baggage that has been accumulated over the first decades of life. A combination of experiences generates fear or a sense of inadequacy. No logic or rational explanation may back up these issues; they just are. And they come with the person.

What have been the experiences my wife has had with the men in her life? Have they been abusive, intimidating, repressive? Have they encouraged thought, development of potential, and social competence? If the latter, the tracks have been laid to a confident and effective adulthood. If the former, the tracks point toward struggle. And the need may be for some amount of protection while the memories of the past are worked through.

Have there been moments of profound humiliation or failure? Deep hurt as a former relationship ended in anger and recrimination? Disillusionment when an anticipated event did not occur? Grief over the death of someone close? The impact of a serious illness or disease?

Four years ago my wife found a lump in her breast. They hoped it would be possible to treat the cancer without taking the breast. But it wasn't, and she had to have a mastectomy. I never realized what a loss it would be for her. She worried that I wouldn't be attracted to her any longer. She mourned some deep loss of her own sense of womanhood. There were many times when all I could do was hold her while she wept. Early on I realized that there were no words that were going to dissolve her grief. So for the most part, I just kept reassuring her about my delight in her beauty and my love for her and then stayed real close.

We've been going through the whole infertility problem. We've waited for a child for ten years, and it's put enormous stress on our relationship. I can't tell you how many times we've come to a month when her period hasn't started at the expected moment, and there's been the slightest hope that we're on our way. Then there's that moment when I hear her weeping, and I know what's just happened. What I've learned is that it's different for men and women. I want a child badly, but nothing compared to her. And there are times when I just don't have the slightest idea what to do. Just be with her, I guess.

We did a lot of making out when we first started going together. And in the first months of our marriage, the sex was terrific. Then one day something happened. She just turned off. At first I thought it was something I'd done. But I couldn't get anything out of her. It really began to affect our relationship. And then it came out. We went to see a counselor, and after a few conversations, she began to tell the counselor and me that there had been an experience of molestation when she was about nine. Her grandfather had done some things to her, and she'd forced the memories down inside for all these years. Then one day she began to feel bad about sex. Now we were beginning to find out why. The fact that I'm willing to go with her every week to therapy has said more about my love for her than anything else I could do. We may win this one if we are patient with the process.

My wife's mother had a way of making her feel stupid all the time. Never seems to have made her feel that anything she did was worthwhile. So she really struggles with a sense of self-worth or that she can achieve something extraordinary. I've had to learn that my encouragement and praise, even for the smallest things, is the most important thing I can give to her. So I pour it on, and I'm ready to cheer anything with the hope that we can erase the old messages and replace them with new ones.

You've just heard from four men who have discovered how to protect their wives in the most vulnerable areas of their lives. We're all in need of protection in one way or another. These just happen to be some of the ways a man's wife may need it. What the men are saying is that protection isn't always muscular. It has to do with assurance, affection, the listening and understanding heart, and the avoidance of any ridicule or impatience. That's another form of devotion.

4. SHE IS CURIOUS ABOUT MY HEART; SHE WANTS MY OPENNESS.

We men have grown up being taught that people want to know us for our skill and our abilities. But down deep inside, most wives want to know something else: the way of our hearts. And this is not easy to give because most of us have never been taught, nor has it been modeled for us, how to give away the key to our hearts.

Because feelings are important to my wife, she wants to know of my feelings. But how can I share my feelings if I have never monitored them? How can I speak of my feelings if, all my life, I have been taught to stuff them, to leave them unconsulted?

My wife wants to know where she can make a contribution to my life. How can she encourage me? What questions nag at me, and can she help me find the answers? She wants to know how I really feel about spiritual matters. Do I trust God?

My wife craves to know what I think. Am I fearful? Do I know where life is going? What are my hopes, dreams, and plans?

> My father was the consummate self-contained man. I never saw him lose control under any circumstances. Never cried, never lost his temper, never showed any emotion. He was not the kind to say "I love you," so I never heard it. I had no doubt that he did, but the fact was that you weren't going to hear it in words. Only in what he did for you. But the point is that I came into married life somehow feeling that this was the way for me to be. And it drove my wife crazy. She was always telling me that there was no way of knowing what I was feeling or what was really bothering me. And she said the same about the positive aspects of life. I didn't show excitement or enthusiasm. And it almost drove us apart. Then I got laid off, and when I told her, a dam burst inside of me. I couldn't pretend that I wasn't devastated. And as I talked through how angry I was, I was surprised at how good it seemed to be that I could share this with her. And she handled me beautifully. The best thing that ever happened to me was losing that job. It taught me that there was a whole new way to live in a relationship. I'm still not real good at opening up, but she tells me I'm doing a heck of a lot better.

5. SHE DESIRES THAT I BLAZE THE TRAIL; SHE WANTS MY LEADERSHIP.

This is not a matter of power or control. My wife has a head of her own. She has dreams, ambitions, and miles to go before she sleeps. But she would like to know that I think like this, too, and that I am willing to be a blazer of the trail when the time comes for that to happen.

In my marriage, I have seen many times that remind me of the flight of Canadian geese, which fly over our home on their way north in the spring and their way south in the fall. I am told that it is the instinct of the geese to rotate the leadership of their famous V-shape formation. The one in front sets the pace, the direction, and creates the windbreak that makes it possible for the others to fly with a little less exertion.

And when the leader grows tired, there is another to replace him while he falls back.

I have accepted the role of the person who blazes the trail. And my wife, Gail, supports that role as long as she knows that I move in accordance with our chosen faith and values. She desires my initiation in thought and choice. She asks only that I honor her responsibility to respond, to build upon whatever idea or dream we are nursing along to a greater level and breadth. That I consider what is important to her and what God may be saying to her.

I do not write these words as if I was a perfect leader in my marriage. Many times I am aware that my wife is light-years ahead of me in various areas of life. Her desire to know God, her care of people, her depth of character, and her commitment to the traditions and values of our family life far exceed mine. And I speak more from truth than modesty.

When a younger married man, I thought that leadership meant taking charge and setting the pace in everything. As an older and somewhat wiser man, I've learned differently. I've come to see that leadership does not mean domination. Rather, it means accepting responsibility for whatever we believe to be the call and the expectation of God upon our lives together. Beyond that, to assure that each of us, working according to our strength and point of competency, is offering inspiration and direction to the other with the intent that together we'll do the right thing.

My sense is that women are far more leadership conscious than men are. It's in their genes to ask in every situation, "Who's in charge here? Who's going to make the right and the best thing happen?" And they are no longer content for the answer to appear in the male gender if the man is not competent. Men can no longer hide behind their ration of testosterone to assure leadership. They must demonstrate their right to exert it. When a man has done that, any wife I know is glad to share the journey.

A man stands at the feedback time of a First Monday session and says,

> I've gotten real lazy about this issue of leadership. I've been letting my wife discipline the kids. I wasn't initiating anything when it came to the two of us having fun together. I didn't take interest in the house so my wife had to keep reminding me about things that had to be done. Then a few months ago she sat me down and read the riot act. She told me that I'd stopped being the man she'd married. She wasn't interested in being my mother *or* my maid. So I had a real serious decision to make, she said. Either get back in the saddle and be what our family needed,

or there could be some drastic changes. So I went out and talked to some guys that seemed to have it together, and they've been kind of mentoring me. It's been hard. Once you get out of the habit, nothing comes easily. But she was right. And the interesting thing is how our marriage is coming back to life.

A man is learning here that the best way to be devoted to his wife may be to let her know that he is willing to take charge of things again.

6. SHE NEEDS TO BE AFFIRMED FOR HER VALUE; SHE DESERVES RESPECT.

My wife has brought a wonderful mind to our marriage. She thinks not always as I think (and I am thankful). She has perspectives, orientations, and experiences that are different from mine. And they are all for her, for me, and for people around us.

Too often I have been in a position to observe marriages where a man has so strangled the mind of his wife that she has stopped thinking. She has no opinions of her own, and if she does, they lie in peripheral matters that he thinks to be unimportant and irrelevant. Sit at the table with such a couple and all you hear is the man talk and offer his opinions. She remains silent, knowing that her judgment is not valued and has not been cultivated.

I might have done this had I not married a very strong and mentally tough woman. I quickly came to realize that she was not going to bow to my thoughts because they came from the mouth of a male. My facts were lovingly challenged; my opinions were tested in debate. My ideas were washed in experience, and little by little, I came to understand something that many in my father's generation did not understand: two brains are better than one.

She wants to be recognized for her deeper or unseen beauty. Not just the beauty of the female face and form (which are certainly there to be appreciated). But the beauty of character and depth. Creativity and competency. A lively soul and strong passions.

When we were newly married, I took Gail to the ranching country of eastern Colorado/western Kansas and plopped her down in a country parsonage seven miles from the nearest paved road and twenty-five miles from the nearest town. Our nearest neighbor was almost a mile away, and rattlesnakes frequented our backyard. I watched her gain the trust and the affection of the ranchers' wives. More than once, when I was gone, she went out in the dead of winter and single-handedly unfroze the windmill. On Sunday she played the piano for the worship service and then rushed back to the baby room to nurse our newborn son, Mark.

Then I asked her to move to southern Illinois and an entirely different congregation where there had been a history of divisiveness and division in the church. I watched her entertain literally hundreds of parishioners in our home as we reached out to know them and love them. I saw her lead Bible studies, counsel women, mentor teenagers, and grow in the process of doing all of it.

Then on to New England, an entirely different style of life. There I watched her raise teenagers, organize several hundred women into an amazing weekly Bible learning experience, write a book, and begin occasional international trips to minister to missionaries and pastors.

For a few years I asked her to travel the country with me as we worked with students and student-workers. I saw her deal with immense disillusionment and disappointment for which she was not responsible. And I saw her walk through a time of withdrawal when we had to seek God about our futures.

On to Manhattan where we lived for several years in the heart of one of the world's great cities. There I watched her mix it up with people of a score of different races and cultures, adjust to apartment living twelve stories up, and learn the ways of the streets—a far cry from Colorado and Kansas.

In all those things I learned the scope of her capabilities, her ability to stretch and meet the extraordinary demands placed upon her. I saw her in moments when no one else could have seen her: when there would have been reason to explode in retribution, when disappointment piled upon disappointment. But in all things she held fast. And I can't think of enough ways to tell her that I respect her.

Respecting her means that I ask her advice and heed it. It means trusting in her decision and choice making. Permitting her rebukes and corrections. Learning that there may be more than a few ways that she can lead me to God. Devotion to her means that I as a husband make these things happen.

7. SHE LIVES A DEMANDING LIFE; SHE NEEDS SOMEONE TO SHARE THE LOAD.

I am old enough to remember the days of "women's work." It consisted of everything under the category of homemaking: cooking, laundry, shopping, tending the children, and cleaning. "Men's work" involved income production, lawn care, and matters pertaining to finance and the car. Jokes were made about women and money, women and shopping, women and talking. Wise and smart men have stopped the joking; boorish men keep telling the jokes.

It's different today. Students of society are telling us that the middle-class lifestyle of the fifties could be maintained with approximately forty-six hours of income-producing work a week. Today, that same lifestyle requires more than ninety hours of income-producing work per week.

The result? In families where there are a husband and a wife, both are probably working. And both must share the load at home. The day of "men's work" and "women's work" has come to an end.

I grew up in a home where I was expected to do "women's work." My boyhood tasks involved a daily dusting of furniture (a necessity with a coal-fired heating system), emptying wastebaskets, cleaning toilets, and vacuuming the carpets. One day my father called attention to the result of halfhearted work: "The next person who comes into this home will look at this dusting job and think it's the way your mother works. You want them to think that of your mother?" I said no and did the job again.

What I learned as a husband was that I didn't mind doing the work about the house. I just didn't see what had to be done. And what's more, I didn't have the natural instinct (do many men?) to put things away after I used them. Result: something like a trail of debris wherever I went.

Slowly, and not without some conflict in which I really hurt my wife, I had to come to the realization that it was *our* home. That its neatness, its tranquillity, and its appearance were *my* responsibility, also.

I wanted my wife on my team. But was I on her team? Picking things up, helping to serve at the table, taking on the kitchen chores, participating in the housecleaning without being begged or badgered. Those were the things I had to learn. And when I did, the response in terms of respect and relationship was remarkable.

A young wife writes,

> I think the thing which hurts me the most (and he never sees this) is that he tells me he loves me all the time but has no idea how deeply I'm hurt when he comes home and shows no interest in our home. From the moment he arrives home he is like one of the children. He leaves things scattered all over the house, never seems to put a thing back where it

belongs. And then it never dawns on him that somebody has to take care of all this. So I feel like I'm nothing but a nag. How do I get across to my husband that his words and his affectionate gestures mean virtually nothing when all he does is add to my work and shows no interest in helping me with it?

8. She Is Willing to Do Almost Anything for Me; She Needs My Appreciation.

The Scriptures say that when God finished each phase of creation, He stopped and looked at what He had done and appreciated it. *To appreciate:* the act of putting value on some thing or some event. *To depreciate:* the exact opposite. Put bluntly, if one does not appreciate, then with silence or neglect, one depreciates.

Most of the women I know (and Gail is at the top of the list) are ready to do anything for the man they love. But their will to serve and support grows thin after a while if there is no response. Much of the fuel we all run on is simple appreciation.

One woman I know made the point this way:

When I worked out in the marketplace, one of the most satisfying things there was to complete a project and have your boss tell you how well you'd done, what difference it was going to make for the organization. You'd go home feeling that your skills and energies were really being appreciated. Then came the day when I got pregnant and was supposed to lay that all aside for motherhood. Isn't that what a lot of preachers say is the thing to do? Well, I was excited about what it would mean to be home with my children and to prepare a place where my husband could come home every evening. And then I began to realize that I'd lost something. *Nobody* took the place of my boss to tell me that my work was appreciated. Sometimes I wanted to grab my husband by the arm when he came home and take him to the kitchen and show him the floor I'd just cleaned. I wanted to say, "There! Take a good look at that floor. What do you think of it?" Someone tell me what a good job I've done.

How does a wife hear appreciation? Cards, small gifts, words? Devotion means that I go out of my way to express thanks for every little thing.

About two years go, out of impulse, I took a little yellow sticky note and wrote, "Into this mirror looks the loveliest woman in all the world."

I stuck it on the upper part of the bathroom mirror that Gail uses every day. Since I rarely use that bathroom, it had never occurred to me until the other day that the note has remained stuck there where she can see it every morning for two years. It's still there! Anyone want to guess what appreciation means to my wife? I guess she hears it as devotion.

9. SHE IS A HUMAN BEING; SHE WANTS TO HAVE FUN.

Twenty-five years into our marriage I learned an important lesson. Gail and I had begun to lose sight of what it meant to have fun together. We loved each other; we were often seen at work together; we shared satisfaction in the structure and solidity of our home.

Our children were teenagers, and that meant that life was full of activity. We stood on the sidelines of every game, appeared at every event that seemed important to them. Our table was often visited by their friends, and vigorous conversations of considerable value were the order of the day.

Then one day the children left us. They left! As they should have done. But when they left, they took a considerable part of our hearts with them. And they took a large parcel of the fun. We awoke one day to the strange conclusion that we had fallen prey to a subtle miscalculation: the fun in our life together had been too wrapped about the children. It was not their fault; it was a rather understandable mistake. We had to learn how to discover fun all over again.

There is a serious danger in the life of married people who have set themselves to high purposes and goals. The development of careers, the desire to serve one's generation, the serious pursuit of a disciplined life—all are noble, lofty goals. But care must be taken to avoid the circumstance in which *life* is sucked out of our central relationships. We become *absent* to each other as we move from one challenge and one obligation to another. Listen to our conversation: it centers on fatigue, why the calendar is too full, why we're going to have to put off something we looked forward to for another month, why we have so few friends, why it's been a long time since we had a laugh.

I know those feelings and thoughts; we've discussed them more than once in our home.

As I look back on those bleak days, I hold myself far more accountable than anyone else in our family. I was at midlife, caught in a turbulence of drives. I wanted to be effective at what I do best, wanted to be the consummate father, wanted to be useful to other people. And I assumed, all the time, that Gail would wait a little while longer until there was time to do the things *we* really wanted to do together.

I found my private thought life often caught up in fantasies of escape: fleeing to Europe for a long walk in the Alps, a sailing trip from Maine to Florida, six months in the forest in New Hampshire without a phone, someplace where there were lots of laughs and few needs. I should have listened to those fantasies; they were trying to send me a very important message. But I was too involved to hear, and besides I walked in a tradition of spirituality that encouraged the squelching of such thinking.

The day came when Gail and I had to stop and reassess the craziness. Life came to a screeching halt, and we had to ask, What have we done to ourselves? It may have been a harsh question for two people who felt they'd worked hard to keep their lives in order, but it was a valuable one. And we came up with some answers we didn't really like. One of the results was the decision: regardless of what anyone says, learn to have fun (in abundance) all over again.

And we have!

Zwolle, Holland. We are in Europe where I am to speak at a conference. In accepting the invitation, we've stipulated that on the day of our wedding anniversary, we have to get away for the day and night. Our hosts have agreed.

So here we are in a lovely Dutch town north of Amsterdam. It's afternoon, and we come across a restaurant, three men in chef's garb sitting out in the sun. I approach them.

"Gentlemen, do any of you speak English?"

"Ja," one of them answers. "We all do."

"I have a problem and need some help. You see, it's our wedding anniversary today, and I want to take my wife here to the best restaurant in all of Zwolle where we can get the very best meal. I'm wondering if this might be the place."

The three men look at each other uneasily. Finally, one speaks, "Ja, you have come to the best place."

"Now we need to be serious about this. We've flown three thousand miles from America because we heard that some of the best food in Holland is served in this town and that it's the best place in the world for a man to take his wife if he really loves her. So you've got to promise me that I'm making a good decision here."

By this time Gail has turned her back on the conversation because she's laughing so hard.

But the three men are very serious about this concern of mine. And they vigorously assure me that I have come to the right place.

"Well, can you show me where my wife and I might sit if we came here tonight?" All three stand up from the resting place, one of them unlocks the door of the restaurant, and soon we are all carefully studying the empty restaurant, discussing which of all the tables is the best for a romantic evening. For several minutes, the men debate this in Dutch before settling on a recommendation.

"Now what would a man order for his wife if he wanted to make sure she was getting the very best meal?" Gail cannot believe what's happening.

The three men pore over the menu, and the conversation in Dutch heats up a bit as they decide what would be the ideal combination of foods for the occasion. And then one of them offers an English description of a multicourse meal they have invented on the spot. They eagerly await my approval. I approve and move on.

"And the dessert?" The same process follows.

"Now I assume that when I bring my wife here tonight, we will have soft music, and you will all be here to give her an enthusiastic greeting." By this time the momentum of the conversation has become so agreeable and they are so anxious to please me that they are ready to say yes to anything.

When we arrived at the restaurant that evening, the entire staff was at the door to escort us to our table. Other diners already at their tables, noting the treatment we were receiving, suspected we were royalty. And we had fun! We really had fun!

I've decided that your wife really knows that you're devoted to her when you give her the message in no uncertain way: *I can't think of anyone else I'd rather have fun with than you.*

10. SHE HAS A NEED FOR GOD; SHE WANTS TO BE "PASTORED."

The word *pastor* is suggestive of the clergy. The word should rather be reminiscent of the shepherd whose task it is to lead, feed, and protect sheep.

There is a sense in which the relationship of a man and a woman in marriage is constantly changing. There are times when a man wants to be "mothered" by his wife. He draws a moment of maternal strength from her nurturing character. This is not a moment for advice giving.

He simply wants to know that there is a sense of the safe place to which he can retreat and find an ounce of peace.

And there is another time when a wife desires to be "fathered" by her husband. She wants to know that someone else has the long view in mind. That her man cares about the spiritual nurture necessary to her and to the family. She desires her husband to want to lead her to God.

Most of us men do not find it natural to lead in the spiritual dimension of life. Spiritual leadership calls for qualities that were not developed in us at an early age, nor has culture placed a value on it.

For more than thirty years I have been involved in Christian ministry in one role or another. I have been expected to lead congregations and organizations in a spiritual manner. I am the one expected to offer the prayers, the sermons, the consolation when someone is in struggle. This long period of involvement in spiritual leadership would lead one to believe that it must be the same in my home. That I have always found it easy to lead my family through the exercises of worship, devotion, and prayer.

But nothing of the sort has been true. I am somewhat ashamed to admit that, apart from the usual ceremonial prayers and religious activities (prayers at meals and festive occasions) of the family, I often neglected my pastoring responsibilities in the first years of our family's life. My rationale was that I was too tired, too preoccupied, too busy to do any more than I was doing. When Gail sometimes wondered aloud why we were not more spiritually active in our private married life, I turned away in silence. I had no good explanation.

All I knew is what most men know. A strange force inside prompted me to resist the simple invitation I should have given to prayer together. I allowed some impulses to lead me away from opening the Scriptures and the devotional literature at the appointed time. Just because one can do these things in public is no guarantee that they can be done as easily in private.

And so the years passed, and Gail waited for the moment when I would hunger to be more of a pastor to my marriage and family.

The wait came to an end through a rush of pain. Migraine headaches with pain so severe that I could hardly stand it caused me one day to cry out for help. "Would you lay your hands on me and pray with me?" I remember saying to my wife. And she came alongside.

Somehow a barrier began to break down in that experience of terrible weakness. The migraines are a long-ago memory now. But I am more than thankful for them because they offered me the opportunity to engage my wife in a dimension of life that is a key delight to both of us today.

It was pain—the pain of migraines, the pain of failures, the pain of pressure—that brought me to an understanding of pastoring my wife. It took years before I found it easy to suggest that we spend time together in the presence of God, that we seek the mind of God for a decision, that we assure ourselves that God was leading in this process or another.

What caused the barrier? I think it had something to do with the age-old struggle that men have with weakness. Spiritual life begins with one's sense of vulnerability; it demands transparency; it causes one to recognize an Authority and Power greater than we are. Spiritual life calls for listening when one would rather act. Spiritual life calls for humility when most of us have been taught to be proud or at least to fake it.

The bottom line is this: spiritual life and leadership ask men to surrender some parts of the image of strength and pride that the culture encourages from boyhood. In the act of pastoring, we fear our loss of masculinity.

Of course, it may not help that some wives listen to our primitive prayers and critique them. Or hold them up to us several days later ("How can you pray and ask God to answer your prayer when you . . . ?"). In ways that I'm not sure I'm smart enough to explain or understand, it is hard to pastor someone you make love to, argue with about money, the kids, or the calendar. Pastoring the person who sees your dirty underwear, has been there when you hit your thumb with a hammer and when you have thrown up in the toilet, is not an easy matter.

Your wife and mine want to know where we're at as we navigate through life at the deep spiritual levels. Are we in touch with God, and are we prepared to offer the kind of leadership that helps them to know God? Or must they go it alone?

BREAKING THE SILENCE

The two Tolstoy quotes hang out there in the darkness for the man who lies close, yet far away, from his wife in the marriage bed. The one quote reveals a man of high aspirations for the human race. The other, a tragic commentary of a wife, disillusioned, empty of spirit, tired of life, sucked dry in a marriage that offered her close to nothing.

The private thoughts rage in the night: *What does she really want from me? Can I give her what she wants? Can we get ourselves out of this awful tailspin that began an hour earlier? Can we come back to the special moments of a day ago?*

Say it. Speak out into the darkness. She's awake. And she's as stubborn as you. Someone needs to break the silence. It might as well be you. Say it: "I've really been wrong tonight." In minutes there are soft words to replace the hard ones. One touch ignites another. And the gestures of love return.

And a man, just before he moves into sleep, once again returns to his private thoughts: *how good the love of this woman beside me; how wonderful the years we have shared; how gracious our walk through life together.*

CHAPTER 10

WHAT STORM SIGNALS MEAN

I'm thinking of an occasion not long ago when the U.S. Navy experienced three serious aviation accidents within the same week. In response, the chief of naval operations called for a complete stand-down of all activity for a period of forty-eight hours. No planes were to fly; ships were to come to a standstill. All naval personnel were to spend two full days studying procedures and searching for evidence of operational carelessness or material defects.

The navy's top officer asked for organizational reflection. Specifically, he wanted personnel to look at the life of the navy and ask, How are we doing, where are we making mistakes, how can we avoid them, what can be done better, and what needs to be changed?

Let me move to a second thought: the pits at Indy. Ever watch a pit crew load fuel, change tires, and check an engine—all in nine and a fraction seconds? It all happens when a shrewd driver decides to temporarily give up the lead and leave the race for a short time and assure himself that his car can finish the race. I'm stretching the point, of course, but what's going on in that pit could be called automotive reflection. It's a checkup and a recharge all in one.

A third thought: a prudent businessman has his books audited and his inventory checked. Why? To make sure everything is legal and profitable. He'll soon be belly-up if he doesn't. Call it fiscal reflection.

A fourth: an experienced wilderness hiker stops frequently to rest and to make sure that he's on the right trail. It's the reflection of an explorer. They'll be sending out the search-and-rescue people if he doesn't do it.

And a fifth: a smart man takes a day off from work and heads for his doctor's office for an annual checkup. It's not fun, to be sure, but the heart and the prostate (and a few other things) need to be examined. A reflection on personal health?

In each of these scenarios it would be absurd if the person in question saw no value in a reflective stand-down. The navy might keep on crashing planes if crews don't search for what's going wrong. The Indy car will never finish if the race is five hundred miles long and the gas tank holds only four hundred miles' worth of fuel. Businesses that permit internal sloppiness (like the bank in England that recently went under) head downhill quickly. And so do hikers without maps and men who neglect their hearts and prostates.

So why would most men agree that the people in these pictures are smart to stop occasionally for the good of their equipment, their organizations, and their bodies *yet fail to see the importance of stopping regularly to take stock of the state of their souls?*

These have been word pictures that illustrate something I'd like to call *reflection*. I've chosen this word to suggest what a man does when he looks within himself and asks questions such as, What do the recent events in my life mean? What is the state of my personal relationships? Why do I have feelings of fear or anxiety in the pit of my stomach? Why am I bored, unmotivated, irritable? Why do I have a longing to make a change, to try something new?

In pursuing answers, the reflective man pulls from the lessons of past experience to know what to say, how to act. He sorts out confusing situations, and he tries to find the source of peace or interior disruption. The man who doesn't know how to reflect, to look within, has forfeited a tremendous resource. What his soul has to say to him. And he should never underestimate what the soul has to say.

Reflection is not natural for some men. It seems easier to just keep pushing on ahead, staying busy, doing what has to be done. As we've already observed, more than a few men have been taught that action alone is where it is. Keep in motion; keep talking; keep doing deals. Maybe something will work out before you have to look inward and do the hard stuff of thinking. Perhaps you can outrun the enemy.

Some of us might prefer to avoid reflection because we fear that a look within might be too painful. We can't afford to discover the possibility that we might be ineffective fathers or husbands. We don't want to face up to the discomfort that our choices are reaping unbearable consequences for us and others. So it's better not to reflect at all. Reflection is stressful for the man who lives in denial.

From my journal:

> At the dinner last night I sat next to F——. He's clearly one of the more brilliant men I've ever met. Highly connected . . . lived everywhere . . . done everything. But then it struck me that he was frantic to keep control of the conversation perhaps so that we wouldn't venture into anything of a personal nature or where he might get blindsided with questions that might make him feel uncomfortable. I'd already noted that his adult children hadn't even bothered to speak to him when he entered the room although they'd not seen him in several months. When asked to give the prayer at the beginning of what might have been a very sentimental occasion, he found it impossible to offer anything but wooden, formal words. When I asked him if what he was presently doing was making him a happy man, he immediately launched into a protest of how pleased he was. Yet it occurred to me that if my marriage was a disaster, if my kids had no respect for me, and if I was unable to express any kind of emotional connection with the occasion we were involved in, I'd probably be off in some corner wrestling with some awfully hard questions rather than up front trying to amuse a crowd with the nature of my personal success.

A strange and destructive reflection comes upon the man who chooses to put the blame for all troublesome things on others or on the system: if I'd married a different woman, if taxes weren't so high, if I hadn't been on the wrong side of the political wind, if it weren't for affirmative action, if . . .

Reflection becomes difficult if a man features himself as being too busy to stop. He fills his life with activity, with the noise of distracting conversation, with things to do and places to go. He becomes uncomfortable with inactivity, with silence. He cannot survive long without the rush of a crammed schedule and people needing and applauding him.

Little by little—because of pain avoidance or denial, or blaming, or busyness—this unreflective man becomes unable to take stock of what is going on *around* him or *in* him. He prefers the company of a noisy television at home or the car radio while on the road. He goes from one thing to another: from work to games to amusement to events and back to work. He does anything to keep from having to look inward.

A look at the life of Jesus gives insight into personal reflection. Mixed with the descriptions of His constant intersection with people are references to the quiet, isolated moments where He withdrew to commune with His heavenly Father. We have this sense of the constancy of the private-thought moments as He determined His pathway and monitored the levels of His endurance and energy. And so we never see Jesus surprised in a negative sense. He was never without the appropriate response. His actions were those of One who understood issues far below the surface at the level of meaning and significance. Result: no wasted time, no bad decisions, a keen focus, and a life in which His mission was fulfilled. Credit a lot of that to His habit of personal reflection. How can we learn from this example?

Even as I write the early drafts of this chapter, a hurricane is making its way toward the eastern coast of the United States. It will hit, the weather people say, about midnight tonight. The storm signals are out from South Carolina to New Jersey. Most people are boarding up their homes and stores, evacuating inland, preparing for the worst.

Technology has helped East Coasters to track this storm for well over a week. Satellites saw it first as it became a tropical depression in the South Atlantic Ocean, and experienced weather people quickly realized that it was more than a generic weather disturbance off the coast of Africa. Then we tracked the storm as it gathered hurricane strength over water and headed directly toward Bermuda. Storm signals sounded, and most Bermudians braced for the blow. They were smart to prepare, and when the hurricane hit, the result was only some minimal damage.

Now, as I write this, we've learned that the hurricane is moving toward the U.S. mainland, and we have reliable estimates of where and when it's coming ashore. Like the Bermudians, many people are getting ready.

But some are not! They don't believe the storm signals. The newspeople always manage to find these folks and interview them. One gets the impression they think a hurricane is an occasion for a party. Some are angry because the weather just might interrupt their vacations. "We're not stopping our vacation for this storm; we'll ride it out," they say. "We stuck it out the last time; we'll do it again." And so by this time tomorrow some may lose their lives, and loved ones will probably blame the weather service for not being rigorous enough in broadcasting its storm signals.

I say all that to offer a metaphor: *storm signals*. The reflective man learns to stop whenever he senses one or more of them. He shuns denial, he refuses to laugh things off, and he doesn't seek escape. He takes storm signals seriously and asks about what can be learned and changed.

Storm signals (like heavy clouds and brisk winds) are rather gloomy in nature. Like the folks on vacation, we'd like to pretend that they'll go away or that they're really misinformation. But the reflective man makes no such assumptions. Like the navy people, he stands down, and he observes and thinks and prepares. Life is full of "tropical depressions" and "tropical storms." We can ride them out. But the hurricanes of personal experience are another matter.

A woman writes,

> As I watch men in action, I am impressed with how few of them ever seem to stop and listen to themselves. Women learn to listen at an early age. They listen to their bodies, for example. They know exactly where they are in their monthly cycles, and they know how much this is going to affect the way they think and see things. They understand that every day is going to be slightly different and that there will be strong and weak moments. And when you know that, you build up a set of initiatives and responses that take you through life reasonably well. And so we learn to listen to every part of ourselves.
>
> But men seem to be another story. I get the impression that they resist listening to anything that comes from within. They talk about playing through the pain, and they seem to think that emotions should never play a role in determining how they're going to function. They avoid the messages of fatigue and wave off the need to deal with things like sadness or fear. My impression is that they get themselves into lots of trouble that could have been avoided if they'd learned to listen more.

So what do we look for when we search for storm signals? Here are some ideas. It's not an exhaustive list, understand, but a representative list that reflective men might want to be in touch with.

MOODS

We watch out for bursts of anger, prolonged bouts of sadness, and continuing feelings of irritation that go beyond the normal. Why do I react with disproportionate feeling toward the guy who cuts me off on the freeway? Why do I assume he did it on purpose when I expect people to offer grace when I do the same thing because I wasn't paying attention?

Why am I irritated at the simplest inconveniences: having to wait in line, reacting to an elevator that takes too long to arrive at my floor, to people laughing too loudly at the next table, to sudden loud noises as children play? What's behind my jitters, my overreactions?

And why am I overcome with feelings of intense sadness? Why am I unable to rejoice with anyone in his success or positive turn of events? Why do I see gloom and bleakness in every possibility? Why has it been days (or weeks?) since I've last laughed? Is there a tendency to avoid the company of other men who seem to have their lives under control, who seem more successful than I perceive myself to be?

The first king of ancient Israel, Saul, was a man who bristled at storm signals. He drifted into a deep melancholy, and his aides found that the only thing that would soothe him was music. That was one of the ways that the young David entered his life. He was invited to the king's quarters to play and sing for him. And it worked. But then Saul would suddenly burst into a frenzy of rage and throw spears at David and presumably anyone else who got in the way.

It would have been a time for Saul to reflect upon his changing moods and what they meant. And it would have been the right moment for a courageous friend to step in and question the king about his moods and his behavior. But perhaps one doesn't do that sort of thing to a king (or a CEO? or a successful athlete? or a guy with a gigantic ego?). And no one did. Before long, the failure to heed early storm signals eventuated in a king gone mad, first chasing David all over the wilderness (as if the young kid was really going to threaten his government), then striking out here and there against perceived enemies until he died a tragic death in a losing battle.

PREDOMINANT THOUGHTS

My wife, Gail, our married children and our grandchildren, and I are in an open sleigh drawn by two huge Belgian draft horses. We are deep in the New Hampshire forest in the middle of winter enjoying a wonderful serendipitous moment. The man who controls the horses warns us that they are about to break into a gallop. "The minute they know they're headed in the direction of the barn, they'll want to run," he says.

Predominant thoughts are like those horses. Give them half a chance, and they begin to race. I'm talking about thoughts that are almost always out of control. They emerge without warning—while we're driving, sitting in church or a business meeting, waiting through a lull in a TV show, lying awake in the middle of the night and returning to sleep seems impossible.

What are these predominant thoughts about? Resentment toward someone who has wronged me? The fantasies of what life could be like if I had more money, lived in a different part of the world, had a different job?

Are they thoughts of escape? A man speaks of issues in his life he thinks are unbearable: "I find myself constantly thinking about how good it would be if the plane I'm on would crash. Or if I could just steer the car into a wall on the freeway. It would be nice to get it over with. Am I suicidal?"

Probably not. It's the mind's way of saying that wearying events are piling up at such a rate that it would be more advantageous to run away than stick around. And thoughts of death are runaway thoughts.

The mind swirls into fantasies, of travel, of pleasure pursuits, of one-night stands. Why? Because a fictional world of the mind becomes more attractive, more stimulating, more manageable than the world we are living in.

A reflective man inventories these uninvited thoughts. Why are they growing in frequency and in variety? What's the underlying message? Why is it easier to take a trip to a mental Disneyland than to deal with reality? Do the predominant thoughts signal that there is something in his life that needs to be challenged, evaluated, changed?

A CHANGE IN KEY RELATIONSHIPS

Storm signals are in evidence when there are shifts (usually negative) in the status of key relationships. Consider this conversation over lunch:

ME: You're resigning from T——?
HIM: Yep! I've had it. Some changes have to be made.
ME: But why? What brought you to make a decision like that?
HIM: A couple of weeks ago I was riding along in the car with my wife and kids. Our son—who's eight now—asked my wife a sports question. And she immediately answered him. And it hit me: I'm away at work so much that the kids have gotten used to getting their needs met without me. It's them and their mother: that's the real functioning family in our home. I'm out of the loop except for paycheck purposes. Here is a simple question that a boy ought to ask his father, but that doesn't occur to him. He asks his mother instead. So I decided that night that I was going to kiss off these

twelve- and fourteen-hour days and do something that will allow
me the time I need with these kids so that they can ask *me*
questions for a change.

There's an example of a man reading a tiny, but significant, storm
signal. It's likely that there had been other signals, and this one acted
like the proverbial straw in a decision process. But he was smart enough
to read a signal that many would have missed, and he realized that some
key relationships in his life were, as they say, going south.

You're probably getting storm signals when your wife says, "If you
loved me as much as you say you do, you'd . . ." Signals are screaming
when you find it easier to lie to your wife than to tell her the truth about
a mistake you've made or something you've forgotten. You know you're
getting signaled when you want to avoid certain friends or their questions. And you want to ask why when you start running from men and
women you've known all your life who show evidences of increasing
spiritual growth.

If I find myself jealous of other people whose fortunes have advanced
beyond my own, if I begin to think of people competitively as better
than or not as good as I am, if I find a cynical or bitter edge in my
general assessment of people, I'm getting some fairly strong signals
that something in my soul has gone sour. If in quiet moments I find that
there is a list of people who, when they come to my mind, stimulate
anger or desires for vengeance, if I find myself plotting how to get even
or to embarrass them, something is wrong. Call these storm signals.

THE USE OF PAIN SUPPRESSORS

A man gets storm signals when he discovers that certain things are
beginning to control the way he lives his life. He begins to increase his
use of alcohol—extra glasses of wine, increased numbers of cocktails at
dinner, growing numbers of trips to the refrigerator for beer.

A man finds himself unable to pass a magazine stand without looking
through a number of "skin magazines." The use of one kind of drug or
another to alter his state of mind becomes increasingly attractive. He
spends every discretionary moment in front of a television watching
sports. He is unable to stop working: the mind on the job during every
waking hour, the feeling of guilt anytime there is a moment of recreation
or play, the sense that he has never done enough.

These signals suggest that some lifelong pain or struggle deep within the soul has never been named and never brought to light where it can be dealt with. It becomes a habit of the heart to suppress it with experiences that create a state of anesthesia. If there's enough alcohol in the system, enough sexual stimulation, enough distraction of work-related issues, he doesn't have to think about the condition deep within. Slam the door shut on what the heart screams out; seek the virtual reality of a more serene state. It works for a while. But the reflective man asks what he might be running from when he prefers the state of anesthesia rather than a clear mind.

The Loss of Focus, Enthusiasm, or Vision

Having been one of those who experienced a total loss of enthusiasm at one time, I can write about this storm signal with feeling. This excerpt is from my journal a few years ago:

> There used to be a day when my dreams were larger than life. Gail used to kid me that all my dreams were expensive. But nevertheless she honored them and listened carefully when I spun them out. But she doesn't have to listen anymore because I'm no longer dreaming. Why? Where did all of this energy go that I once had? I remember how I used to smile at the guy who said, "When I started out in life, I resolved to hit a home run every time I came to bat. Now I'm in the seventh inning, and all I want to do is get through the game without getting beaned." I don't smile at that anymore because I understand exactly what the guy was saying. I guess the question of the day goes something like this: If you've lost your enthusiasm, can you get it back? Can you dream again? Is vision-lost, vision-never-to-be-found-again? If so, life is too long.

When a man begins thinking like this, he better interpret the words as storm signals because that's exactly what they are. And unless he moves into motion rather quickly, the perspective expressed in the words will become a permanent view of personal reality. A man's life becomes reactionary rather than one of initiative or creativity. The mind and the deeper parts go on hold, a devastating paralysis to the spirit.

I am a man who is grateful that the words from my journal describe a bleak time in the past, not the present. The answer to my own question: yes, it is possible to dream again; it is possible to regain vision; it is possible to become enthusiastic, in love with life. God makes this a gift to the man who reads the storm signals for what they are and chooses to seek the kind of restorative help that renews and redirects.

The ancient psalmist is no stranger to these feelings when he writes,

> I cried out to God for help;
>   I cried out to God to hear me.
> When I was in distress, I sought the Lord;
>   at night I stretched out untiring hands
>   and my soul refused to be comforted.
> I remembered you, O God, and I groaned;
>   I mused, and my spirit grew faint.
> You kept my eyes from closing;
>   I was too troubled to speak.
> I thought about the former days,
>   the years of long ago;
> I remembered my songs in the night.
>   My heart mused and my spirit inquired:
> "Will the Lord reject forever?
>   Will he never show his favor again?
> Has his unfailing love vanished forever?
>   Has his promise failed for all time?" (Ps. 77:1–8).

The psalmist is not content to remain engulfed in this personal misery. He reads his own storm signals and resolves to make a break with the status quo.

> Then I thought, "To this I will appeal:
>   the years of the right hand of the Most High."
> I will remember the deeds of the LORD;
>   yes, I will remember your miracles of long ago.
> I will meditate on all your works
>   and consider all your mighty deeds (Ps. 77:10–12).

The man has done the right thing. He's gone back to the place where he lost his focus and his perspective. And the result is a new spirit, a new enthusiasm. But it would not have happened if he hadn't first confronted what many men would have liked to avoid: the fact that the spirit was empty, devoid of the spiritual energy that keeps a man moving strong.

SLEEPLESSNESS

A man is probably getting a storm signal when the body cries for sleep and the mind won't permit it to happen. It's time to ask *why*. Why am I going to bed, sleeping for an hour, and waking for hours at a time? Why do my thoughts spin almost out of control as I toss in my bed and finally rise to walk the halls and rooms of my home? Why is there anxiety boiling in the pit of my stomach?

The ancients had a strong respect for things that happened or did not happen in the night. They took sleeplessness seriously and, when sleep did occur, listened carefully to their dreams, seeking the messages that they believed came from the gods or from the depths of their own being. They saw the messages as potential storm signals impelling them to actions of one kind or another. When did men stop treating the signals with the seriousness of our ancestors?

> In the second year of his reign, Nebuchadnezzar had dreams; his mind was troubled and he could not sleep. So the king summoned the magicians, enchanters, sorcerers and astrologers to tell him what he had dreamed. When they came in and stood before the king, he said to them, "I have had a dream that troubles me and I want to know what it means" (Dan. 2:1–3).

If the quiet messages of the soul are resisted in the daytime hours, it is not unusual that the soul will speak more persistently in the night-time. In the tossing and turning of the sleepless hours is a signal to which a man needs to listen.

DEFENSIVENESS

We are dealing with storm signals when we react to difficult moments with defensiveness, complaining, or whining.

I am defensive when I resist any attempts to evaluate my work or my life—performance. I refuse to listen, to consider that anyone might offer a different outlook on what I am doing or becoming. Thus, I become angry or make excuses or try to deflect the blame to someone else.

During a recent season of professional football, a large number of New York Giants fans pelted the visiting San Diego Chargers and their coaches with snowballs from the grandstands. Several dozen were ejected from the stadium, and many lost their season tickets. One snowball thrower found his picture on the front of a sporting newspaper the next day. There he was in full color, his arm extended in the familiar follow-through position just as he'd released a snowball. When the authorities advertised a $1,000 reward for identifying the man in the picture, fifteen people called to offer his name. He was subsequently charged with disorderly conduct.

When interviewed on television, he gave these various explanations for his behavior:

1. When in Rome, you do as the Romans do.
2. I was simply throwing a snowball back at other fans.
3. Things got out of hand.
4. Why did I get singled out when so many were doing the same thing?
5. The whole thing could have been avoided if the snow hadn't been there.

In recent days I have had some intense visits with a young pastor who is struggling to gain the loyalty and respect of his congregation. As I listened to his account of relationships between his lay leaders and himself, I began to recall a conversation that probably did more to shape my life as a pastor than any other.

I was (at one time) a very young pastor, and each Monday I met with the chairman of the church's board. In the middle of one such meeting, the chairman, a wise and rather tough man, suddenly waved his arm as if to call time-out to our conversation.

He said, "Pastor, I need to tell you something. I've met with you week after week and noticed that you have a difficult time ever listening to difficult news. You want to give one excuse after another. You spend more time trying to explain yourself than you do listening and asking where the point of truth might be. You better beat this one, or you're never going to be an effective leader."

He had pointed up a storm signal. My defensiveness was an indicator of just how unsure of myself I really was. On the surface, I tended to act as if I had everything under control, as if I knew exactly what was happening and should happen. But the truth was that I didn't know half as much as I tried to pretend. And my defensiveness when caught and critiqued was the evidence. Every pastor (every leader) needs a man like the one who pointed up my patterns of defensiveness to me.

It was time to become a reflective man. To have reacted angrily to his comments would have been to forfeit one of the great learning experiences in life. But to stand down, as I did, and think deeply over this exposure of a dangerous tendency in my leadership style made all the difference.

Some men need to listen to their prevailing tendency to whine or complain about everything that appears to go against them. The attitudes (poor me, everyone's against me, no one understands, I need better breaks) that attempt to garner pity are merely signposts, or storm signals as we've been saying, to trouble on the interior. And when we listen to ourselves and hear the childish tone beginning to enter our speech, it's time to become the reflective man who asks why.

GUILT

Perhaps no other storm signal is meant to give a more urgent warning that something is wrong and needs to be addressed than what we call the power of guilt. It is a message that comes deep from the soul saying that something is terribly wrong.

More than a feeling or an emotion, guilt is the pain message of the soul crying out that there has been a violation of God's law or principles that we or our base community has created by which we should live.

Guilt is an unpopular subject for many people. And so we hear someone say, "You're putting me on a guilt trip," or "All he does is raise your guilt level."

Gail and I once visited a village deep in West Africa where most of the people were sick with leprosy (sometimes called Hansen's disease). People who have read the Bible are very familiar with the condition. Nerve endings are deadened so that a person never really feels pain at the extremities. Burn the fingers, get an infection in the foot, take a bite from a poisonous spider on the nose, and never feel a thing. Sound good? Not really! When you see people with leprosy whose limbs are rotting away, falling off because they've had no pain to warn them of trouble, you give thanks for the pain messages of the physical system.

Guilt is the pain message of the spiritual system. It speaks to the person on a divergent path from God. It calls attention to choices and values that are likely to be destructive and harmful. It warns when someone is on the verge of breaking or has already broken covenants and trusts.

The pain message of guilt as a storm signal does not last indefinitely. It appears that men can outlive guilt by ignoring it or rationalizing that its message is untrue or unreliable. Many men live beyond guilt, and they generally pay a strong price for it.

Recently, an American Airlines 757 crashed into the side of a Colombian mountain. At this writing, all signs point toward human error as the reason for the accident. Nine seconds before impact, an instrument in the cockpit began to sound the loud audio warning that the plane was flying dangerously low. This is what guilt is supposed to do: warn us that we are walking (or flying) into danger, that we must pull up before disaster strikes.

My longtime publishing friend Victor Oliver tells of a time when he was the guest preacher in a midwestern church: "As I sat waiting to preach, I felt a strong inner message from God that I should convey to the congregation at the beginning of my sermon. So when I was introduced, I said, 'Perhaps this will seem strange, but I feel the Spirit of God telling me to say to someone in this congregation that you are guilty of gross fraud and need to stop what you are doing this very minute and make amends. And if you do, God will enable you to escape from your trip. I don't know who this person is, but I feel that I must deliver His message.'"

Oliver went on to preach his sermon and to return to the hotel where he was staying. Later that afternoon a man approached him in the hotel dining room and asked if he might spare a minute: "I'm the man you were speaking to this morning when you said you had a message for someone who was guilty of fraud. Thank you for speaking God's message to me."

One wonders how many men are living with the secrets behind guilt, this most powerful storm signal that seeks to warn us. Rather than fight the message of guilt, it would be a wiser thing for a reflective man to recognize the gift of this interior spiritual system.

David, author of many of the psalms, gives us a vivid description of the guilt experience when he writes,

> When I kept silent,
>   my bones wasted away
>   through my groaning all day long.
> For day and night
>   your hand was heavy upon me;
> my strength was sapped
>   as in the heat of summer.
> Then I acknowledged my sin to you
>   and did not cover up my iniquity.
> I said, "I will confess
>   my transgressions to the LORD"—
> and you forgave the guilt of my sin (Ps. 32:3–5).

The message behind guilt is one of *repentance,* an ancient word that basically means "to turn around and choose another direction." That's a hard thing for a man to do, especially if it challenges his pride and self-image. But I know of nothing more powerful when it's done.

My grandchildren play about our home with an energy level that often invites bumped heads and scratched knees. We are not the first to call these injuries boo-boos. And our grandchildren are not the first to discover that one of the important points in the healing process is for a grandparent to kiss the boo-boo. As our grandchildren move through their twos and threes we have kissed a lot of boo-boos. Something beautiful happens almost every time. The magic of the kiss seems to make most of the pain go away.

There is magic in the grace of a God who offers the perfect response to guilt. He, too, kisses the boo-boos of the heart when a man becomes man enough to acknowledge the fact of his guilt and the causes behind the message. What a man names before his God and others who have been offended, God covers with restorative kindness and forgiveness. And like the pain of a bumped head or a scratched knee, the guilt goes away.

We have looked at several storm signals. There are many, many more. The reflective man takes these signals with optimum seriousness. Like the navy, he takes the time to stand down. Like the racer who can read the gauges on his car, he heads for the pit. Like the businessman, he examines the books. Like the hiker, he frequently checks his location. Like the smart businessman, he makes an appointment for his annual physical. And when the message comes that something is amiss, he responds accordingly with self-examination and change.

Some time ago I came across a description of the sinking of the *Titanic* that seized my attention. The words come from Richard Mayhue, a California pastor, in *A Christian's Survival Guide:*

> At 2:20 A.M. on April 15, 1912, the impossible happened. The unsinkable ship [the *Titanic*] sank. The most celebrated cruise ship in all of history nose-dived to the Atlantic bottom. It had sailed four days earlier from North Hampton, England on its maiden voyage en route to New York; no expense had been spared to make it the most gala cruise ever. All went according to schedule until Sunday night when the *Titanic* sailed into an ice field.
>
> She had received four warnings of impending danger that day from ships who were in the midst of the ice, but she chose to ignore all four—

several did not even reach the bridge or the captain. At 11:00 P.M. that Sunday night the wireless operator, John Phillips, received a direct warning call from the *California* which was ten miles away in the midst of some very large ice.

Phillips was tired, having sent messages all day to America. So that night he cavalierly tapped back, "Shut up, shut up, I'm busy." Forty minutes later the beloved ship of the White Star Line collided with an ice behemoth.

Within hours she rested in her watery grave along with 1,500 passengers and crew, certainly one of the world's great human disasters.

Figuring out the message in this story is, as they say, a no-brainer.

"It is with the heart that one sees rightly; what is essential is invisible to the eye," wrote Antoine de Saint-Exupéry in *The Little Prince*. Reflective men understand this. And although a few men may be behind the curve in understanding the nature of reflectiveness, they work at it. Taking the time, the effort, the opening of the ear and eye to hear and watch the storm signals that send their messages to him that something is wrong, that something needs correction, that something needs assistance. In so doing the hurricanes are tamed, and life goes on in greater fullness and maturity.

CHAPTER 11

THE
MANAGEMENT
OF SELF

He could be one of the great competitors of his time," the play-by-play announcer remarked, "but he doesn't know how to manage himself." That was said as a television camera focused on the figure of a mammoth football player, ejected for fighting, heading from the playing field to the locker room. It was the fourth time in as many games that he had lost his temper and picked a fight. And all four times he'd gone to the showers.

He doesn't know how to manage himself. The words stuck in my mind, and I identified them with one of the private-thought themes of many men: the ability to bring all parts of one's life under personal control and to live in a personal harmony that is economic (not wasteful), effective (not weak), and satisfying (not guilt-producing). Some people relate this to the notion of self-discipline.

Control has always seemed a central issue in the life of a man. The control of events, the control of things, and the control of other people are general examples. In one of Paul Newman and Joanne Woodward's finest movies, *Mr. and Mrs. Bridge,* the Bridges sit at dinner at the local country club. When warnings come that a tornado is approaching, all the guests in the dining room head for the shelter of the basement. All, that is, except for Mr. and Mrs. Bridge. Mr. Bridge insists that they remain where they are and continue their dinner. The silent message is clear: he knows better than the weatherman on the radio, and he and he alone, not the club manager, will determine if and when they should seek the safety of the basement. Even though the lights go out, glass is heard breaking, and trees are falling, Mr. Bridge will not budge. "I see no need to scurry into a hole," he says to India, his wife. And she, totally abandoned to his influence, is afraid to protest and so continues to sit at the table pretending to enjoy her meal.

"Where are the Bridges?" someone asks in the basement. "He doesn't know the meaning of the word *retreat*," comes the answer. "He is like one of Napoleon's fourteen-year-old foot soldiers." Upstairs, as the storm worsens, Mrs. Bridge finally gains the courage to ask if they should not reconsider and go to the basement. "Now look here, India," he says, "for twenty years I've been telling you when something will happen and when it will not happen. Have I ever, on any significant occasion, been proved wrong?" As she weighs her answer, the lights suddenly come back on, and the storm seems to instantly diminish. All becomes quiet. There is no need for Mrs. Bridge to commit herself. Like it or not, her husband's point seems to have been made. Mr. Bridge seems the consummate man; he is in control of everything. But even the weather?

I saw the will of a man to control a couple of years ago when Gail and I were walking along a New Hampshire country road. Suddenly, a huge, very ugly dog came running at us, growling and barking from a cabin nearby. There was nothing friendly about his approach. Instantly, I reacted, pointing my walking stick toward him to let him know that I was "armed" and that I wanted some distance between us. At that moment a bearded man appeared from one side of the cabin and shouted angrily, "You hit that dog, and I'll break the stick over the top of your head!"

The man was both my age and my size. But he was angrier, and I was not interested in testing his resolve. But then I didn't want Gail or myself bitten, either. Control became the issue: Whose way would the situation be handled? It was clear that the dog's owner wanted the control more than I did, and he was prepared to assert himself in whatever way necessary to make sure that it was his. My mind raced, seeking an appropriate response. I found in the darker side of myself a desire to win the confrontation, but in the better side a more powerful desire to settle it without doing something that invited craziness.

I'm not sure my response accomplished that, but I stood still, staring at the man, and said as firmly as I could, "Call off your dog!" He did, and the dog bounded to his side. Crisis defused! I stood for a moment staring at him, and then I turned my back on the situation as if I hadn't heard his earlier words and walked on. Which man controlled? I'm sure he thought he did.

Take a former government official, Alexander Haig, secretary of state at one point for President Reagan. When the president was shot and had to undergo surgery, Haig immediately convened a news briefing. Since the vice president was away from Washington, a reporter asked, "Who's in charge?" Wanting to reassure an anxious country and, at the same time, wanting to assert himself, Haig looked into the cameras and said, "I am in charge." Although the U.S. Constitution saw things differently, Haig nevertheless wanted to convey a message quite in keeping with the masculine temperament: *I am in charge.* Alexander Haig never lived that moment down.

The need to control is not virtuous, but it nevertheless remains a male fantasy. To know, to influence, to be on top of all things. Our childhood perception of our dads is that they could do anything; they knew everything; they had (or could have) everything. Or so we thought.

Most men would like to control at least a piece of the world around them. They admire football coaches because they appear to be in charge. Coaches send personnel into the game, and they pull them out. They decide which plays will be run. Within the confines of the playing field, they play a man's game. They say what goes. Men would like to have something of the same influential "word" in the life of a family or with their close friends. They want to be heard and respected. If they feel they're being ignored or defied, they feel a definite threat to the notion of manhood.

But the most important kind of control is the control or management of self. And when it becomes clear that a man can't even bring parts of himself under management, his personal morale, his self-esteem, hits bottom. That kind of control, what I have called the *management of self* (or self-discipline), is most significant.

My journal carries a frank account of a day when I was not properly managing myself. Days before, I'd made a decision to lose a bit of weight that I ought not to be carrying around. I'd been doing well for several days, and then I went on a speaking trip and slipped:

> At breakfast I broke the rules and ate twice the amount of pancakes and pure maple syrup that I should have eaten. And I must add for the purposes of honesty that there was a large bowl of pure whipped cream on the table that I could not resist. My personal commitment simply wasn't strong enough. So I freely ate because *everyone else was doing it,* and (in the absence of inner restraint) no one was there to remind me that I shouldn't. Then at lunchtime when I got to the airport, I had nothing

better to do because planes were delayed. So I went up to the restaurant and ordered a cream-pasta dish, which came with an overload of Italian bread and *real butter*. And I ate it all! Now I not only had no one to remind me of my weight-loss commitment, but I also had a waiter who wanted to help me out in this downward spiral. I was idle and my desires to eat just took over. The same conditions prevailed at dinner. I ended up at a McDonald's, *and I ordered the largest of all the cheeseburgers and fries.* And, again, ate it all!

I'm ashamed of this! It's a defeat of the will. I had made some great progress for several days, but now I am back to square one. This seems to be a personal metaphor for a lot of things in my life that want to resist permanent control. Today I'm in a repentant mood, and it's clear that something deep within me wants to deal with this.

The concern for the management of self covers a large personal span of things. The management of thoughts, feelings, desires, choices, deeds. Can they ever be brought into harmony? Or must I feel that I am in constant battles with this part of the self or the other? Why this anger, this foul mood? That sexual temptation? These struggles with ambition, laziness, envy, jealousy, resentment? Why couldn't I have said no? Why that choice? Why can't I get this thing done? What was behind that wasted time? Why was it impossible to say, "I'm sorry," or "I love you," or "You're absolutely right," or "I need some help," or "What we are talking about here is absolutely wrong!"?

Thomas Kelley had these internal struggles in mind when he looked at the inner life of a person and wrote in *A Testament of Devotion,*

> Each of us tends to be not a single self, but a whole committee of selves. And each of these selves is a rank individualist, not cooperative, but shouting out his vote for himself when voting time comes. And even when a consensus is taken, the disgruntled minority agitates on the streets of the soul.

More than a little time of private thoughts centers on this wish. What would it take to bring these "selves" under control? What do I have to know? What are the steps? Does anyone have the secret?

I see these questions written on the faces of scores of men who go off on men's retreats, attend Promise Keeper conventions, or come to something like our own First Monday in Lexington, Massachusetts. They have a picture in mind of what a self-managed man looks like, and they're looking for a way to make it happen.

This kind of thinking is often stimulated in a moment of self-loathing. Something has gone wrong, the result of mistakes, laziness, lack of thoroughness, or poor discipline. My journal entry is a good example. Worse yet, it's something that seems to happen over and over again. Thus, a man drifts into an inner reverie: Why can't I bring this thing under control? Why am I not in charge?

What often results is one more *intention:* the promise that something is going to be different. Tomorrow, I am going to start losing weight (and this time I'm serious!). When we get through this business project, I'm going to start being more attentive to my wife; this marriage is going to get better. Starting next quarter, I'm going to lead the regional sales team because I'm going to discipline myself to make more calls. Next time I get into this kind of situation, I'm not going to let myself get drawn in the conversation to the point where I lose my cool.

Over the years I have visited with many men about their private thoughts regarding self-management. But no conversation stands out more than the one I had with a man in his early fifties whose perception was that his life was one long string of failures. I don't think he was correct, but he was convinced that he'd never finished anything of significance, never reached any of his goals, never been able to shape his character to the point where he might be satisfied with himself. He saw only bad choices, bad actions, bad relationships. Suddenly, he totaled up the score, and as far as he was concerned, he perceived himself as a big zero. He put his face in his hands and said over and over again, "I'm so disappointed. I'm so disappointed. I'm so disappointed."

Private thoughts that center on the in-charge question begin to make headway when a man first asks himself, How do I handle the truth about myself? What is my reaction when and if the score adds up, and I find myself losing ground? Is there denial, blame, victim talk, whining, or quitting? Or am I like the real pros who, having lost a game on Sunday, head for the practice field on Monday determined to drain every ounce of valuable experience out of the losing effort so that next Sunday is different?

I'm thinking of Ahab, one-time king in biblical Israel. He complained about a prophet, Micaiah, one day and revealed his bias when he admitted, "I hate [Micaiah] because he never prophesies anything good about me, but always bad" (2 Chron. 18:7). He couldn't handle the truth about himself, which is the first step toward the mismanagement of self. Another Hebrew king, Jehoiakim, received a searching letter from the prophet Jeremiah, and when his assistant read a portion Jehoiakim didn't like, "the king cut [the piece] off with a scribe's knife and threw [it] into the firepot, until the entire scroll was burned" (Jer. 36:23).

On the other hand, I don't think there is a biblical personality, outside of Christ, who models the management of self better than Daniel of Babylon who has an Older Testament book named after him and his story. The man lived a long way from his home where family, friends, customs, and cultures could have partially explained his noble behavior as both a private and a public person. He worked for pagan kings whose ethics and morals were considered vile (if you were Jewish), and yet Daniel never capitulated to their pressure or their influence, even when his life was at stake.

Early in his youth, Daniel was enrolled in a West Point-like academy for training in leadership. The menu at the dinner table included the finest foods and wines. Everyone was expected to accept the king's hospitality. A man would have been a fool, so it seemed, if he didn't. Daniel didn't! He said no, having found somewhere deep within the resolve to reject outside influences. We read this simple story and immediately see right through it to the deeper point: that the battles for the management of self—who's in charge—are won on these small playing fields. Say no or yes to the little things, and you set the stage for the day when you'll need the courage and the wisdom to say yes or no to the bigger things. And Daniel did that. Result: we never see him out of control.

So as we reach back to the ancients, we have a couple of extreme models: Ahab who never said a useful no to himself in his life, and Daniel who never got himself into a spot he could not handle. On the spectrum between the two extreme models, the question hits: Where are we?

Private thoughts that center on the management of self have no value if they are not founded on the truth about oneself. And that requires three perspectives.

1. WE NEED TO RESOLVE OUR PAST HISTORIES

One day I picked up a box of books at a library sale in a New Hampshire town. Among them was a book published in 1947, *The Mature Mind*, by a then well-known psychologist, Harry Overstreet. As I thumbed through the book, I caught this comment:

A human being does not grow beyond a problem that has deep emotional significance for him until he comes to terms with that problem: until he understands it; accommodates it in his life arrangements; if possible, resolves it entirely. Instead of growing beyond such an unresolved problem—and of growing beyond its power to hurt—*the individual becomes fixated at the point of development where he encountered the problem* (italics mine).

These words, written fifty years ago, speak right to the situation of more than a few men. A man cannot control what he hasn't named.

As some of these chapters have been written, we have watched NATO troops entering Bosnia on a peacekeeping mission. There are occasional reports of sniper bullets coming from hidden sources and land mines hidden beneath the surface of roadways. These hidden sources of danger threaten the lives of servicepeople every day. And until the shooters are identified and the land mines located, the danger will persist.

What occurs to me is that same sort of thing exists far beneath the surface of a man's life. The bullets and the explosives of past events that remain unnamed, unresolved, unconquered. With some regularity their effect is felt in the reactions and patterns of life he now follows.

Back to weight control as an example. A man I like speaks of his struggle with eating: "When I was a boy, my mother would put a spoonful of sugar in my mouth every time I felt bad about something. I have come to realize that long ago I began to associate bad feelings and stress with feeling better by tasting something sweet." It's taken thirty years to unearth this land mine of motivation at the root of a weight struggle.

What is the truth about ourselves in the past? The answer to that question lies in looking back to at least four sources of shaping experience, four dimensions of personal history that often converge to bring either conflict or harmony.

The first dimension is (buckle up for this) theological or biblical in character, and I feel an obligation to begin with it. So stick with me! *Each of us is made in the image of the God of the Bible.* At the core of ourselves we are made to echo the essentials of divine character: love, wisdom, justice, righteousness, compassion (to name just a few). The deepest parts of us long to be in tune with this godly personality and groan in soul-pain when we are not. Unless we deliberately and tenaciously manage to cut off these signals from the inner parts, we will always be uncomfortable with choices that deviate from the character of God, which He has stamped upon our nature.

Second, *we carry within us the major themes of character and experience of our family lines.* These are mysteries also difficult for me to understand, but there is no doubting that we also reflect the long-haul image of our family line. The older we get, the more we see how much we look like and maintain the characteristics of our fathers. It's scary the first time you look in the bathroom mirror or a storefront window and see your father's expression or hairline. Or sometimes it's that of an uncle or a great-grandfather. It's there in the genes, and we cannot deny it. Only with bursts of sustained energy can we disown the weaknesses and strengths of our families.

Third, *we carry within us from the past the direct messages of our birth parents.* The effects of their parenting in the first years of life are powerful, often indelible. Early religious leaders well understood that the first seven years of a person's life are the most significant in forming character and faith.

It is suggested that even our basic perceptions of the kind of God there is in heaven are formed by our earliest perceptions of our parents—specifically our fathers. If a father is or was an angry man, it will be hard not to think of God in the same light. If a father is dominating or highly controlling, one has a similar impression of God. Weak father, weak God. And so the impression forms the notion of the divine until we deliberately choose to reengineer the impression.

Finally, as we look back into our personal histories, *we carry within us the accumulation of our life-experiences:* the accomplishments; the disappointments, embarrassments, and failures; the strange moments of learning that stick with us for the rest of our lives. We really can't disown them. We can shed a few of the past events and experiences perhaps; but the chance of running away from the past is virtually nil. It's always there, and it always seems to be a nagging reality somewhere just beneath the trapdoor of our minds.

At the age of six, I once went to the butcher for my mother and refused the penny change when I paid the bill. When the butcher told this to my mother—folks did that in those days—she sternly rebuked me. "Never forget to bring home the change, even if it's a penny. Every penny is important!" And I never have forgotten again. To this day I find myself waiting, no matter how long, for even a penny or two of change that I have coming to me. I don't think it has anything to do with greed. It's just that my mother ground it into me at a strange and impressionable moment of learning.

Private thoughts about personal history become far more directed and useful when you refuse to let your mind wander and you channel it toward answering questions such as the following. Call them a personal historical inventory, and ask yourself,

- Who have been the formative persons in my life who have orchestrated the "strange moments of learning"? And what did they teach?
- What have been my key failures and disappointments in life, and what has been their long-term effect?
- What is my history of personal relationships? Have I used people or given to them? Do I withdraw from people or go toward them?
- What are the key areas of my character or personality that I dislike and desire to change? (A friend says to me: "I began to study Paul's 'fruits of the Spirit' last night. You know those qualities he says ought to belong to every follower of Jesus: love, joy, peace, patience, etc. I realized as I studied them that I'm not a very kind man. I've got to treat my son and my wife differently.")
- What unhealed or open wounds am I living with?
- How accurate or trustworthy are my feelings? Am I in touch with them at all?
- What is my starting point for beliefs and values? Who or what do I openly reverence? (Some months ago I toured the St. Stephen's Cathedral in Vienna. A sign said that there was a surveying stone in front of the cathedral that marks the point for all surveying measurements in the country. That night I wrote in my journal about the necessity of knowing what was the starting ground for all measurements in my life's choices and relationships.)
- What have been the dominant themes of your life that keep returning again and again?

These nosy questions force open the filing cabinet of the past life. They cause us to go back through the files of experience and begin the task of bringing life up to date. Overstreet is correct: "A human being does not grow beyond a problem that has deep emotional significance for him until he comes to terms with that problem: until he understands it; accommodates it in his life arrangements; if possible, resolves it entirely."

And what do we do with such files? Some need to have "forgiveness" stamped on them. Others need to be reinterpreted in the light of what we know now. Still other files need to be thrown away because they have no relevance or significance any longer. We cannot afford to let them dictate who or what we want to be in the present.

The point: management of self begins with a bold searching of the past and the settling of issues that have often been fountains of shame, embarrassment, fear, or inadequacy. For the man who prays, God helps here.

2. WE NEED TO KNOW WHERE WE ARE NOW!

In a set of essays entitled *The Way of Man,* Martin Buber relates the rabbinical story of an older man who was chronically forgetful. He would awaken in the morning but forget where he'd put his clothes. He would spend the entire day, the rabbis said, seeking out his clothes, and by the time he found them, it was time to go back to bed. Years went by, and each day was one of total futility: get up, look for your clothes, go back to bed. Until the older man had an idea. As he went to bed, he proposed to himself, he would write down where he put his cap, his shirt, and his pants. That would cut down on the time needed for the daily search. It worked!

The next morning when he got up, he located his clothes immediately, thanks to the bright idea of the night before. But having dressed, he suddenly had time for a question he'd never asked before: "Now that I've found my clothes, where am I?"

The rabbis understand something that many people do not. They perceive that human beings can be so busy pursuing foolish things (like finding clothes) that they never have to ask, Where am I? So don't be surprised, the rabbis would say, if the question stumps you when you ask it.

Some years ago I authored a book entitled *Ordering Your Private World.* The preponderant number of responses to that book came from one chapter that describes people in one of two categories: called or driven. Somehow the questions that were included in that chapter caused a large number of people to sadly conclude that their lives were far more marked with a sense of drivenness than any sense of calling.

If there were questions that might help you identify the issues of the past, there are also questions that might help you map out the present in your life.

Ask questions such as,

- Who am I trying to please?
- What am I trying to acquire that defines security for me?
- With whom am I competing?
- What am I running from?

- What would I die for?
- Who are my friends?
- To whom am I accountable?
- Do I have any sense of goodness about myself?
- In the eyes of others, what am I valued for?
- Does death have any relevance in my thinking?

Stephen Covey tells the story of a young man who became disillusioned, so he said, with the American way of life and all of its success orientation. Against the wishes of his parents, he left the country and traveled to Japan where he joined a commune. In the days that followed, his parents received glowing letters from him about life under the guidance of a guru. He had found the peaceful way. Then one day he excitedly called home to report that he was doing so well that he was about to be named the second in command of the commune.

The point of Covey's story is that you can think you're going to bring about a renaissance in self-management by changing jobs, changing friends, changing locations, changing families. But usually, there is no change. The real changes are not "out there"; they are "in here" (I'm pointing to my heart)—the part we carry with us day and night no matter what the external changes.

3. WE NEED TO KNOW WHERE WE ARE HEADED

The management of self demands a vision for where we are going and what we wish to be.

Again, I want to turn to Martin Buber. In another place the man wrestles with the notion that we can sum up the totality of who we are with three penetrating questions:

1. What am I thinking, and what do my thoughts mean? It occurred to me that he's dealing with the issue of a person's *convictions:* the set of values and beliefs that flows out of a relationship with the divine. No one can experience closeness to God and not come away with a strong sense that some things are right, others wrong; that eternal facts call upon us to be unique people and behave in unique ways.

2. What am I saying, and do my words accurately express my thoughts? I hope I'm not being too cute (I do some public speaking and like occasional alliterations) when I suggest that the question refers to our *confessions,* the statements that identify or describe where we're going in life, why we're going there, and what we think it all means.

3. What am I doing, and do my deeds conform to my words? I seized upon the word *contributions* because that's what I think life is all about at its highest level: contributing—giving rather than taking, adding value rather than slashing it, building rather than destroying. To come to the end of my life and know that someone saw me as a contributor, well, that's about as high an aspiration as I might ask for.

So I like these questions and the kind of thinking they make possible. They force me to build upon my reflections of the past and the present and to become intentional about the years of the future. A man cannot pretend to think himself under personal management if he does not do this. Like a set of lined-up dots, these three questions—thinking, saying, and doing; convictions, confessions, and contributions—suggest a harmony of the total man.

Some of us nurse strong convictions within, but we may not say much about them (confession) or do much about them (contribution). Some of us may be avid talkers (confession), but our inner lives are bereft of conviction, our performances absent of contribution. And some may appear to be a flurry of activity, but you never know what they really believe (confession) or why (conviction). Think about that before you read farther.

When there is such a discontinuity in the dots, problems are inevitable. That was one of the major struggles of Simon Peter (the heavyweight disciple of our Lord). His thoughts, words, and deeds didn't always line up. The colossal failure in his life best known to us was built on the disharmony of his thoughts and words on the one hand, his deeds on the other.

The impetuous disciple could promise the world. But one never knew whether or not Simon's words accurately reflected his convictions and whether or not they would lead to real contributions. He seemed unable to deliver when the time for action arrived. Thus, the man who said he would dare to die for Jesus (confession) ended up disowning Him when crunch time came (contribution). The particular event seemed a defining moment for Simon, for his courage quotient climbed considerably after that humiliation. The dots began to line up more and more, and you got the feeling that he steadily gained new levels of management in his life. Which, by the way, is comforting because the change came a few years into his adult life. In other words, a man can change.

But the point is this: alignment of conviction, confession, and contribution plays a key role in the management of self. And sometimes it takes a crisis of some sort to drive us toward realignment.

Many years ago I spent some time in the Ecuadorean jungle. Each day I was flown to various villages of Indians who lived in places so remote that only a plane could reach them. We would drop down out of the sky onto rough landing strips (barely wing wide) carved out from the tall forests. Each "airport" was more terrifying to me than the one before it. The daily ordeal of takeoffs and landings began to adversely affect me. Within a short time, I became convinced that there was going to be one flight too many and that the pilot and I were going to die in a flaming crash. Thus, I became preoccupied with my pending death. But I was a man, and most men do not like to admit to such inner struggles. So I deceived myself and others, telling everyone what a great time I was having when, in fact, I would have paid dearly to have been back home.

Each night I returned to the jungle base and withdrew to my room in the guest house. With the aid of a candle (electricity was in short supply) I opened my journal and wrote long, morbid, heart-searching letters to my wife, Gail, and our children, Mark and Kristen. It seems silly now, but I felt at the time that I was writing the words of a soon-to-be dead man. And what did I write about? My love for my family. My hopes and dreams for our children as they grew up without their father. My regrets of things not done, words not said. And one more thing: my sadness over intentions I'd never fully realized. The writings were filled with a sort of spiritual will and testament: what I believed (my convictions and confessions) and what I wished I could have done (my hoped-for contributions).

"When a man knows he is to be hanged in a fortnight, it concentrates his mind wonderfully," wrote Samuel Johnson. And so it was with me. I was dealing with these three questions—my dots.

Those pages remain in my journals some twenty-five years later. Obviously, I survived the jungle flights, but I never completely forgot the private thoughts, especially the ones about the future I'd never expected to see. It is only one of two times when I completely lost assurance about tomorrow, and it was instructive to me to see what became important in the light of an anticipated shortened life. I gained insight into the areas that are significant if a man is to ever come to a point where he is in reasonable control of himself.

The managed life, then, is first of all a life that is founded on something (conviction), something that is fixed and nonnegotiable. This makes measurement of progress and direction possible.

In the movie *Apollo 13,* Tom Hanks plays the role of astronaut Jim Lovell. The space vehicle he commands has been crippled by an explosion, and it becomes increasingly questionable that he and his fellow astronauts can get back to earth. There is one crisis after another as equipment fails, batteries run low on power, and freezing temperatures threaten the ability of the men to function. In the midst of all the pressure there is a moment when they must make a midcourse correction and position the spacecraft more precisely for a safe reentry into the earth's atmosphere. Blow this procedure and they burn up or they skip back into space never to return.

Hanks looks out the window, sees the earth, and realizes that it is his only point of reference in an otherwise very dark sky. "All we need to hold our attitude [a space term] is one fixed point in space," he radios Houston. And that will have to be the earth itself. There is a tricky thirty-nine-second "burn" of the attached lunar module's rockets. "We're dancing all over the place," one of the astronauts complains as they work together to keep the earth in their crosshairs. They are successful, and when the thrusters are shut down, *Apollo 13* is on its way home.

And here's the message in the story: if you want to bring your future under management, you've got to have a polestar (for Hanks it was the earth), a fixed position by which the journey into the future is measured.

Another way of making this point is to recall a second movie: *Superman*. Lois Lane is falling through the air, and Superman swoops in and scoops her up. She's never met him before, and to say the least, she's kind of startled.

"I've got you!" he says. (Remember Alexander Haig to the nation: "I'm in charge!"?)

"You've got *me?*" Lois Lane cries out in panic. "Who's got you?"

Reasonable question! For Superman—and for you and me.

In a famous biblical storm scene Paul, a prisoner of the Roman government, stood on the deck of a boat in the midst of a furious gale. Smart, experienced men on board knew that they were minutes away from disaster, and sailor and soldier alike were thinking death thoughts. But Paul shouted to them,

> I urge you to take heart, for there will be no loss of life among you, but only of the ship. For there stood by me this night an angel of the God to whom I belong and whom I serve, saying, "Do not be afraid, Paul; you must be brought before Caesar; and indeed God has granted you all those who sail with you." Therefore take heart, men, for I believe God that it will be just as it was told me (Acts 27:22–25 NKJV).

The apostle's faith was strong, and he had enough of it for everyone. They all survived. He had a fix on Someone greater than himself. And it was adequate not only for him but also for all who were with him. Using Lois Lane's language, "God's got him!"

I have to wonder about men who never bother to fix their sights on Someone greater than themselves. They seem to get away with it for extended periods of time until something like a storm in life rocks the boat beyond a point of tolerance. Then they want to hear a reliable voice, feel a strong hand, or see a dependable signpost.

For people of faith, that fixed position is Christ. "I will never leave you or forsake you," Jesus said to men who were mapping out their future-oriented questions. "Take My yoke upon you," He commented to people who were not sure they had the energy to keep going. "Follow Me," He proposed to those who felt the uncertainties of the future. They were not forsaken, their burdens were lightened, and they never lost direction, which is to say that they came to an experience of self-management that was really Christ-management. "What is the fixed position by which you reference all things?" the man of faith is asked. "Christ," comes the answer out of a man's private thoughts. It's his *conviction*.

Then there's a second question: What am I saying (my confession), and do my words accurately express my thoughts? What vision do the people around me have of the state of my heart (my convictions) on the basis of my words? Is there a connection?

The writer of the Proverbs declared, "A wise man's heart guides his mouth, and his lips promote instruction" (16:23). For more than a few of us, the control of the tongue and the quality of its messages is a major challenge. The words that we speak form a powerful connection between our convictions and our contributions. Our words (or lack of them) give us away. If they are angry, superficial, cynical, or arrogant; if they are shrill, flattering, vain, or relentlessly critical, they reveal a heart absent of useful convictions.

Here is another excerpt from my journal:

An interesting lunch with A—— yesterday. Every time I've been in a group with him, I've noted that he made a joke out of everything. And he really is very funny. No one can be around him for very long without doing a lot of laughing. Then our conversation yesterday. I asked him a question and he evaded it with a silly joke, and I called him on it. I said,

"A——, I have this impression of you: that you love to keep people laughing so that we will never really know what's going on in your heart. It's a terrific defense! So tell me 'cause I really want to know: what's going on inside of you that you don't want any of us to find out?" He looked like I'd shot him. There was some silence, a drained face, a tear (I think), and a muted voice. And then he began to tell me. . . .

My words can . . . well, let me go back to the biblical proverbs: "Pleasant words are a honeycomb, sweet to the soul and healing to the bones" (Prov. 16:24). "The tongue has the power of life and death, and those who love it will eat its fruit" (Prov. 18:21). That sort of says it. The man who has his life under management appreciates the power of words. How they can lift a child beyond the wildest of dreams or, conversely, crush her. How words can make a wife feel loved and valuable or cheap and exploited. How a working teammate can be elevated to the highest potential or reduced to ineffectiveness.

Always, a man's words reflect the energy and quality being developed out of his interior life of conviction. If the convictions are founded on a fixed position of eternal truth, the words are capable of being truthful, gentle, resourceful, encouraging, directional, and pleasant. The words need not be brilliant, only wise; need not be funny, only cheerful; need not be saleslike, only motivating.

Listen to yourself, the older mentor tells me. Never forget that in any personal world where you are regarded as the highest authority (a father, a boss or foreman, a group leader), people will analyze every one of your words to see how it affects them. Don't speak cheaply or impulsively. Your words carry too much weight.

The man interested in living the self-managed life regularly prays that the God who connects with his interior life will so bathe his words that they reflect clearly and cleanly what is going on within.

Finally, the third question: What am I doing, and is my performance in conformity with my convictions and confessions? It's the issue of contribution. Later in this book I want to comment on the subject of legacy (a major private thought for most men). But here it seems appropriate to suggest that contribution begins with great goals. The goals are formed by the words (confessions) that reflect the life of the soul (convictions).

As I've tried to say elsewhere (i.e., *The Life God Blesses* and *Ordering Your Private World*), goals tend to concentrate around seven themes in life: (1) my physical life, (2) my primary relationships, (3) my vocation, (4) my use of money, (5) my intellectual life, (6) my recreational life, and (7) my spiritual disciplines. Good goals are informed by my convictions. And management of life requires goals. Otherwise I am like the moron who shot arrows into the air, painted targets around the spot where they landed, and proclaimed himself a skilled archer.

In a less complex time, men did not always have the "luxury" of defining goals. In effect the goals were stated for them: survive, keep safe, warm, reasonably well fed. A man got up each morning and tried to do whatever enabled life for the next twenty-four hours.

But most of us are in a different world where we assume survival for a while. There are food, shelter, and safety in reasonable amounts. So we have gone to a myriad of options, so many, in fact, that we have to make choices. And the choices may not be easy.

The life brought under management will have to get used to selecting and deselecting, saying yes to the best and no to things that seem good. There can even be disappointment that I cannot do everything I'd like.

Choices emerge out of convictions and confessions. To be fully active, they are translated into goals: I will do this by such and such a time, and when I've done it, the result will be. . . . Some men embrace this notion of goal setting and maybe even overdo it. In other words, they become goal-driven. That's not a good extreme. Other men eschew goals as too guilt generating, not liberating enough. That's also not a good idea. Clearly, balance is the ideal: directions and measurements that do not enslave us but do guide us.

Again, read a portion of my journal:

In one day I have had two insightful moments. In a conversation with Paul Borthwick [one of my lifelong teammates in ministry], we talked about what he has learned through his experience with diabetes. "When you face all the downsides this problem can possibly produce, you make some new choices in life rather quickly." Weight-loss (Paul's way down); regular exercise (he swims five times a week); regulation of diet (Paul's off ice cream and brownies); spiritual discipline (Paul is newly aware of his mortality and that the future is always uncertain). So he has made some hard choices and set some rigorous goals. Then I had dinner with Bruce Wall [an urban pastor and city leader in Boston]. He's dropped at least forty pounds since his heart attack. He's got goals too. He's rearranged his schedule from its old frantic pace to one where he's with his wife and kids in far greater dosages of time. He raised his hands in utter delight when I asked him about the state of his soul. And he's redefined his priorities so that his worklife is productive but not excessive. You look across the table at this man and you recognize that he has brought his life under as much control as it is possible for a man to do. A heart attack initiated this. And he lives by his goals.

Selection and deselection: we will do some things, and we will not do other things. And some of the things we will not do are just as good as the things we choose to do.

Goals reflect these choices. In pursuit of a life under management, a man will take the necessary time to work on them.

Somewhere Machiavelli wrote, "Whoever wishes to foresee the future must consult the past; for human events ever resemble those of preceding times. This arises from the fact that they are produced by men who ever have been, and ever will be, animated by the same passions, and thus they necessarily have the same result."

I'm not confident that Machiavelli had the same thing in mind that I have as I bring this chapter to its conclusion. But if he was writing about the management of a great nation, he also was speaking to the principle of managing a great life (and all lives are potentially great). The past is our doorway to a present life where we have the capacity to stop and think about where we are and what ought to change. And the present is an opportunity to forge a new future. I am confident that new futures are possible, and that we can be different men tomorrow from what we are today.

The man on television who is embarrassed by his gray hair can darken it with something called Grecian Formula. It's okay by me if he wants to do that. But coloring the exterior only falsifies reality. And that's the trap a lot of men fall into. They go for a "look." And they hope that the "look" will convey the notion that life is under management and doing well. But the coloring on the surface quickly washes away in the hour of loss, pain, struggle, or challenge.

"He could be one of the great competitors of his time," the play-by-play announcer remarks of the athlete headed for the showers, "but he doesn't know how to manage himself." The man who has learned to manage himself (the Bible calls it self-control) stands in contrast. He knows where he's come from; he knows who and where he is; and he knows where he's going and what he wants to become.

Incidentally! Simon Peter, the guy with all that trouble with self-management? Later on after he'd gone through some rather tough reality checks, he wrote the following. Read it with the ideas from this chapter in mind:

His divine power has given us everything we need for life and godliness through our knowledge of him who called us by his own glory and goodness. Through these he has given us his very great and precious promises, so that through them you may participate in the divine nature and escape the corruption in the world caused by evil desires.

All that sounds like a self-management issue to me. He went on:

For this very reason, make every effort to add to your faith goodness; and to goodness, knowledge; and to knowledge, self-control; and to self-control, perseverance; and to perseverance, godliness; and to godliness, brotherly kindness; and to brotherly kindness, love. For if you possess these qualities in increasing measure, they will keep you from being ineffective and unproductive in your knowledge of our Lord Jesus Christ (2 Peter 1:3–8).

God smiles with lots of grace upon men who think like that.

CHAPTER 12

THE FORMATION OF CHARACTER

The Boston Marathon is one hundred years old. One hundred races make it possible to hear some breathtaking stories of courage and heroism. There are stories of men and women drawing upon the last drop of strength in order to persevere and finish the race. You'll hear about athletes in wheelchairs, their shoulder muscles painfully cramping, driving for the tape. And you'll pick up some not-so-appealing tales that show off the darker side of human beings.

The last category brings Rosie Ruiz to mind. Charging down Boston's Commonwealth Avenue a few years ago, she crossed the line, an apparent winner in an impressive time. But something was wrong, and it didn't take long for the evidence to mount that she'd joined the race only in its last mile or so. Cheating became the dominating story of that year's marathon. And it was a character issue. The subject of character is always in play when attention gets focused less on the *product* (in this case a trophy and crowd recognition) and more on the *process* (how and why you got to the finish line). If we don't hear enough about character these days, it's because, as a society, we've become more results- or product-driven than process-driven. Process and character are topical bedfellows.

Character is a prominent theme for men in private thoughts. You're into it when you start asking questions like these:

- What is more important: the truth about myself or my surface appearance?

- Are there things I would do if I was guaranteed perfect anonymity that I wouldn't do if there was a chance that Mother might just come around the corner?
- What would I be willing to die for? What would I be willing to risk the loss of my job for?
- Would I ever lie to my wife?
- If bending a few rules during income tax preparation might save some bucks, what would I do?
- If I knew that I would never be found out, if no one I knew would be hurt by my action, would I take something that didn't belong to me?
- How powerful is the drive within me to keep promises, vows, and covenants?

The question—what am I really made of?—will most likely be asked on a day when you face a significant test. I have been betrayed, cheated, misled. How will I respond? I have been told that I have prostate cancer. How will I handle it? I believe an injustice has been done. Will I speak out against it? I have a chance to gain something at someone else's expense. Will I take advantage of the situation? Excuses and/or opportunities suddenly appear that tempt me to break a commitment and seize hold of an advantageous or pleasurable situation. What's my decision?

A movie star thousands of miles from his girlfriend has an idle moment and picks up a prostitute. A mergers-and-acquisition man worth tens of millions of dollars breaks the laws about insider trading because he'd like to accumulate a few million more. A witness perjures himself before a congressional panel. A military officer requisitions a huge jet to transport him, a friend, and a pet halfway across the world at taxpayers' expense. Are these evidences of character issues?

"He has character," we say. And everyone assumes that we are speaking of a good man. If we mean something else, we usually add adjectives or descriptors. "Frankly, he's of questionable character," someone comments, or, "I'd say he's got some character flaws." Not much else needs to be said. A man reputed to be of good character quickly gains our trust. One of dubious character makes us instantly wary.

Character is always being tested. In his book *The Heart Aroused,* David Whyte tells of his friend Joel Henning, a consultant who one day was summoned by the CEO of one of his most lucrative accounts. Henning rushed to the palatial office. Soon he was locked into a conversation in which the CEO asked him to use his position as a consultant to persuade a manager in the company (who was also a friend of Henning's) to accept a transfer that he was reluctant to accept. Immediately, Henning demurred, saying that it would be an abuse of his position and the friendship. The CEO responded, "I don't find that remark helpful for my purposes, *or* for your *future* with this company."

Joel Henning told this story repeatedly to teaching seminars, David Whyte writes. And on each occasion he asked his audience to feed back to him what they thought would have been his response. Invariably, they shouted back things like, "You told him you weren't going to compromise your ideals"; and "Of course, you refused!" Clearly, everyone anticipated an attractive and noble ending to the story.

Whyte's book records his actual response: " 'No, no, no,' says Joel almost in triumph. 'I said, George, *now* I understand what you wanted me to do. I'll talk to Robert over lunch, *today.*' "

And Whyte's point? Almost every one of us, sooner or later, faces such a moment in which character is on the line. Sooner or later, almost every one of us is blindsided or pressurized or persuaded in such a way that we make choices revealing the inevitable defects of our character. In other words it's possible that every one of us has a breaking point where our character defects show themselves. And we need to be very careful lest, in commenting on the character flaws of another, we find ourselves an inch away from the moment when our unique flaws will be revealed.

It's several years ago. I'm in a car rushing from the Minneapolis airport to a convention center where I've been asked to give a speech. We're in the middle of downtown traffic stopped at a light two cars back from the intersection. A homeless man, clearly drunk, staggers across the intersection and then lurches down the middle of the street toward the car in which I'm seated. He reaches the front of our car, my side, and falls. I can see his chin hit the pavement. Instantly, there is a fierce flow of blood. I open the car door, stand up, and look down at the man. Several thoughts race through my mind. I'm in a strange town; I'm wearing a brand-new suit; I'm on the verge of being late for my speech; this man is drunk, dirty, and beyond my ability to help. And I remain immobilized, just standing there, looking, giving other people enough time to take over and offer the help I will not now have to give. Within a minute or two I am on my way to the convention center to give my speech.

Did my choice (or nonchoice) say something about my character? In the months after that event, I came to the conclusion that it did. The event (or nonevent) suggested confused priorities and convictions about what was most important: the genuine need of a human being in my path and the doing of my job. The ultimate irony of the story would be greater if my subject at the Minneapolis convention center had been the parable of the good Samaritan. Think about it!

Character—the composite of a person that shows moral and spiritual structure in action—is perhaps the most potentially beautiful thing in all the world. Most of us thrill to the tales of people who reveal great character in the crunch moment.

A man I know and highly admire was married to a woman with severe mental problems. Her illness caused her to frequently disappear for long periods of time. In so doing she inadvertently made my friend's life as difficult for him as anyone could ever imagine. I suspect that every friend he ever had would have completely understood if he had dissolved the marriage. But he chose not to. In the years of the life of that marriage, I never heard him say a negative word about his wife who, because of her sickness, made his life so harsh. He chose to dote on the good memories, the infrequent moments when things went well. And when she disappeared for the last time, he remained faithful and hopeful. And not in an unrealistic or a naive way. He understood exactly what he was doing. When the word came that she had been found dead, we all searched for ways to convey to this man our profound admiration and reverence for the way he had conducted this part of his life. The word *character* was frequently used.

We admire the character of people who blow the whistle in companies that wink at illegal or unsafe procedures. Like the engineers who risked their careers when they warned that the O-rings on the *Challenger* booster rockets would be only marginally reliable in cold temperatures. We admire the Dr. Kings who are prepared to risk jail or assassination to raise consciousness on social issues like racism. And we marvel at the accounts of Herr Schindler who put his life on the line as well as exhausted his wealth during World War II in order to keep Jews out of the death camps. We hear his haunting, wailing words at the end of that amazing movie: "I should have done more; I could have done more."

But character is seen in a thousand small bit parts that never get written up. How I react to the guy behind me in the jetway at the airport who thinks I'm moving too slowly and says, "Why don't you get out of the way and let the rest of us get by?" What I choose to do when the clerk gives me change that is five dollars over what I really had coming. What I say when a man shows up who wrote me off ten years ago but now wants me to provide some financial support for his beleaguered organization.

Sometimes character shows up at a ball diamond. A Little League game is in the last inning with the score tied. There is one out. The team at bat has a man on third, and the batter hits a catchable fly ball. The boy on third base tags up and is waved home; the fielder flings the ball at the catcher. The runner slides just as the ball arrives. There's lots of dust. The umpire bellows "out!" And two partisan crowds erupt: one cheering, the other protesting. Fathers and mothers, coaches and players, rush the field to celebrate or to argue.

Suddenly, the catcher, a small eight- or nine-year-old boy who caught the throw and tagged the runner, approaches the umpire and says, "I dropped the ball!" Everyone is incredulous. Depending upon what side you're on, this new information is a bombshell. For most people it speaks to the outcome of the ball game. But the discerning spectator sees character at home plate: character forming in the heart of a boy who one day will be called upon to speak up for even more significant truths. And one has the feeling that if he does it today, he'll probably do it the same way tomorrow, no matter what the cost.

Character describes the inner soil out of which actions and words grow. Character is formed out of a lively conscience, powerful and influential models of behavior, sound teaching, and a realization that we are accountable to God.

When the Midwest sustained terrible flooding a few years ago, the U.S. Corps of Engineers assured residents along the major rivers that levees and dams were built to hold up to 100-year floods, in other words, the worst predictable floods on record in a century's time. The problem was that the flooding fit a 500-year specification, and the 100-year floodproof levees weren't good enough. Character (good and otherwise), like levees, shows itself most clearly in the stormy moments.

It is difficult to find a satisfactory definition for the word *character*. The temptation is to say that you know it when you see it. And you know what it's not. We live in a world adept at building the image of a man. And image will stand up and look good as long as the weather is sunny. But when the 500-year storm hits, image is as worthless as a levee built of sand. The only thing that stands up under such pressure is genuine character.

Character might be noted as the collection of traits and behaviors that reflect the spiritual orientation (or its lack) of a man's life. But even that short sentence leaves me cold. Because we have this sense that the word contains a lot more meaning than that.

Raise the subject of character, and most people immediately think of someone they know who reflects it. And their "someone" is not always well known or eminently successful as he or she would be if the issue was image. More often than not people think of someone in a modest situation, a somewhat obscure person who is always there, doing the right thing, making a steady difference.

When asked why such a person was selected as a model of character, people would likely tell a story of a moment where wisdom was required to make a decision or where an issue of moral significance was at stake. People of notable character are described as having done something that may have been to their own disadvantage or at risk to their security or safety to come to the aid of another person. Sometimes the illustration of character has to do with the steady, consistent life of a mother or a grandfather.

In the Scriptures, you will probably find no one who revealed what we like to refer to as sterling character better than Joseph, son of Jacob. His whole life seemed one endless test of character, and his response to each situation suggested the depths within the man's heart.

As a boy, he was the family whistle-blower when he went to the fields—they were in the grazing business—and discovered that his brothers were running a scam that somehow cheated the father of all that was coming to him. His "ill report" resulted in a sharp deterioration in brotherly relations that cost Joseph dearly. But we see the formation of character, as in the case of the Little League catcher, that would qualify him later in life for a job in the palace of the Egyptian pharaoh that would have destroyed any person who was open to bribes and corruption.

Joseph's well-known stint in the home and business of the Egyptian Potiphar was another testimony to sterling character: "Joseph found favor in his sight, and served him. Then he made him overseer of his house, and all that he had he put under his authority. . . . [Potiphar] did not know what he had except for the bread which he ate" (Gen. 39:4–6 NKJV). You don't hand over the keys to the house, the PIN number to the charge cards, the right to hire and fire, and the authority to invest and liquidate to a man unless you have been overwhelmed by the power of his character. You simply know that everything is in good hands.

Probably everyone knows about the third test of Joseph's character when Potiphar's wife visited him "every day" proposing a tryst (Gen. 39:6–10). Her invitation—"Come to bed with me!"—had to have had some kind of effect on him. And his words—"How then could I do such a wicked thing and sin against God?"—revealed a man who thought that sort of thing through and understood where genuine yeses and noes came from: a heart fixed on the pleasure and commandments of the Everlasting Lord.

Thrown into jail on trumped-up charges (of attempted rape no less), Joseph overcame the temptation to descend into self-pity, bitterness, or termination of will and purpose. He showed his character when he became "first" prisoner:

> The LORD was with him; he showed him kindness and granted him favor in the eyes of the prison warden. So the warden put Joseph in charge of all those held in the prison, and he was made responsible for all that was done there. The warden paid no attention to anything under Joseph's care, because the LORD was with Joseph and gave him success in whatever he did (Gen. 39:21–23).

That was the man who, a few years later, was suddenly brought to the pharaoh's palace and given an opportunity to help the most powerful man in the nation figure out the meaning of dreams and the appropriate response. When Joseph offered a strategic plan for an impending national economic predicament, the pharaoh conferred with his advisers and engaged in a national search for a czar who could manage the crisis: "Can we find anyone like this man, one in whom is the spirit of God?" (Gen. 41:38). We get the feeling that they liked Joseph but realized that he wasn't one of them, an Egyptian. Interesting! They couldn't find anyone. So Pharaoh said, "There is no one so discerning and wise as you. You shall be in charge of my palace, and all my people are to submit to your orders" (Gen. 41:39–40).

From the tent of a sheep grazer to a slave/executive to a prisoner/ manager, Joseph made the trip to chief of staff in the Egyptian palace. And he did it all on character. He was marked with an uncompromising sense of right and wrong, an impeccable honesty and dependability, a wise and discerning mind, a strong moral compass, a soul free of bitterness and vengeance, and a courage to speak and act out the truth. This is a fairly complete menu of what character looks like.

One of the most significant books I have ever read is *Shantung Compound* by Langdon Gilkey. I have frequently quoted from it in my talks and in my writings. And on this matter of character it once again offers lessons that fit with my purpose.

In his remarkable book Gilkey writes of human behavior during World War II as he observed it in a detention camp in northern China. Two thousand citizens from most of the Western nations were held by the Japanese in a small hospital compound where space, food, fuel, and comfort were scarce. The question the book asks is this: How do people act under conditions of extreme and prolonged stress? Gilkey, a prisoner himself, begins the retrospective admitting that he anticipated the best of behavior in people and soon became disappointed:

> The camp was an excellent place in which to observe the inner secrets of our own human selves—especially when there were no extras to fall back on and when the thin polish of easy morality and of just dealing was worn off.
>
> Strangely enough, I still kept expecting the opposite. For one of the peculiar conceits of modern optimism, a conceit which I had fully shared, is the belief that in time of crisis the goodness of men comes forward. For some reason we think that when there is little food or space among a community of people, they will be more, rather than less, apt to share with one another than in the ordinary well-fed existence. Nothing indicates so clearly the fixed belief in the innate goodness of humans as does this confidence that when the chips are down, and we are revealed for what we "really are" we will all be good to each other. Nothing could be so totally in error.
>
> What is unique about human existence "on the margin" is not that people's characters change for better or for worse, for they do not. It is that the importance and so the emotional voltage of every issue is increased greatly. Now much more vulnerable than before, we are more inclined to be aware of our own interests, more frightened if they are threatened, and thus much more determined to protect them. *A marginal existence neither improves men nor makes them wicked; it places a premium on every action, and in doing so reveals the actual inward character that every man has always possessed* (italics mine).

So we know that the makeup of a man is not in his physical strength. Nor is it in his ability to bluster about and intimidate weaker people through the strength of his personality. And the makeup of a man is not ascertained by his sexual prowess, his financial statement, or his ability to shoot ten successive three-pointers.

Thus, we look at what is within and ask what forms this thing called character that sums up a man. This is what a reflective man looks at late at night when he inventories his thoughts and actions. If in such moments a man wants to assess his character, he might check out these benchmarks.

CHARACTER IS DEFINED BY A MAN'S SENSE OF DIRECTION

This is what David, king of Israel, had in mind when he gave his son a challenge for his life:

> You, my son Solomon, acknowledge the God of your father, and serve him with wholehearted devotion and with a willing mind, for the LORD searches every heart and understands every motive behind the thoughts. If you seek him, he will be found by you; but if you forsake him, he will reject you forever. Consider now, for the LORD has chosen you to build a temple as a sanctuary Be strong and do the work (1 Chron. 28:9–10).

Character is meshed with a man's highest ideals and purposes. A man's sense of direction is both a reflection of his character and a determiner of the depth of that character. In Solomon's case, his sense of direction was highly influenced by his father's challenge. This is typical of things in the ancient culture where direction in life was passed on from generation to generation. A young man took very seriously his father's blessing. In that sense character was already in formation as he set out to please his father and continue the family's character.

We do not live in such a cultural orientation today. But a man's sense of mission and purpose (direction) remains just as important.

It is said that an ancient Greek traveler, seeking directions, met Socrates by the side of the road. "How can I reach Mount Olympus?" he asked. If we expect a profound answer from the philosopher, we are rewarded. For Socrates replied, "Just make every step you take go in that direction." Hmmm. A noble sense of direction always opens the door for noble events and words along the way.

CHARACTER IS DEFINED IN THE QUALITY OF A MAN'S CHOICES

When God called the Hebrew nation out of Egypt, among the very first things He did was to establish a basis for their choices. We know that basis as the Ten Commandments. The commandments are the short form of the law that was designed in part to help a nation become holy in its character. Holiness would be in the choices.

Do you know anyone who has visited the Great Wall of China? The structure once designed to defend against invaders from the north is so enormous that I have read it can be seen from the space shuttle.

But the wall was merely technology, and it was a failure. It failed at least three times to keep out the enemy. Not because it was poorly designed, but because the adversaries outside the walls bribed the gatekeepers. In regard to computers technicians say, "Garbage in; garbage out." It's the same with a mighty technology like a wall: no character at the gate of the wall; no enemy stays outside the wall. In a sermon, Harry Emerson Fosdick reflected upon this bit of history and said, "It was the human element that failed. What collapsed was character which proved insufficient to make the great structure men had fashioned really work."

CHARACTER IS DEFINED BY HOW A MAN HANDLES HIS FAILURES

We have been told over and over again that men learn more from their failures than from their successes. We dare to think that an essential part of maturity may be a passage or two through the fires of failure. We wonder about the character of a man who has never failed, or acknowledged failure. We admire him. But we secretly wonder—as they do of a boxer who has never been hit hard—if he has a glass chin. Will he collapse the first time the heat turns up?

We ask if a man listens and learns in a time of failure. Does he quickly own up to his complicity and culpability? Does he come out of the struggle with an awareness of what happened and why? And does he turn his terrible moment into a kind of strength?

CHARACTER IS DEFINED BY HOW A MAN RESPONDS TO ADVERSITY AND DISAPPOINTMENT

Different from failure, adversity describes conditions when a man faces things that are said to be out of his control. His body fails on him; an economic downturn costs him his job; a loved one dies.

I have seen adversity in the lives of the farmers whose church I once pastored as a very young man. I have stood with a man as a hailstorm blew in from the west, destroying his wheat crop a week before the scheduled harvest. On the other side of the section road, another man's crop went untouched by the capricious storm. Result: another year of income loss, of expenses and interest payments. Another year of hard work wiped out in minutes.

How does a man act in such a moment? Curse God? Quit? Get drunk? Hit his wife? The man I was with quietly said, "The Lord gives, and the Lord takes away. Blessed be the name of the Lord." And life went on.

I have long admired a Salvation Army evangelist by the name of Samuel Logan Brengle. And part of my admiration stems from the way he learned to handle adversity and disappointment. He always knew how to squeeze something positive from the worst moments. Somewhere in his middle years when he was in Boston, Brengle was hit on the head with a brick by a drunken man. For the rest of his life he fought massive headaches and occasional depression. But he never complained. Perhaps the character to handle the adversity came in his younger years when he learned to live with harsh moments.

Take, for example, the time when he was a young Methodist minister, and he craved an opportunity to be the pastor of a prosperous church with a beautiful manse. In his youthful enthusiasm, he was sure that he would gain the bishop's approval for the appointment, but at the last minute he was denied, and he ended up with a circuit of country churches. Looking back years later, he wrote,

> Losing that city church was the best thing that could have happened to me. If I had gone to that appointment to work among those cultured and refined people, I should have swelled with pride, tried to show off my spread-eagle oratory, and doubtless would have accomplished little. But out among the comparatively illiterate and uncultured farmers of my circuit, I learned the foundations of true preaching: humility and simplicity.

CHARACTER IS DEFINED BY HOW A MAN RESPONDS TO HIS ENEMIES AND HIS CRITICS

Love your enemies, Jesus taught His followers. Not a simple prescription, particularly when said to people who were the product of a vengeance culture (an eye for an eye). Not that easy even today after nineteen hundred years of accumulative learning.

Jonathan Edwards, the outstanding theologian of the eighteenth century, decided to make his critics into "friends." In 1722, he wrote in his journal,

> Considering that by-standers always espy some faults which we don't see ourselves, or at least are not so fully sensible of: there are many secret workings of corruption which escape our sight, and others only are sensible of: resolved therefore, that I will, if I can by any convenient means, learn what faults others find in me, or what things they see in me, that appear in any way blame-worthy, unlovely or unbecoming.

The central character in Victor Hugo's awesome novel *Les Miserables* is Jean Valjean. During a time of severe famine, he was arrested for stealing a loaf of bread to feed his sister and her many children. His sentence to five years at hard labor was extended to nineteen years when he was caught trying to escape. When released, he was given the yellow passport or identity card that marked him for life as an ex-convict. In that miserable condition he entered the home of Monseigneur Bienvenu, a Catholic bishop who had taken a vow of poverty and lived in such simplicity that Jean Valjean did not know he was in the presence of an influential man of the church.

Invited to eat and stay the night, Valjean came to the table. There he saw the two things the bishop had kept for himself over the years: valuable silver cutlery and two silver candlesticks, a gift from his great-aunt. The temptation to steal them was too much, and while the household slept that night, Jean Valjean placed the cutlery in a basket and, leaving the candlesticks, escaped out the back of the home and over the garden wall.

But the next morning, Valjean was back, this time in the hands of the police who had arrested him with his silver booty because he looked so suspicious. The police were proud of their "collar," and they expected the bishop to identify the stolen goods and press charges. But they were mistaken.

The bishop stepped forward and said to Valjean: "Ah, there you are! I'm glad to see you. But I gave you the candlesticks, too, which are silver like the rest and would bring two hundred francs. Why didn't you take them along with your cutlery?"

The police *and* Jean Valjean were dumbfounded. "Monseigneur," said one of the policemen, "then what this man said was true? We met him. He was acting like a fugitive, and we arrested him in order to find out. He had this silver."

"And he told you," said the bishop, "that it had been given to him by a good old priest at whose house he had slept. I see it all. And you brought him back here? It's all a mistake."

That was the beginning of the reclaiming and changing of Jean Valjean's life. It had taken the remarkable love of a man, the bishop, for his enemy. Such is the possibility when a man has character enough to renounce the right to vengeance and to offer his best to the one who wished his worst.

CHARACTER IS DEFINED BY HOW A MAN RELATES TO THE WEAK AND HELPLESS

Somewhere in the darkness of the hearts of most men there is a desire to dominate, to control. John Bramlett was a football player in the old American Football League, and in an entertaining account of his playing days called *The Taming of the Bull,* he writes,

> I learned to read the [offensive] formations, then let my instincts take over. When the ball was snapped, I didn't think about what to do, I just did it, using my body for a battering ram. I could lay a man out with a forearm, or come up under him with a head block that would loosen his teeth. The idea in football is not just to hit but to leave an impression. Once you get people looking around to see where you are, they don't have time to look for the ball.

Obviously, Bramlett's opponents hardly qualify as being among the weak and the helpless, but Bramlett's words, nonetheless, reflect the mindset of the consummate intimidator, the bully. Is there any hint of a "Bramlett" in each of us looking at life in the way he looked at a football game and his adversaries?

You see character in motion when a man has such opportunities but renounces the temptation to take advantage of them. Rather, he becomes the advocate of those who are weak and helpless. You see it in how he is gentle with children. How he comes alongside the errant teenager, the brother who is broke, the aged man who seems to be of no use to anyone. How he is the fierce defender of the person spit out by the system, the one with ears to patiently hear a story that is of no interest to others.

When I lived in New York, I came to know a laboring man of another race. We would often exchange words of greeting and simple conversation when our paths crossed. Then one day I realized that I'd not seen him for some days. I found one of his fellow laborers at the job site and commented that I'd not seen N— lately. "Oh, he got mugged about ten days ago. Really beaten up. They say it's gotten to him. He'll be back, though," said the laborer.

A couple of weeks later N— was back on the job, and I greeted him. I could instantly see that he was a changed man. His face was drawn, lifeless. His posture was slumped. He was a beaten man, more than physically beaten.

I asked N— if we could have breakfast the next morning: "Gail will fix us a good breakfast. We've got to talk." He nodded that he'd come. And the next morning he arrived at our apartment door.

When we had finished our breakfast and Gail had left the room, I said, "N—, I'm looking into your eyes and I don't see any life." He quietly nodded, looking down.

"I want you to tell me the whole story of what happened."

And he did. He described the horror of being attacked from behind by two men who pushed him to the ground, kicked him, and stomped on him until he was virtually unconscious. Then they robbed him. He described how bystanders left him lying for many minutes until he finally regained his senses, staggered to his car, found an extra set of keys, and drove home.

When he finished the story, I said, "Tell it to me again." He did.

And when he finished, I asked him to tell it again. With each telling I could sense that he was flushing out the awful pain of the story. Now there were some tears. When he had finished a fourth telling, I said, "N—, when my friends have trouble, the best thing I can do is pray for them. I lay my hands on the head, and I ask God to wash away the pain of the body and the heart. And I'd like to do that for you." He nodded his assent.

I went over to where he was, and I held his head in my hands and began my prayer. I asked God for his healing, his courage, his relief from bitterness. I prayed that he would be delivered of bad memories and, most of all, that God would put the light back into his eyes. When I finished, I was hugged by a man who seemed to feel that I'd saved his life.

Months later N— invited Gail and me to his home for a family dinner. When we arrived, we realized it was not a dinner but a banquet, and fifty family members were there. The food reflected his ethnic identity, and it was delicious. I'd expected to eat, and I'd expected to meet people, but I didn't expect the introduction that came at the end of the dinner.

"My family, I'd like you to meet Gordon and Gail. They saved my life." And he went on to tell the story of our breakfast and my prayer. And the words he used and the things he recalled and told his family left me speechless. He remembered everything. And he lavished his affection on those who'd come to his side when he was helpless.

I have often doubted the depth of my character when it comes to caring for and advocating for helpless people, but that night I delighted that at least some part of me had been touched by God and had come to believe that there is no better thing in life than to be in a place where you can be brother to a wounded man.

G. K. Chesterton's famous biography of St. Francis includes this observation:

> To him a man stays always a man and does not disappear in a dense crowd any more than in a desert. He honored all men; that is, he not only loved but respected them all. What gave him extraordinary personal power was this: that from the pope to the beggar, from the sultan of Syria in his pavilion to the ragged robbers crawling out of the wood, there was never a man who looked into those brown burning eyes without being certain that Francis Bernadone was really interested in him, in his inner individual life from the cradle to the grave; that he himself was being valued and taken seriously and not merely added to the spoil of some social policy or the names of some clerical document. . . . He treated the whole mob of men as a mob of kings.

CHARACTER IS DEFINED BY HOW A MAN PERFORMS WHEN NO ONE IS LOOKING

"I'm in London on a business trip a few weeks ago," a man tells me. "I have some free time, and I'm walking through the city when suddenly I see a theater that's showing a porno movie. I'm alone. I'm lonely. No one's looking, and something inside me says, 'Do it!' In a minute I'm standing in line behind these other guys waiting to buy a ticket.

"All kinds of rationalizations are running through my mind. I've never seen a movie like this before. It can't hurt anyone when you're this far away from home. Who's going to find out? And then an old song we used to sing in church begins to play in my mind: '*I would be true, for there are those who trust me; I would be true, for there are those who care.* . . .' You have to picture this: the line is moving now, one side of my brain is telling me to do it, and the other side is singing this song louder and louder. I buy the ticket and start in the door. But the song is now so loud I can't hear anything else. Shoot, how do you beat a song? So, I finally turn around, walk out the door, and rip up the ticket. Wasted money, but a reasonably clean soul. I'm sure glad I didn't go in."

It is a relatively easy thing to live like a noble man when he is surrounded by the restraints of custom and acquaintances. Temptations there may be, but they are considerably lessened when he is in familiar company. But when a man is alone, on a business trip away from his home, in a crowd where no one cares, he has only character to guide the way and offer the resolve to stay true. And character is not formed on the spot. Bottom line: you know the depth of your character when you're alone and your mother isn't around.

CHARACTER IS DEFINED BY WHAT A MAN DIES FOR AND HOW HE DOES HIS DYING

In the play *A Man for all Seasons,* Mr. Common Man steps out at the end of the play after Sir Thomas More is killed, and he comments on what the audience has seen: "I'm breathing . . . are you breathing, too? It's nice, isn't it? It isn't so difficult to keep alive, friends—*just don't make trouble*—or if you must make trouble, make the sort of trouble that's expected. Well, I don't need to tell *you* that" (italics mine).

Most of us do not know what we're prepared to die for. We've not lived in a time or a circumstance where death was required. The closest some of us have come to such a gutsy decision might be to lay a job on the line when a matter of ethics or legality is at stake.

Dietrich Bonhoeffer died for what he believed. Character for him was what was formed in his childhood days at his father and mother's table when they studied the Bible, sang hymns, and affirmed the creed. Deposited into his soul at the deepest levels was a belief that people should be free, that oppression should be fought, and that God was a man's highest authority.

That was why it wasn't hard to understand Bonhoeffer's choice when in the late 1930s, he chose to leave a professorship at Union Seminary in New York and return to his German fatherland and almost certain persecution. His friends begged him not to go, as the friends of St. Paul had once prevailed upon him not to go to Jerusalem. But he insisted that Hitler-dominated Germany was where he belonged.

During the early war years, Bonhoeffer's convictions led him to believe that the only way to stop Hitler was through a plot to take his life. And he became party to a group of people who laid the tracks for Hitler's assassination. When the plot failed, he along with others was arrested, harshly interrogated, and transferred from prison to prison. His letters to Eberhardt Bethge and to his fiancée chronicled the agony of those days. At one point he wrestled with the genuineness of his character in a marvelous poem:

> Who am I? They often tell me
> I could step from my cell's confinement
> calmly, cheerfully, firmly,
> like a squire from his country-house.
>
> Who am I? They often tell me
> I would talk to my warders
> freely and friendly and clearly,
> as though it were mine to command.
>
> Who am I? They also tell me
> I would bear the day's misfortune
> equably, smilingly, proudly,
> like one accustomed to win.
>
> Am I then really all that which other men tell of?
> Or am I only what I know of myself,
> restless and longing and sick, like a bird in a cage,
> struggling for breath, as though hands are compressing my throat,
> yearning for colors, for flowers, for the voices of birds,
> thirsting for words of kindness, for neighborliness,
> trembling with anger at despotisms and petty humiliation,
> tossing in expectation of great events,
> powerlessly trembling for friends at an infinite distance,
> weary and empty at praying, at thinking, at making,
> faint, and ready to say farewell to it all?
>
> Who am I? This or the other?
> Am I one person today, and tomorrow another?
> Am I both at once? A hypocrite before others,
> and before myself a contemptibly woebegone weakling?
> Or is something within me still like a beaten army,
> fleeing in disorder from victory already achieved?

Who am I? They mock me, these lonely questions of mine.
Whoever I am, thou knowest, O God, I am thine.

Dietrich Bonhoeffer died on the gallows at Flossenburg prison. Had he lived a few more weeks, he would have enjoyed liberation from the advancing Allied armies. Those who were there the morning he was hung said that he was escorted from his cell to the prison yard. There he commended his soul to God and died bravely. There was character in his behavior and attitude all the way to the end.

Philipps Brooks warns that this building and alteration of character is heavy-lifting work:

> Someday in years to come you'll be wrestling with the great temptation, or trembling under the great sorrow of your life. But the real struggle is here, now, in these quiet weeks. Now it is being decided whether, in the day of your supreme sorrow or temptation, you shall miserably fail or gloriously conquer. Character cannot be made except by a steady, long-continued process.

Bonhoeffer would have agreed.

There are many stories from the Boston Marathon's hundred-year history. The stories of bravery and courage. The stories of the weak-hearted and the deceitful. The race brings it out—whatever is in the heart. So do the stories of life. Sooner or later character shows.

When a man sits in the late night hours and tabulates the day, the questions he is most likely to ask have to do with character. The older he gets, the harder it is to alter character. But if it must be altered, it is never too late to start, and the sooner the better. As far as I'm concerned, that is where the power of God comes in.

```
┌─────────────────┐
│   CHAPTER 13    │
└─────────────────┘
```

THE MEANING
OF WORK

Austrian psychiatrist Victor Frankl was among the millions of Jews arrested during World War II and sent to the death camps. Deemed healthy enough to join the work gangs rather than be sent to the gas chambers, he managed to survive the unthinkable horrors and, at the end of the war, to record his observations and conclusions about how people cope under such extremes.

In his remarkable book *Man's Search for Meaning,* Frankl details the first hours of his ordeal when he and the other newly arrived prisoners were stripped of everything by their Nazi guards and capos (turncoat prisoners). Everything! First their clothes and then their possessions: personal effects, watches, and jewelry. Some of the more unsuspecting prisoners begged to keep a wedding ring, a medal, or a good-luck piece. At least something! "No one," Frankl writes, "could yet grasp the fact that *everything would be taken away.*" The author was no exception to this incredulity:

> I tried to take one of the old prisoners into my confidence. Approaching him furtively, I pointed to the roll of paper in the inner pocket of my coat and said, "Look, this is the manuscript of a scientific book. I know what you will say; that I should be grateful to escape with my life, that that should be all I can expect of fate. But I cannot help myself. I must keep this manuscript at all costs; *it contains my life's work.* Do you understand that?"
>
> Yes, he [the capo] was beginning to understand. A grin spread slowly over his face, first piteous, then more amused, mocking, insulting, until

he bellowed one word at me in answer to my question, a word that was ever present in the vocabulary of the camp inmates. [expletive deleted] At that moment I saw the plain truth and did what marked the culminating point of the first phase of my psychological reaction: *I struck out my whole former life* (italics mine).

I have read this passage in Frankl's book many times. With each reading, I am newly captured by a sense of revulsion. I remind myself that more than a few men (and women, of course) feel they have gone through a parallel experience.

Think about it! Your work! The thing that represents the latest, the best, the sum total of all you can do, all you feel (rightly or wrongly) you're worth. In Frankl's case it was a book, the magnum opus of his life's work and professional thought. If it had been another person, the magnum opus might have been a piano concerto, a massive marketing report (a year in the making), a complex software program, a complex mathematical formula: anything that represents long, hard work, anything that represents the substance of what a man does best when he is using his gifts. This function or product—this thing we do best— reduced to a single expletive, stripped away and flung into a fire and, to compound the indignity, flung perhaps by a stranger who cares nothing about the person he or she terminates.

Again, a lot of men I know think they've shared a version of Frankl's experience. They awake one morning to hear that their company has been sold, merged, reorganized, or forced into bankruptcy. A few at the top have bailed out with golden parachutes; the rest have thirty days of severance and their pension accruals (if they're "lucky"). Careers are trashed overnight, the news perhaps delivered by some organizational executive who flies in from another part of the country. In effect a job, a sense of contribution, is confiscated. A person and his contribution are no longer considered essential. So he is fired, laid off, swept away in keeping with the language of restructuring, downsizing, reengineering, and modernizing. These antiseptic words, easily spoken if you're a stockholder, come from the business literature and amount to one thing: someone no longer counts!

"SO WHAT DO YOU DO?"

When men think private thoughts, the subject of work—what I do— comes into play as frequently as any topic I've tried to write about in this book. Men think about work because it has been their essential definition for almost two hundred years. Once warriors, men became farmers and craftsmen and merchants, mostly peasants identified by their family line and the place where they lived more than anything else. But then came the industrial revolution, and men (and, again, not a few women) headed for the factory and became workers. During the next two centuries, they became managers, tradesmen, executives, professionals, technicians, entrepreneurs, researchers, consultants, and analysts.

Once upon a time, many men derived their names from their work: Miller, Smith, Shoemaker, Rider, Joiner. Today, titles of power or achievement can be as important as the names once were: product development manager, executive vice president, CPA, associate professor, Certified Life Underwriter, foreman, director, systems engineer. Titles become a key to identity. *This is me,* the title implies. *I'm significant, needed.* Today, work often dominates the first questions we ask of each other when we meet: "So what do you do?" It's a question that generally comes before where are you from, what's your family like, and what do you believe? We exchange business cards, E-mail addresses, and promises to lunch. We network with other "titles" so that we're sure our contacts are fresh if we ever have to launch a job search.

The only seeming problem with this process is what you feel like when the question—so what do you do?—comes and you don't have an answer, or just as bad, you aren't proud of your answer. You aren't doing anything at the moment; you're embarrassed by the thought that what you do isn't impressive enough. Bad solution: you begin to avoid groups of people most likely to ask the question.

A man's work may be centered in an office, on the floor of a manufacturing plant, in a lab, or on an airplane while traveling from city to city. But no matter where it is located, work is almost always in a man's mind, and it remains prominent among the private thoughts during each working hour. If work is going well, the mood can be light; if work turns sour, a darkness can pervade all other aspects of life.

Like the proverbial gunfighter always keeps looking over his shoulder, a man keeps asking questions about his work: How successful am I perceived to be? Is this all there is? Do I enjoy what I'm doing? Why do I hate this job? Does it get any better than this? How am I going to handle the guys who want my job? Will the union protect my seniority? How can I stand up to a boss who seems bent on making my life miserable? Can I keep pace with the changing state of the art? Will I survive the next round of layoffs? Who is watching out for me in the process of restructure? How much longer can my body (my mind) keep up this pace? Will my legs, my back, my stomach hold out? What do I do when the guy at the top wants to bend rules and procedures that violate my standard of right and wrong?

Think these thoughts too often, and it isn't long before work begins to define the center of gravity of a man's life. It makes little difference what the other sectors of life look like. Work begins to dominate. If permitted, it becomes the final arbiter of the meaning of a man's life. And when the work ends (retirement, termination), there is nothing left to continue the defining process. That is why a significant number of men cave in physically, many prematurely dying, when forced into retirement. So attuned to their work, they had nothing else to seriously live for beyond the office, and they had not prepared to define themselves in other ways.

At one time in my life I went through this awful moment. I recall the evening three couples came to visit us. One man was an eminent surgeon, another man was a successful lawyer, and the third was a highly esteemed educator. Suddenly, I realized that they were successes, and I wasn't. They were employed, and I wasn't. They were in the fast lane of life, and I was on the shoulder of the road. No, I was really in the junkyard. As much as I loved and revered them, I wanted them all to go home.

Ralph Branca, the Brooklyn Dodgers pitcher who threw a home run ball to Bobby Thompson in the 1951 National League championship play-off game, can attest to how one pitch can define a life. So can Boston Red Sox first baseman Bill Buckner, who let a World Series–ending ground ball slip past his outstretched glove. Both men have spent a lifetime atoning before an unforgiving public. Or perhaps I should put it this way: they *seem* (my judgment) to be atoning. No law I know demands that they do this. It's a self-prescribed one. And they are not the only ones, not by a long shot.

However, that's not the case for Rocky Rhodes who, at the age of forty-one, made a choice to redefine his life of work. Rhodes was a cofounder and (a title) chief engineer of Silicon Graphics. In 1994, the *Wall Street Journal* noted, he had a chance to be a founder in the start-up company Netscape Communications, a "Wall Street darling."

But Rhodes must have been doing some private thinking because one day he suddenly said no to a career-defined life, deciding to cut back to a part-time schedule that "baffled acquaintances and left him adrift at the margins of the company he helped found, casting about for projects that fit his oddball hours."

"Why," Sue Shellenbarger of the *Journal* asked, "would anyone make such a choice?" Why would a man accustomed to seven-day (one-hundred-hour) workweeks suddenly reorganize his entire life? "He loved his work so much that he sometimes awoke at night with an idea and ran into the lab to execute it."

The life-changing decision began to take shape in 1987 with the birth of his first child. As he said to the *Journal*, "[life became] a constant battle, a struggle against the ability of my work life to totally consume me and, on the other side, this blossoming family life that I felt was more important."

Somewhere during this period Rocky Rhodes, along with his wife, Diane, decided to redefine priorities. The *Journal* noted that you'll find their "reengineered" life described in four words written on a Post-it Note on the refrigerator in their kitchen: *God, family, exercise,* and *work.* Based on that sequence, Rhodes said, "My working priorities were upside down." So life changed.

> Mr. Rhodes wouldn't mind a stampede of imitators, but he is more interested at the moment in "getting all the bugs out" of his own schedule, he says. His new situation still creates tensions as he tries to allocate his time among job, volunteer work for a children's museum and his church, and his kids—launching model rockets with Dustin, eight; helping five-year-old Bianca with phonics; and watching Ninja Turtles shows with Gabriel, three.
>
> "I don't know if working half-time will catch on," he says. "But it would be nice if more people gave more thought to things they hold dear."

Time for a reality check! Most of us can't make the same decision Rocky Rhodes made. Some of us would like to. I would—and may in time. Rhodes apparently had unique financial freedom, we correctly observe. We mutter, "If I had [our assumption] his money, I'd be following right in his path." Would we? Think about it!

This paragraph can be found in a journal entry for the same week that I have been editing the final copy of this book:

> Yesterday I had a wonderful visit with D——. We haven't talked in several years since he graduated from college. He has a lovely wife and two small children, and I have seen him regularly at worship on Sundays. So a couple of weeks ago I asked if we could get together. Yesterday was the day. D—— has chosen to stay in the "waste management" business. Specifically, he collects garbage. And he is proud of what he does. He

works about 60 hours a week, and he works hard. Told me that he really feels it in his shoulders and legs.

What drives him? D—— told me that he decided several years ago that he would view his job as merely a means to gain income. That his real priority would be his family and their life together. So he earns a pretty good income but he's home for the best hours of the day when his kids can enjoy having a father around. He told me, "While I'm working, I see all these husbands and wives leaving their apartments with their briefcases and their kids on the way to day school, and I don't envy them a bit. They alway seem tired and hassled. And I wonder if they ever get to enjoy their personal lives and their families as much as I do." I thought about how often we've used the metaphor of the garbage man as the low end of the job market. D—— talks a lot more intelligently about real purpose and priority in life than most guys I've listened to who think that their jobs are the most important in the world. I learned something from D——. I really admire him.

I'm reminded of a scene at the Harvard Club in New York City. I often went there when we lived in the City, not because I am a Harvard graduate (or a member of the club) but because I had friends who were. One morning I'd been invited to breakfast. My host had not yet arrived, and the lobby was empty. The doorman and I were the only people there. I'm not sure he was aware of my presence. He went about his work while I scanned the *New York Times*.

The quietness of the moment was rudely interrupted when a man, obviously quite agitated, stomped down the stairs into the lobby. He clearly intended to make an intimidating entrance, and when he saw the doorman, he erupted in anger over the fact that a suitcase had not been brought to his room.

You would have thought that the suitcase contained uranium, $50 million, or a rare Egyptian antiquity, which, since it was the Harvard Club, might not have been an impossibility. Anyway, the outraged overnight guest assailed the doorman with his words, some of which were quite un-Harvard-like (I think). And when he offered the doorman the piece of his mind that I felt should not have been shared, he stomped back up the stairs.

The doorman, seemingly unaware that I was in one corner watching all of the action, suddenly commented on the experience, growling profanely to himself at a volume level that enabled me to know how angry he was, "I wish I could win the lottery. I'd be out of this place in a minute."

My intuition is that he spoke the private thoughts of more than a few million men who would like to make the Rocky Rhodes decision but can't or won't.

"Americans work so hard that we often put work at the emotional and spiritual center of our lives," writes Jeffrey K. Salkin. He goes on to quote John Updike: "We may live well, but that cannot ease the suspicion that we no longer live nobly."

Salkin comments in the *Wall Street Journal* on Updike's observation:

> I hear this on the ball field from other parents. I hear this in my study. I meet many people who are spiritually burned out from work. I meet many disillusioned with their professions. We sense that we are spiritually damaged by the pernicious cycle of working, wanting and having as ends in themselves.
>
> Workaholism and its handmaidens, careerism and materialism, are not only social issues. They are religious issues. . . . Work becomes an end in itself, a way to escape from family, from the inner life, from the world.

Sometimes life presents a wake-up call that this is happening. An event becomes an intervention into one's private thoughts, offering a chance to rethink priorities and definitions. From the *Wall Street Journal:*

> On May 6, 1993, James Houghton, chief executive of Corning Inc., stepped off a curb into the dimly lighted streets of Williamsburg, Va., and was hit by a car. The impact knocked Mr. Houghton out of his shoes, crushing his right leg and throwing him headfirst to the pavement.
>
> He survived and has healed well, except for a slight limp when he is tired. . . . And yet, the events affected Mr. Houghton more profoundly than people knew. He came perilously close to death. As if to underscore his own mortality, a close friend and confidant died of a heart attack soon afterward at the age of 50.

In my book *The Life God Blesses,* I called these *disruptive moments,* moments of life-storms when there is a chance to rethink the map of personal experience and direction. In Mr. Houghton's case, his near death accident caused him to evaluate his entire work life. The result? A shift of power to other Corning executives and a set of decisions that made him plan an earlier retirement and involvement in community organizations where his skills and contributions could continue. He said, "I feel very good about my management team, and if I walked out of here tomorrow, everything would be fine. If something happened to me tomorrow, retirement, or getting hit by a truck, they'd be ready to step in."

"I hated all the things I had toiled for under the sun, because I must leave them to the one who comes after me," wrote the teacher in Ecclesiastes. "And who knows whether he will be a wise man or a fool? Yet he will have control over all the work into which I have poured my effort and skill under the sun. This too is meaningless" (2:18–19).

LESSONS FROM THE STORMY MOMENTS

So in the stormy moments you learn several things.

First, *you do not let work pass judgment on your self-worth.* Because when "the job goes down the toilet, you don't want to be going down with it."

Back to Victor Frankl who, in *Man's Search for Meaning,* describes a day on the work gang in the death camp. Watch worth come under fire here:

> Another time, in a forest, with the temperature at 2° F, we began to dig up the topsoil, which was frozen hard, in order to lay water pipes. By then I had grown rather weak physically. Along came a foreman with chubby, rosy cheeks. His face definitely reminded me of a pig's head. I noticed that he wore lovely warm gloves in that bitter cold. For a time he watched me silently. I felt that trouble was brewing, for in front of me lay the mound of earth which showed exactly how much I had dug.
>
> Then he began: "You pig, I have been watching you the whole time! I'll teach you to work, yet! Wait till you dig dirt with your teeth—you'll die like an animal. In two days I'll finish you off! You've never done a stroke of work in your life. What were you, swine? A businessman?"
>
> I was past caring. But I had to take his threat of killing me seriously, so I straightened up and looked him directly in the eye. "I was a doctor—a specialist."
>
> "What? A doctor? I bet you got a lot of money out of people."
>
> "As it happens, I did most of my work for no money at all, in clinics for the poor." But, now, I had said too much. He threw himself on me and knocked me down, shouting like a madman. I can no longer remember what he shouted.
>
> I wanted to show with this apparently trivial story that there are moments when indignation can rouse even a seemingly hardened prisoner—indignation not about cruelty or pain, but *about the insult connected with it.* That time blood rushed to my head *because I had to listen to a man judge my life who had so little idea of it* (italics mine).

Rightly or wrongly, if you're a man, it's likely that your work defines a lot of what you think you are, what you think you're worth. And if your work disappears? Well, perhaps you understand what Frankl felt like the day his manuscript was snatched from him by a man who passed judgment on the masterpiece of his professional life with one barnyard expletive.

"You take over," wrote St. Paul to his disciple Timothy. "I'm about to die, my life an offering to God's altar. This is the only race worth running. I've run hard right to the finish, believed all the way. All that's left now is the shouting—God's applause. Depend on it, he's an honest judge. He'll do right not only by me, but by everyone eager for his coming" (2 Tim. 4:6-8 *The Message*). In that way, Paul made it quite clear to any interested party that his work did not define his worth. Only God's opinion of him counted:

> So then, men ought to regard us as servants of Christ and as those entrusted with the secret things of God. Now it is required that those who have been given a trust must prove faithful. I care very little if I am judged by you or by any human court; indeed, I do not even judge myself. My conscience is clear, but that does not make me innocent. It is the Lord who judges me. Therefore judge nothing before the appointed time; wait till the Lord comes. He will bring to light what is hidden in darkness and will expose the motives of men's hearts. At that time each will receive his praise from God (1 Cor. 4:1-5).

The apostle's point was evident. His worth as a man did not depend on a title (*servant* was quite adequate for him). His worth did not depend on the opinions of others who might comment about his work. And his worth was not even held hostage to his own ups and downs as he labored each day. His worth was established at the throne of his Maker.

Here is a second idea about stormy moments in your work life: *you must discipline yourself not to let work define your sense of success in life.*

A professional baseball player signs a contract that offers $34 million for five years. In a radio commentary the other day, someone estimated the thousands of dollars this man makes each time he comes to bat even if he takes three strikes and returns to the dugout. You don't want to know the number!

Our cultural temptation is to label him successful because of the bucks. We're also tempted to do that when we see a five-star general alight from a military jet, an executive step from a stretch limo with a beautiful model thirty years his junior, and an entrepreneur dive off the back of his white ocean-rated yacht. These symbols suggest that work has paid off, that it's really important work—we analyze the symbols and reach a conclusion. Success, we say.

Success, the wordsmith informs, is the attainment of a goal and, it is assumed, the enjoyment of the fruits of that achievement. Unfortunately, we are too quick to focus on the fruits instead of the quality of the attainment. And we are often tricked both by the fruits and by our misunderstanding of what the goals were.

Is a man a success who displays the so-called material fruits of success if these fruits are more the result of clever financing and indebtedness than they are of the payoff of hard work? Is a man a success if the fruits are more inherited than earned? And is a man a success if he has done his work while forfeiting any sense of satisfying relationships in the process? If he has failed to make useful contributions to his community of intimates? If along the way to his "success," he left, as we are wont to say, bodies in his trail?

As ancient kings often did, Babylon's King Nebuchadnezzar pronounced himself a success: "As the king was walking on the roof of the royal palace of Babylon, he said, 'Is not this the great Babylon I have built as the royal residence, by my mighty power and for the glory of my majesty?'" (Dan. 4:29–30).

"The words were still on his lips," the writer of the book of Daniel records, "when a voice came from heaven, 'This is what is decreed for you . . .'" (4:31). The next seven years were the most miserable of Nebuchadnezzar's life. He learned that success was not just in the attainment. There were deeper issues, and one of them had to do with his character. In his own eyes, he was a success, but in God's eyes, it was another story.

My friend David Ryder is a pretty successful man. He spent thirty years building up a business that sells coffee and the hardware for brewing it in offices and factories all over eastern New England. He was a director in a local bank, dabbled in real estate investments, and generally had that businessman's Midas touch. Most men would like to enjoy the relative prosperity David and his wife, Betsy, have gained from their hard, hard work.

I have watched the Ryders raise their family, each son or daughter going on to a highly contributive lifestyle. I mean, there are churches, communities, and companies a lot better off because of David and Betsy's kids. They are unmistakable assets in a human sense.

One day the Ryders said "enough." David stepped out of his company's day-to-day management and the activity of income production and came to work with me on our pastoral staff at Grace Chapel in Lexington, Massachusetts. He took enough courses (and continues to do so) to become proficient in caregiving. Today, he heads up a large pastoral care ministry in our church. Scores of people now visit in hospitals, provide pastoral care to struggling people, and are available for long-term encouragement because of David and his wife, Betsy. He used to sell coffee; now he trains and motivates people.

David does all this on a full-time basis without benefit of income from the church. He does this because he made a decision to pursue a different kind of success that work as he'd known it was not going to provide. There had to be something more. And there was. I have become used to David sticking his head in my office door and saying, "Aren't we having a lot of fun?" Thus, success for David has been measured not merely in bucks but in people trained, folks cared for, a community knowing that it will be supported in rough moments.

"Do we need, like some people, letters of recommendation to you or from you?" Paul asked in a letter to the Corinthian church (2 Cor. 3:1). In his own way, he was talking about success. He was telling us that applause, material assets, and even appreciation were not his definition of success: "You yourselves are our letter, written on our hearts, known and read by everybody" (2 Cor. 3:2). In other words, Paul decided that success would be defined not by the work but by the opportunities he had to serve and please the living God. And it was all he needed: symbols of achievement or not.

Third, *you also learn in stormy moments not to permit work to define your concept of personal influence.* Most men live with the temptation to control. In many and very subtle ways the male has been encouraged to take charge, to control things and people from the earliest days of his life. He is easily fascinated by the men who run the bulldozers, pilot the planes, pull the levers that make the crane lift and lower things, jackhammer concrete into little pieces, and direct traffic. And in play he is seen pushing model trucks around the floor while he makes engine sounds with his voice. Unless he is discouraged, he plays with toy guns. Why? Because they are all symbols of control, of the exertion of influence. This, of course, is also true in the new craze of computer games, which may even exacerbate this feeling of control.

Some of us begin in the later years to measure our lives in terms of what we can control through our work. The climb up the career ladder may or may not be a pursuit of the symbols of success; it may or may not be an attempt to prove self-worth. Perhaps it is a search for a place to control people and events. Talk to the politician, the surgeon, the military officer, or the quarterback about the feeling that one's word or gesture plunges people into action, that it changes things. What I am calling influence or control, some people call power.

In *Inside the Third Reich,* Albert Speer, Hitler's celebrated architect, wrote of his years at the side of the führer. What drove him; what were his motivations; what blinded him to the realities of what was happening? In part it was his lust for power, being near the control center, and he couldn't bear to be separated from it:

> I realized that the desire to retain the position of power I had achieved was unquestionably a major factor. Even though I was only shining in the reflected light of Hitler's power—and I don't think I ever deceived myself on that score—I still found it worth striving for. I wanted, as part of his following, to gather some of his popularity, his glory, his greatness, around myself. . . . I had been bribed and intoxicated by the desire to wield pure power, to assign people to this and that, to say the final word on important questions, to deal with expenditures in the billions.

Said to the extreme perhaps? But spoken in the extreme, it points to the way many people look at their work as an opportunity to control. Know anyone like that? Am I motivated at hidden, darkened levels by this drive as I give my talks, write my books, lead a staff? It's a question worth daily examination. For if a man's life is defined by his work alone, it will not be long before his will to power (the words of the philosopher Nietzsche) will be likely to show.

It seems to me there is one more thing you must not let your work do. And this is a corollary of the strange flirtation with the meaning of success. If I have emphasized a concern for not letting work define you, let me suggest a fourth idea: *you must not let the work become a controlling factor in your life because of a fear of failure.*

In an earlier chapter I referred to the tragic story of Martin Siegel as described in James Stewart's *Den of Thieves*. I go back to Siegel because, in a few words, Stewart describes what motivates some men to cross the line into impropriety and make the choices that lead to big trouble.

> As Siegel's career took off, trouble developed in the rest of his life. His father's business [was in trouble]: Siegel flew to Boston almost every weekend to help. His marriage suffered . . . Siegel . . . gave [his wife] little support. In February 1975 they separated.

Stewart goes on to describe the business failure and bankruptcy of Martin Siegel's father. And then this:

[Siegel's father] became, at 47, a broken man. He tried selling real estate; that didn't work out. He tried doing house repairs. Finally he landed a job selling roofing at Sears. Siegel watched with alarm as his father seemed to give up on his own way of life. He noticed the older man beginning to live vicariously through the sons and daughters he had never had time for.
Siegel was haunted by the possibility that something similar might happen to him. He vowed he would never wind up a broken man (italics mine).

Two lessons from this excerpt provoke me. The first is the description of Siegel's father's slide into personal defeat. A slide perpetuated, I suspect, because he had pegged his life and its worth against success in work. When the work went, the man slid.

The second lesson is "Siegel was haunted." Having seen failure and its effect, Siegel was virtually obsessed with the notion that it should never happen to him. And that notion formed the frame around his choices and actions. "After his father's misfortune," Stewart writes, "Siegel plunged himself even more completely into his work, frequently logging 100-hour weeks."

I cannot define my worth; I will not let it define my ultimate contribution or success in life; work cannot be used to control people for my own ends; it cannot be pursued out of a fear of failure. In the stormy moments, the disruptions, we find out if any of these are happening.

Jerry White, president of the Navigators, a highly admired organization committed to the Christian development of people, lost his adult son one night in a senseless murder. It seems almost trivial to call the murder of a man's son a disruptive moment, but it certainly qualifies to illustrate the point I'm making. White's wife, Mary, wrote a searching book called *Harsh Grief, Gentle Hope* in the aftermath as she described their experience in grief. In a brief ending statement, Jerry White wrote,

On my personal journey in the first months following Steve's murder, I found myself not caring about much of anything except getting through the next day. As challenging and exciting as my task of leading the worldwide Navigators organization is, I found that it faded into the background, crushed by the weight of grief. Any thoughts of ego or pride stemming from my position became virtually inconsequential. I had to rebuild my thinking, my motivation—and to some degree, my [theological] beliefs.

But the process was good. The wounds of my life gave others the chance to help me and to see more of my inner life and my weakness.

I'm moved by White's comment. At tremendous personal expense he tells us about something that more than a few of us will face before our lives end. A breaking experience. Something totally out of our control. And it is likely to affect some or all of our view of work.

An elevator door opens and a man drags himself out. He is well dressed. He carries all the markings of a once-proud man who has had a stroke and is a shell of his former self. I wonder how he handles the fact that he can no longer think as long and as hard as he once did, that he can no longer maintain the caseload of past times, that he can no longer talk in complete sentences. With his work disrupted, is he still a man? Only he knows.

The skills of a man become obsolete overnight because of a new technology. He has to go backward in income production and in recognition in terms of title. Can he do it?

It wasn't the drop in pay that bothered me, Gordon; it was the loss of the personal parking place, the corner office, the two secretaries, and the knowledge that when people called me, the first thing they heard was "This is Mr. G——'s office." Now I walk a block from the general parking lot, sit at a work station, and answer my own phone. That really bites! I just never knew how important those little trinkets were to my view of myself. I'd worked all my adult life for those things; the money was almost an afterthought.

The market slumps, and a guy who has built fine houses all of his adult life can't scare up the simplest renovation job. He sits at home making calls, waiting for calls, while his wife goes off to develop the income. "I'm nothing without a hammer in my hand," he says. "She doesn't know how often I've cried while she's backing out of the driveway. Take away my work, man, and I'm just a big zero."

THE CLOUD OF WITNESSES

When a man thinks private thoughts about his work, and if he has made the choice to organize his life about the Bible, he needs to press his mind toward the perspective of biblical heroes. We do not find it easy to think of these men as working folk, but they were. In the Older

Testament, Abraham was in the grazing business, Joseph an administrator, Moses a nation builder, Joshua a general, Daniel a government official. In the New Testament, Simon Peter was in the fishing business, Paul of Tarsus a maker of tents, and Jesus a carpenter (which some believe means that He was actually a stonecutter). Each man was a member of that so-called cloud of witnesses of whom the biblical writer speaks.

The cloud of witnesses offers us some lessons in work life that transcend the centuries. Each story has stood the test of time. To use Harvey McKay's terms, these men swam with the sharks. And if they were "bitten" at any point, some ultimate benefit convinced them that the bite was worth it. But each of them reminds us that work, in its place, offers great reward. But they might also say that life is bigger and more significant than just a man's work.

Abraham taught us that there comes a moment when a man has to say no to accumulating more advantages. Rather than seek the lush pastures where his herds could expand and he could become more prosperous down near Sodom, he moved happily toward the hill country where grass was more sparse but where he could find God and where he could increase in the kind of character and faith that God was asking of him. Result: he became known as God's friend, which is one giant step better than getting a Malcolm Baldrige National Quality Award.

Joseph had something to say about a man's dependability. Work for your father; work for a slave owner; work for a prison warden; work for a pharaoh. It was all the same in Joseph's eyes: you do what you have to do, you do it right and well, and you commit to making your boss or your organization a success. Ultimately, everyone wants to have you around.

Moses was a nation builder. His was the work of taking an ungrateful, disorganized, small-thinking tribe of people and teaching them how to think, how to work together, how to become guided by the laws and the love of the God of Israel. Under his leadership they enjoyed some brilliant moments. His life suggested that a man's work has to line up with God's purposes, an everyday pursuit. And he made that happen whether it was the matter of pursuing water and food, fighting off an enemy, organizing for the purpose of communication and settling disputes, or making strategic plans about the future and where they were going to live.

Joshua did the work of a military officer. A friend of mine says that Moses was fine for desert life, but it took a Joshua to lead people through a dangerous military campaign. Joshua demonstrated the value of a man organizing his life around a book, Scripture, which he constantly consulted. He was instructed to meditate on it day and night. And he found his encouragement in the contents of that book. It was more important to him than what he might find in awards, raises, or the praise of people.

Daniel worked in a hostile government environment. We have to believe that the kings he served were wicked to the core, although brilliant and shrewd. We have to believe that Daniel saw more than one decision go down that was entirely contrary to what he believed. But it was clear to him that he was in a strategic position to leverage a government when it came to the purposes of God. So he didn't flinch when it came to saying hard things and calling kings to account. When his critics and his enemies did a witch-hunt to discredit him (the kind of thing that would make a modern investigative journalist or a Senate panel green with envy), it was said that they could not find a detail that would suggest the misuse of influence or funds. If he was going to go down, they said, it would be the result of a collision between the king's god and Daniel's God. That was arranged, but Daniel and his God won. When it comes to integrity, all men are called to be Daniels in their work; some men, like Daniel, may end up in the lions' den. And history suggests that the results are not always peaceful. But in eternity, they are!

The work of Simon Peter is instructive. What first comes to mind is the fact that every time we see Peter at work, he isn't catching anything. Presumably, we don't have the whole story, or he and Andrew and the others wouldn't have stayed in the business. Fortunately, every time we look in on him through a biblical perspective, Jesus came along and solved his immediate problem. Fishing was hardly a glamorous business, and Simon came as close as anyone in the Scriptures to being what we call a blue-collar man. And that's important. If the New Testament proclamation of the gospel is represented in the lives of two men—Paul and Peter—do not forget that one, Paul, was essentially an intellectual and the other, Peter, was a man who made his living working with his hands. I have no doubt that he would have easily blended into a construction crew building a warehouse, would have fit into a group of guys topping off a truck on a loading dock, and would have been quite at home with a team of men hauling garbage. He reminds me that work is hard, exhausting, and full of opportunities to interface with good people.

And he reminds me never to fall for the fantasy in society that God cannot use a rough-and-tumble guy out of the trades to change the world. It happened then! It can happen now!

Charles Cowman was a railway telegrapher when God put a hand upon his life. It was not a task likely to be written up in *Inc.* magazine. Nevertheless, Cowman ended up connecting with men all over the world who knew Morse code. It enabled him to cross cultural and language barriers. Strangely enough, his job laid the tracks for his later life as a missionary to Japan and his cofounding of the Oriental Missionary Society, which became one of the notable missionary ventures of the twentieth century.

Cowman was a Peter type, I think. He was also a hard worker. In his later years he wrote,

> Let me die working,
> Still tackling plans unfinished, tasks undone.
> Clear to its end, swift may my race be run.
> No laggard steps, no faltering, no shirking;
> Let me die working.

I think most of us would have liked the man.

Paul was indeed an intellectual. And that mind was put to work to achieve world-changing things. But he also funded himself by making tents. He never seemed to ask anyone for anything. If someone gave him a buck, he was grateful, even enthusiastic. But he was not going to ask. He would rather make tents than ask anyone for freebies. He teaches me a lot about work: toughness, perseverance, sharp thinking, fearlessness (most of the time), purpose-drivenness, compassion. He was a man worth knowing!

Finally, Jesus. He was a carpenter for at least fifteen years and, as I said, perhaps a cutter and shaper of stone since the word *carpenter* apparently meant either one who worked with wood or one who worked with stone. It doesn't seem to dawn on many people that Jesus made a living, supported His mother and brothers and sisters, and pretty much stayed around home for lots of years before He headed out on the part of life about which we know the most. That was significant! The Lord knew how to make a living.

Jesus, it is said, found favor with both God and man. That is, He was an asset to His community before the healing and teaching ever began. Smacks of all the qualities we've seen in the other biblical workers. But additionally, it's clear that He was a servant—always reaching out to look into another man's (or woman's) heart and seeking the best for that person. I can learn that from Him as I enter my world of work.

So this cloud of witnesses teaches many things. No one defined his worth by his work. No one pinned his success in life on his work. No one misused power or sought control for the benefit of his ego. And no one ran from failure. Each man knew where his center of gravity was to be found when he headed for the office each day.

Sir Leonard Woolf, a prominent British politician for more than a half century, ended his autobiography this way:

> Looking back at the age of 88 over the 57 years of my political work in England, knowing what I aimed at and the results, meditating on the history of Britain and the world since 1914, I see clearly that I achieved practically nothing. The world today and the history of the human anthill during the last 57 years would be exactly the same as it is if I had played Ping-Pong instead of sitting on committees and writing books and memoranda. I have therefore to make the rather ignominious confession to myself and to anyone who may read this book that I must have in a long life ground through between 150,000 and 200,000 hours of perfectly useless work.

Woolf says what frightens most men who think private thoughts: that they might come to the end of a work life and reach the same conclusion. That fear often captivates the mind at the end of a workweek in commuter traffic, during the stormy moments when, as in Frankl's horrific experience, work is snatched away. It's what a man fears when he looks down the trail and sees something called retirement coming at the speed of an express train. Some will delight in the flight to Florida or Arizona, but many will wish that there was more time to make a difference or a buck.

When Orson Welles, perhaps one of the greatest American actors and movie producers of our century, was interviewed toward the end of his life about his choices of work, he made some revealing comments. He made one of the most controversial movies of the century, *Citizen Kane*, and he suffered terribly at the hands of his critics and his enemies. In a rambling comment about his choices, he said,

> I think I made a mistake in staying in movies [but] it's a mistake I can't regret making because it's like saying I shouldn't have stayed married to that "woman." But I did because I love her. I would have been more successful if I'd left movies immediately [after producing and acting in *Citizen Kane*], stayed in the theater, gone into politics, writing, anything. I've wasted the greater part of my life looking for money and trying to

get along trying to make my work from this terrible expensive paintbox which is a movie. And I've spent too much energy on things that have nothing to do with making a movie. It's about 2% movie-making and 98% hustling. It's no way to spend a life.

Back to World War II and the tragedy of the death camps. I began this chapter on work with a man, Victor Frankl, who'd lost everything; I end it with the experience of a woman: Corrie ten Boom. Almost everyone knows the remarkable story of this woman who, well into her eighties, toured the world talking to crowds of people about the importance of forgiveness, of loving and serving God. And she had a platform of amazing experiences from which to speak.

Pamela Rosewell, who traveled with Corrie during the last five years of her life, wrote in *Five Silent Years* of the pressure, the hard work, and the intrusions upon privacy that Corrie ten Boom never resented. Here is a case in point:

> One afternoon, two days before our planned departure [on a speaking tour], my list of top priorities had doubled in size. I did not see how I could get everything ready in time. Papers needed to be finalized, passports, visas, and tickets needed for final checking, suitcases readied, notes gathered for upcoming speeches. We were about to set to work on these items after a full morning of interruptions, when the telephone rang yet again.

Rosewell answered and heard the voice of a young man pleading to see Corrie later in the day for some advice "concerning the future direction of his life." She admitted that she did all in her power to prevent the interview from happening. But Corrie insisted that they see the young man even at the expense of their own privacy and workload.

When Rosewell later protested, Corrie ten Boom responded,

> "Child, you have to learn to see things in the right proportions. *Learn to see great things great and small things small.* . . . When you stand at the gate of eternity, as I did in concentration camp, you see things from a different perspective than when you think you may live for a long time. Every time I saw smoke pouring from the chimneys of the crematorium I asked myself, 'When will it be my turn to be killed or die?' *And when you live like that every day, in the shadow of the crematorium, there are very few things that are really important—or only one—to share with as many*

people who will listen about the Lord Jesus Christ who is willing that anyone who wants to can come to Him."

I wondered if it would ever be possible for me to see things as simply as she did. I continued my work, stopping to receive our young visitor that evening. And I had to admit that, although people continued to stream through the house, everything that had to be accomplished somehow did get done. It seemed so odd that I, as a young person, had to learn how to be as flexible as this woman fifty years my senior (italics mine).

I compare Sir Leonard Woolf's 200,000 hours of work to Corrie ten Boom's way of working. In my private thoughts I prefer the latter.

CHAPTER 14

THE SIGNIFICANCE OF LEGACY

How much do you think he left?" It's the kind of gossipy question we are likely to hear when news spreads about the death of a rich man. It certainly doesn't say much about the classiness of the person who asks it, but the question does remind us that our perception of a legacy or an estate—what a person leaves behind when he passes—is usually measured in money, things, and property more than anything else.

It's kind of sad because I can think of some men in my world who died leaving another kind of legacy of spiritual and moral currency that will be felt for generations. My great-great-grandfather, Thomas (whose name is my first name), was one of them. Born in 1832 in the Midlands of England, he made his way as a young teenager to the city of Hull on the English Channel where he went to work for a company that processed and sold whale oil. He climbed the organizational ladder as something of an engineer and inventor and reached the topmost rungs. Somewhere along the line he came to an experience of personal faith. The change of orientation caused him to become a lay preacher of the Bible. He must have been very good at what he did (preacher and professional) because when he died in 1913, an enormous crowd of people whose lives had been touched by his nobility turned out for the funeral and formed an impressive parade to his grave site.

Today, I gain inspiration from a man I never knew but whose characteristics lie somewhere in my gene code. I sense his call to me to keep persevering, pushing ahead, making something of the gifts and capacities I have, being a pleasure to God. And occasionally when I feel a keen sense of satisfaction about something, I hear myself say, "I think old Thomas must be cheering."

I contemplated his significance to me not long ago when I stood at the ancient baptismal font where as an infant he was presented to God by his parents. A few paces outside the door of the old English church where he worshiped as a boy is his grave. Thomas, of course, is not there; he's with his Father. But his legacy is in my soul.

When men think private thoughts, it's not unusual to ponder the nature of our legacy. First thoughts are usually oriented about money. What am I going to leave my wife and children? How will they manage in my absence? Is there enough for college? Can the family keep the house?

Then thoughts might wander farther. Would my wife say that she was glad that she shared life with me? What will my children remember most? Is the community, our church, the company I've worked for, any better because I was here?

And legacy thoughts might expand beyond that. Have I made any kind of a difference? Has my life contributed anything to the general welfare of my generation? Will I be remembered as a giver or a taker?

Earlier I referred to a few lines of my favorite Matthew Arnold poem, "Rugby Chapel." In another part of the poem, Arnold ponders things such as personal significance and legacy with these words:

> What is the course of the life
> Of mortal men on the earth?—
> Most men eddy about
> Here and there—eat and drink,
> Chatter and love and hate,
> Gather and squander, are raised
> Aloft, are hurl'd in the dust,
> Striving blindly, achieving
> Nothing; and, then they die—
> Perish; and no one asks
> Who or what they have been.

Legacy thoughts are usually stimulated by some crisis event that intrudes upon our lives. We hear that a friend from school days has cancer and there isn't much time left. A nationally known celebrity who has been around all of our lives suddenly dies. We reach the same age our father reached when he died.

There are other possibilities. A physician does an annual checkup and suggests a return visit because the EKG wasn't flattering. An employer discreetly (or not so discreetly) inquires about the possibility of our taking an early retirement, and we get the message that we're not so important to the company's future after all. The sexual dimension of the marriage goes on hold. A lot of things once cared about seem less important.

There are other more subtle stimuli to legacy thoughts. I become aware of a younger generation that seems more visionary, more creative, and certainly more energetic than I am. In other words, younger people read *Wired* magazine, know what's at the top of the music charts, and seem to think that tiny wire-rimmed glasses are terrific (and I don't). My wife speaks with increasing and infuriating frequency about my gray hair and her own encroaching wrinkles. I am receiving regular solicitations for membership from the American Association of Retired Persons. The young woman at the theater asks if I want the senior citizen discount. All police officers, most physicians, and almost every pastor look like kids barely out of high school. At a wedding the mother of the bride seems more attractive than the bride.

These are samples of the things that spawn private thoughts. This time, thoughts about what the end game in life is going to be like. How will I die? Do I have some tough years ahead of me where my life will be under the control of others? What about the possibilities of a catastrophic illness? What will it be like when one of the two of us dies? How do you say good-bye to someone with whom you've spent fifty-plus years, who has put up with your idiosyncrasies, your defects, your dreams; whom you've held in your arms in your moments of euphoria, fear, and exhaustion; who has kept you going in the toughest moments, told you the facts when no one else would, and laid her hands on you when you needed prayer?

And after that litany of morbidities, there are these extra thoughts: When I'm gone, will I be mourned? Remembered? Valued because I stood for something, because I made someone's life better, because I lived a quality of life that made a difference? Now we're getting down to what I think is the real legacy.

These words are written during the course of my fifty-seventh year of life. Clearly, I am aging. And my private thoughts are shifting from one center of gravity to another.

It seems as if yesterday I was in my twenties. In fact (and keep this quiet), I still think and I feel as if I am someone in his thirties, and I'm occasionally dismayed that others do not see me in that light.

When I was actually back there (in my twenties and thirties), my private thoughts centered on career (choice of), marriage (who, and, later, how to make it work), identity (who I was becoming), establishing myself as a man who might be taken seriously (difficult, if not impossible). Then, too, there were the nagging thoughts of self-doubt (am I good enough?), sexuality (am I man enough?), and a limpid faith (am I growing enough?). In those days when private thoughts inclined toward the wildly ambitious, it was hard to think that there wasn't anything I couldn't do if I wanted to do it badly enough. Unless forced, I did not muse on the possibility of health problems, the probabilities of failure, the probability that somewhere along the way the "system" might randomly deal one or more crippling blows. I, for one, expected to participate in the changing of the world. And (speaking more than thirty years later), change it we have—but not as we intended.

Is it all over? No way. Like you, I live in a world where men and women my age can dare to talk about new careers. In the past fifty years the life expectancy has grown by ten years (more years for women, which does not seem fair). There is a gradual realization that sixty-five is not a legitimate retirement age and that work can take on different forms as a person moves through life. All this creates quite a bit of enthusiasm in me for the future. Until God says otherwise, I intend to assume that I have lots more years ahead when I just might get a few things right and make up for some of the blunders of the past.

So I think in new ways now. I am not plagued by the anxieties of my twenties and thirties: Who am I, will I be successful, will anyone like me, and can I ever get the issues of faith straightened out? Today, I'm interested in a new set of questions, and I'm looking at reality with different eyes. There's great value in the new perspective.

In a chapter of my book *The Life God Blesses*, I took on the question, What kind of an old man do you want to be? In the writing I became enamored of Caleb, the Older Testament sidekick of Joshua who, at the age of eighty-five, asked if he might lead the charge on Israel's hill country where the giant Anakites were said to live in walled cities.

I tell you, Caleb was not a man headed toward Florida and the golf course. He had a lot of living to do. A pension check was not his concern. He seemed to have been convinced that his legs could keep going. But maybe it was really the enthusiasm of his heart. Anyway, Caleb is my inspiration. I like the way he thinks. Young men would not understand him or the significance of what he is saying.

In my first years as a young pastor, I remember thinking once or twice about how few older men ever talked to me about their personal lives. It made me uneasy and caused me to wonder if there was something deficient in my pastoral abilities. Now I understand that those men who never discussed their personal lives suspected that a thirty-year-old couldn't think the thoughts of a man in his fifties or sixties. They saw me as I now see police officers and physicians and most pastors.

I am a four-time grandfather now. My first books were written at the time that our two children were preteens. Now they have left the homestead, married, and presented their mother and me with these four delightful grandchildren, three of whom are already old enough to call me on the phone several times a week and tell me what they've done with their day. "Hi, Papa! How are you?" they cheerfully begin, and my day picks up color. Their joint decision to call me *Papa* has given me my final name. *Papa*, I like it.

The passage of the years has taken me from being Gordo as a small boy to Gordie as a prep-school athlete to Dad as a father to Pastor Mac as a minister to Papa as a grandfather. All five names in their appropriate hour have brought me consummate satisfaction.

Unless there have been dramatic, life-changing moments in earlier years that leave him uncertain and unsettled about the future, it is in the Papa stage that the private thoughts of a man begin to generate the legacy questions. Private thoughts turn away from ambition and acquisition to the issue of what he could conceivably leave behind when the end game is completed.

One day while living in New York City, I passed a wall splattered with graffiti. A young teenage friend was with me, and I pointed at the splay of names, slogans, and symbols and said, "You've lived in the City all your life. Do you have any idea why some people enjoy messing up walls like that?"

"Sure," he answered quickly. "They want to walk by here each day and think, *Hey, man, that's a part of me up on that wall. I did that. That's my name. Or that's my lady's name. Or that's my artwork. That stuff proves I'm alive and I've been here.*"

My mind did a quick jump to a World War II fad. Wherever you went, you saw the words *Kilroy was here* written on walls, on rocks, in the dust on the back of trucks. You could go to the most remote places and find those three words written someplace. Strangely enough, no one was really sure of their significance. No one even knew who Kilroy was. He was just there. The best explanation I ever heard was that Kilroy was a shipbuilding inspector, and as he went from place to place inspecting ships under construction, he wrote in chalk on the bulkhead *Kilroy was here*. As the ships made their way all over the world, servicemen got used to seeing the phrase, and they in turn replicated it wherever they went.

So the ghetto kid and Kilroy have this in common. They want people to know they were *here*. Isn't that why an artist puts his or her name on a canvas, why a craftsperson puts initials on the bottom of a piece of furniture, why it means a lot to me to see my name on the jacket of a new book? Each of us has a desire from deep within to say, "I was here!" I made, created, offered, contributed something. This is a part of my legacy. In the Papa years we can't help counting up the score. What difference have I made, and will it be remembered when I am gone? Where is my graffiti?

Andrew Carnegie who, more than a century ago, made some amazing comments on the subject of philanthropy gave serious thought to the question of what might be left behind. He was sure of at least one thing. When he died, he would not leave any undesignated money behind. Thus, he spent the last third of his life giving his money away. He determined that his financial legacy would be fashioned in libraries, concert halls, universities, and other things that would add cultural value to scores and scores of American communities. We are the better, the much, much better, because of the legacy of his philanthropy.

As I wrote earlier, in the biblical culture, there was much ado about legacies. Generally, they were noted as blessings. A blessing was the effort to press something of value from one life into the life of another. Scripture has any number of examples. In the Older Testament, Isaac blessed his son Jacob (at the expense of Esau who never quite got his act together). Jacob blessed his two grandsons (the sons of his favorite son, Joseph). Moses blessed Joshua; Samuel anointed (a form of blessing) David; David blessed Solomon. In the New Testament, Simeon blessed Jesus; Jesus blessed the children; Paul blessed Timothy. And that's just a sample. We get the impression that blessing was big business in those days.

And this is no cavalier statement. In each case where the "blesser" was extending the legacy to the "blessee(s)," something more than just a fond Hallmark-type wish was being offered. A torch was being passed; authority was being transferred; a vision or destiny was being perpetuated. So people both gave and sought the legacies of others. Supremely, they craved the legacy of God and were only too glad to receive it when anointed.

Now, in these Papa days of mine, the ancient question of legacy begins to focus on me and on men like me. What will be the messages that establish the fact that I was here? Surely, I will leave behind more than a bronze marker in a cemetery or a few ashes in an inexpensive urn. I hope I will leave something behind more valuable than an insurance policy and a bunch of books and papers.

My private thoughts have generated a possible legacy that breaks into seven themes. If carefully sketched out during the days I have left, they will provide a legacy that will live far beyond my time and in the following generations. So in my private thoughts, this is what I think about.

1. MY MATERIAL LEGACY: WHAT WILL I DO WITH WHAT I HAVE?

Our century has known some amazing transfers of money from benefactors to colleges and universities. The *New York Times* noted a $20 million gift to Spellman College and a $100 million gift to Glassboro State College in New Jersey. Gifts of $25 million to Harvard do not seem to be unusual. Recently, $120 million was given to the University of Pennsylvania. When they settle the estate Gail and I leave behind, we will not be mentioned in this league. But there is still hope.

As the *New York Times* declared one day, these gifts pale in contrast (on the basis of sentiment, anyway) to one of $150,000 given by Osceola McCarty, an eighty-seven-year-old African-American woman, to the University of Southern Mississippi. "In the case of Ms. McCarty," the *Times* said, *"it is the heart behind the gift, and the lifetime of effort that went into it"* (italics mine).

The *Times* went on,

> Ms. McCarty . . . earned her money washing clothes for people in her hometown of Hattiesburg, Miss., which is also the home of the university. With no husband or children, no travel or expensive hobbies to claim the dollars and change she earned, she just continued to save it up over the years. After taking out what she needs to maintain her modest lifestyle, she is donating $150,000 to the university for scholarships for black students.

The editorial in the *Times* concluded, "[McCarty] exemplifies donors who struggled to achieve a measure of success in one generation and then reach forward to help the next generation." Man, that's graffiti at its best.

That's what we must contemplate—reaching forward—if we want to leave a legacy. Reaching forward with money we have earned and using it for better purposes than enlarging our perimeter of comfort or opulence.

Andrew Carnegie warned against putting large sums of money in the hands of one's children. He was sure, and history has demonstrated his wisdom with scary frequency, that bequeathing wealth to one's children was quite similar to something we learned as kids: if you assist a butterfly with an early release out of its cocoon, you doom it to weakness and death. If there is something to leave, make sure that it is to the spiritual benefit of the next generation, not to their demise.

A friend once managed a portfolio of family wealth that had been passed through three generations. His position afforded him a view into the life of an extended family who had never had to seriously work for their living or gain their social position through the development of servantlike disciplines. As I remember his commentary, it had to do with the soullessness that occurs when a generation is given everything with no strings attached.

Today, some speak enthusiastically of planned giving. This is the thoughtful and prayerful distribution of resources so that another generation is enabled to grow. It means that you don't wait to give until you are "pitched" by an organizational development person. It means that you don't respond to the most emotional or high-pressured development campaign. It also means that you don't force organizations to attract your generosity by personal visits from their presidents or invitations to their expensive programs. Rather, it means that you've thought through what you have to give and the places that would most benefit because God has convicted you of the necessity of that effort.

"A generous man will prosper; he who refreshes others will himself be refreshed," the Proverbs compiler said (11:25). I have not met an overabundant number of people who have adopted the concept of a giving plan (for both before and after death), but I can tell you that I've never met anyone in this category who wasn't perfectly delighted and fulfilled with what he or she was doing.

I came very close to leaving college for lack of funds. If the U.S. Air Force had not decided that I was too color-blind to get into flight school, I might have pursued an entirely different direction in life. Having been refused by the air force, I looked to see what other options might be out there. In that hour of youthful despair, I received a phone call from Virgil Brock, a hymn writer who had written a famous song, "Beyond the Sunset." In his aging years he had married an old friend of my family, and they were coming through my college town on their honeymoon. Could they stop and see me?

Frankly, I was in no mood to meet two older people, and I came within a whisper of finding an excuse with which I could say no. But I met them. As we visited, they quickly discerned my financial plight. Before the end of the visit, I heard Virgil Brock say, "I have always made it a point to use my money to help young men and women complete their education. I think we could be of help to you." A couple of weeks later I received a check for a substantial amount of money. It underwrote two years of my college tuition and book costs, and as a result, I got my degree.

The Brocks have been gone for many, many years now. But they passed on a legacy to me. Money translated into education translated into ministry. Today, I do not fly jets; I preach the Bible and try to invest myself in younger men and women. The legacy continues.

I was not raised to be, to think, to act "wealthy." My wife and I have prepared ourselves with some care for the older years. Not that we might be comfortable but that we would be able to serve in the kingdom without the anxieties of income production. Along the way I have tried to learn the lesson of generosity (Gail has already learned it). And our hope is that this lesson, once learned, will continue when we are gone.

We want to offer help to the grandchildren of our family who will face the expense of education and getting started in making a difference in their generation. We want to assure that a sound educational institution has received the benefit of our generosity. And we desire to make sure that we've acknowledged the disadvantaged people of our time. Planned giving is of immense importance. It's part of the legacy.

2. MY LEGACY OF AFFIRMATION: WHO WILL FEEL THE MORE COMPETENT BECAUSE I'VE SPOKEN?

A legacy of affirmation means that there are a few people left behind who have begun to reach the fulfillment of divine purposes for their lives because I helped them discover their potential and their value.

St. Paul said to Timothy, "Fan into flame the gift of God, which is in you through the laying on of my hands" (2 Tim. 1:6). Jesus said to His disciples, "Greater love has no one than this, than to lay down one's life for his friends. You are My friends if you do whatever I command" (John 15:13–14 NKJV). You see it all over the pages of human history, the moments when someone gives the blessing to another: you are special, and you are loved.

All over the world men (and not a few women) will tell you that their service in the kingdom of God is a result of the affirmation legacy of Vernon Grounds, now in his eighties, the former president of Denver Seminary. I am one of them. We count ourselves most fortunate to be graduates of the Grounds school of affirmation. Ask any of us, and we will tell you of the many breakfasts in Denver restaurants where he patiently listened to what we thought were larger-than-life issues and then assured us of God's loving attention. And then, picking up the check (always picking up the check), he would send us on our way with an embrace of affection and a word of assurance and benediction that was close to papal: "You are God's chosen instrument; He's going to do great things through you." What we heard again and again was that he believed in us. We needed nothing more.

In my twenty-seventh year, my graduation year from seminary, I happened to be with Vernon Grounds as he gave a lecture at a camp in the Rocky Mountains. When the lecture was over, he said to me, "There are some men who would like to talk to me about finding a pastor for their church. I have a bit of a headache. See if you can take my place. Oh, and tell them that I think you're the man for the job."

With the exception of the last, I did as I was told, assuring the inquirers that Dr. Grounds would be glad to consult with them at another time about possible candidates. I'm sure I managed to inform them just a bit about myself because before the conversation was over, they had invited me to come to their church and preach—but only as a guest. I told them to send me a letter and I would gladly accept if my schedule (can you believe I actually said this?) wasn't too crowded on that weekend.

The congregation of several hundred members was the kind that young seminary graduates almost never see. A few weeks later the invitation to preach came. And there was the hint that if the weekend went well, the leaders of the church might consider me as a candidate for their pulpit. My wife, Gail, was hesitant. "Do you really think," she asked Dr. Grounds, "that my husband should take on a responsibility of that size?"

I'll not forget his words: "Gail, if God chooses to fill up your husband's heart, as I think He is doing, then there's nothing he cannot do. The two of you will do just fine in that church." His legacy of such affirmation has "followed us all the days of our lives," to borrow from the psalmist. At every turn in our road of life—the good ones and the very difficult ones—Vernon Grounds has been there (as he has been for others) with affirmation: you can do it; you're capable; great things are ahead. When (and I am tempted to add *if*) God calls this man home to His heaven, the legacy of affirmation this man will leave behind will far surpass the value of any money he could have made in a lifetime and given away.

For years the Reverend E. K. Bailey has been the pastor of the predominantly African-American New Concord Missionary Baptist Church in Dallas, Texas. Some years ago I responded to his invitation to preach to his congregation. It remains to this day one of my most memorable experiences.

I came to his church that Sunday evening in a state of exhaustion. He seemed to sense it from the moment I arrived. He took me to his office. The rather large room was filled with twenty well-dressed men who quickly stood to honor my entrance.

"Gentlemen," Dr. Bailey said commandingly, "the man here is *tired*. We've got to pray some power into him."

Apparently, the men knew exactly what their pastor was saying because they moved toward me and soon we were into something that resembled a rugby scrum with me in the middle, their hands on my head, shoulders, and back. From around the group came prayers on my behalf. And that went on for about twenty minutes.

When we finished, Dr. Bailey said, "When Mr. MacDonald preaches tonight, I want some of you on the front row, some of you on either side, and the rest of us will be in back of him. You know what to do."

And they did. When it came time for me to preach, the twenty men became a cheering section. They prayed; they shouted; they urged me on. Never had I enjoyed preaching the Bible with more vitality and verve. I preached for forty minutes, and they wondered why the sermon was so short.

Later Dr. Bailey and I sat and talked together.

"Where did you get those men?" I asked.

"Oh, they're *my* men. I'm with them every Saturday morning for four hours. I'm making men out of them. Men of God."

"But," I asked, "don't their wives object to their spending so much time here at church on a day off?"

"Listen," Dr. Bailey leaned forward, put his hand on my knee, and grinned. "The other day one of the women called me and said,

'Preacher, I don't know what you're doing to my man each Saturday, but if you want him another day of the week, you got him.'"

A great legacy of affirmation was being set in place there.

I find few things sadder to hear than the statement: "My father could never bring himself to say anything good about what I was accomplishing. He just didn't know how to let me know that he was proud of me." Or the statement: "My boss doesn't know the meaning of the words *well done*. He's quick to comment when we mess up; he's slow to note the good things that happen." Or the words: "All he can talk about is himself: his goals, his achievements, his ideas. It never occurs to him to turn the attention on anyone else and to inquire about whether the person has anything to say."

3. MY LEGACY OF CHALLENGE: WHO WILL REACH NEW HEIGHTS BECAUSE I SHOWED THE WAY?

We leave "graffiti" on the life of someone else when it is said, "He showed me the possibilities and got me going."

Read again the words of one-time Green Bay quarterback, Bart Starr, who played for Coach Vincent Lombardi:

> I wasn't mentally tough before I met Coach Lombardi. I hadn't reached the point where I refused to accept second best. . . . [He] taught me that you must have a flaming desire to win. It's got to dominate all your working hours. It can't ever wane. It's got to glow in you all the time.

You and I are reading the words of a man who lived under the legacy of a remarkable leader. Years later, Starr would say how his entire life was changed due to his experiences with Lombardi. His perspectives as a businessman and a community leader were profoundly affected by what he'd learned from a man who left a legacy of challenge: a flaming desire to win.

These were the words of God to Moses on Mount Pisgah when Moses wanted to linger in leadership over Israel. It was understandable that he wanted to enter the Promised Land as a leader of his people. The answer was no. The alternative was a legacy of challenge: "Commission Joshua, and encourage and strengthen him, for he will lead this people across [the Jordan River] and will cause them to inherit the land that you will see" (Deut. 3:28).

I had the privilege to preach to the congregation of the Hollywood Presbyterian Church in California. On the day before worship, Gail and I led a seminar for men and women in the Henrietta Mears Education Center. As I read the inscription on the building, which was dedicated to Miss Mears, I recalled all over again the legacy of this woman. Unattractive by modern standards of good looks, tough, pushy, more influential than women have been permitted to be (unfortunately) in most parts of the Christian church, Henrietta Mears was one of a kind. She had a knack of spotting men and women with potential. And like a pit bull, she held on until she had you convinced that God had something special for you.

Some of the most outstanding names in evangelical Christianity, including Billy Graham, Robert Munger, and Bill Bright, will tell you that Miss Mears was a major key to their courage to step out and do extraordinary things. Hers was a legacy of challenge. All over the world are men and women with the Henrietta Mears graffiti on their souls.

I have given a total of fifteen years to a New England congregation known as Grace Chapel. When my wife and I first went there, we were struck by the unusual number of men and women of enormous faith. Some of them were highly educated and highly placed in business and the research and development industry.

But one of them was not so lofty when it came to career matters. In fact, I'm not sure I ever knew exactly what he did because when I met him, he was already retired. His name was Roland Redmond. Roland loved God, and his affection for the church and its ministry was clear to everyone.

We were a young congregation of just a few hundred in those days, and we began to experience extraordinary growth for a New England church. It seemed as if every time we held a congregational meeting, it was to vote on a new staff member or a new building program. Every vote demanded new leaps of faith for which most people had no precedent. Frankly, I disliked almost all business meetings. I was uncomfortable as people would debate and sometimes even descend into what I thought was pettiness to make their points.

On more than a few occasions our meetings lurched toward stalemate on issues that called for greater and greater expansions of our budget and commitment. Sometimes I was sure that we were going to go home either defeated or stymied. But almost every time there would come an almost magic moment. If there were two sides to an issue, they would finally grow quiet, even a bit tired of hearing themselves talk.

At that very moment, almost as if he knew the exact second, Roland

Redmond would stand and face the congregation. He was an older man, and his maturity always commanded reverence. He would cross his arms and almost glower at the people in front of him. He'd look from one side to the other, from the front to the back. And then he would begin with a loud "Hmmph!" We knew we had better give attention.

"I'm a bit disappointed in you," he would begin. "You need to have been a part of this church when it was just getting started. When a mere handful [his voice would begin to rise] of people faced challenges that make what you're facing seem like nothing. They would scrape their money together; they would pray all night if necessary; they would settle in and work hard. And God would give them what they asked for. Now I ask you, Are you going to do any less than they did?"

He'd pause at that point and look around to see if there was an answer to his question. But no one dared move. No one dared say a thing.

"Now I want you to think this over. Is this thing too hard for God? Is it too hard for a people who say they have faith and really care what God thinks? I think it's time that we saw some real faith around here." And Roland Redmond would sit down.

The moderator would stand and say, "All in favor say, 'Aye.'" And everyone would say, "Aye." Our congregation has experienced some great moments (glory to God) because of the legacy of "Papa" Roland Redmond. He made us wiggle and squirm in our weak faith, and he challenged us to get off the dime.

In an age of planners, demographers, market analysts, sociologists, number crunchers, and systems engineers, we have somehow diminished the role of the man with the challenge. Roland Redmond died years ago, and I conducted his funeral. I talked about his legacy. His tiny house, a simple New England cape, probably could not have accommodated a party of more than eight people. He drove an old car. And when he and his wife went to heaven, the funerals were simple in terms of ostentation, but powerful in terms of thanksgiving and praise. He wasn't the only giant in our congregation's history, but he was among the great ones. His was a legacy of challenge.

4. MY LEGACY OF INSIGHT: WHO MIGHT BENEFIT FROM WHAT I'VE LEARNED?

A man accumulates a lifetime of learning. And in the morass of all that input come a few insights over the years that ought never to be hidden under a bushel. Stephen Covey quotes Alfred North Whitehead:

In a sense, knowledge shrinks as wisdom grows: for details are swallowed up in principles. The details of knowledge which are important will be picked up ad hoc in each avocation of life, but the habit of the active utilization of well-understood principles is the final possession of wisdom.

There's the opportunity for a legacy. The painting of the graffiti of wisdom and insight learned at a high price: through struggle, pain, exhaustion, defeat, and victory.

You . . . know all about my teaching, my way of life, my purpose, faith, patience, love, endurance, persecutions, sufferings—what kinds of things happened to me in Antioch, Iconium and Lystra, the persecutions I endured.

So Paul wrote to Timothy as he handed on his legacy of insight. He continued,

But as for you, continue in what you have learned and have become convinced of, because you know those from whom you learned it, and how from infancy you have known the holy Scriptures, which are able to make you wise for salvation through faith in Christ Jesus (2 Tim. 3:10, 14–15).

Perhaps it is late at night when the private thoughts of a man range to and fro across the experiences of life and struggle with the question: What has God taught me that has value for others? And what might these insights be? The gaze inside things and events that are ordinarily too difficult for others to see the first time. A man often needs a guide into the interior places. Unfortunately, the guides too often withdraw, go to warm and sunny places, get ignored in the rush of busy schedules. And legacies that could have been incalculable are lost.

A scandal of sorts is brewing in Switzerland. It is said that the Swiss banks possess the legacies of many Jews who died in World War II concentration camps. Sensing that they were about to lose everything, they found ways to transfer their holdings to secret Swiss accounts. And then they died. Now, fifty years later, the legacies lie untouched in the banks, no one to identify them, no one to put them to use.

The sadness of a lost legacy of insight emerges when the older man does not speak and the younger man does not listen. And such legacies are not in great abundance. We have many strong, powerful, and communicative people, but relatively few insightful people. And what a legacy they have to offer! "Listen, my son, to your father's instruction," the

Proverbs say, "and do not forsake your mother's teaching. They will be a garland to grace your head and a chain to adorn your neck" (1:8–9).

In an essay in *An Invented Life,* Warren Bennis mentions writer John Leonard who, in a television commentary, had spoken of his mother and mother-in-law in glowing terms. During the course of their lives, Leonard observed metaphorically, the two women had been pushed out of the windows of a lot of burning buildings. "I need to know," he said, "how they learned to bounce."

So, what has God taught you? And to whom does this insight need be offered? Many years ago I made my only trip to Japan. One afternoon my host and I walked down a country road. We came upon a very old man who was carefully cultivating small trees. It suddenly hit me that the man would never live to see the trees in their prime, and I said so to my host. I've never forgotten his response: "He does not expect to see the trees in their prime. He is not planting them for himself, but for his grandchildren. That is the Japanese way."

5. MY LEGACY OF A MODELED LIFE: WHAT DO OTHERS SEE IN MY WAY OF LIFE THAT IS WORTH PERPETUATING?

I want to leave behind a life so lived that it becomes a reference point for another generation. This is the opportunity to offer a model from which others can profit. The nephew of Henry Venn speaks of the noble men and women of the Clapham Sect, the eighteenth-century group that gave England amazing leadership in its antislavery efforts:

> These men never endeavored to mold our informed opinions into any particular mold. Indeed it was needless for them to preach to us. Their lives spoke far more plainly and convincingly than any words. We saw their patience, cheerfulness, generosity, wisdom, and activity daily before us, and we knew and felt that all this was only the natural expression of hearts given to the service of God.

I have often thought myself to be something of a composite of the men and women who went before me. If I have a hunger for learning, it is because a few good people did not preach at me but showed me how much fun it was to learn. If I have any desire to serve people, it is not because someone offered me a job and a paycheck, but because some men and women, by their example, demonstrated that it is better to give than to receive and that one felt a whole lot better as a result.

If I have chosen not to fight back against my enemies, it is because I watched a few folks who were under fire from critics and competitors and who chose to keep silent and faithful. If I have learned the value of spiritual discipline, it is because I got into the lives of some holy people who made it clear that the quiet, purposeful, prayerful life is far superior to anything I see out there in the traffic of modern achievement. And if I have ever come near to God, it is because I saw how it was done by a handful of saints. If I offer others mercy, it is because others first offered it to me.

A few months ago Gail and I spent the better part of a day with Kathleen Chambers, the only child of Oswald Chambers. In her older years, she lives alone in a working-class neighborhood in the north of London. We had planned to visit her for just a few minutes, but she insisted that we remain for lunch and more hours of conversation. We did to our delight.

As Miss Chambers and Gail fixed us a light lunch, I was directed to a room in which Miss Chambers had stored all of her father's memorabilia. I held his treasured poetry books in my hands and saw the comments and markings he had made almost a hundred years ago. I saw his magnificent paintings. And then I discovered a small brown notebook, one like a schoolboy would carry. When I opened it, I found every page filled with names. They were the names of British soldiers stationed in the Egyptian desert and to whom he ministered during the Great War. Each name was carefully written and beside it a phrase that would identify how the man should be prayed for. There were scores of names, page after page of names. And here and there a check mark to suggest that a prayer had been answered.

I held a legacy in my hands. I was awed by the memento of the diligent prayer life of a man who lived long ago and died at a premature age. Although I'd known that Oswald Chambers was a man of prayer, I saw the proof in my hands. It has made a profound impression on my life. That's modeling.

6. MY LEGACY OF MEMORIES: WHAT WILL WE DO TOGETHER THAT WILL BE WORTH REMEMBERING AS A LIFE-GIVING EXPERIENCE?

Making memories! It's a concept that my wife has taught me over the years. Times when you do things together that will create a bonding never to be forgotten. The gift of time and mutual experience.

Our son, Mark, and I will always share a trip around the world at the time of his sixteenth birthday. Our legacy is bound in remembrances of entering China when few others had done it, crossing into East Berlin through Checkpoint Charlie and listening to East German pastors talk about ministry under unfriendly political situations, exploring the British Museum and the Tower of London.

My daughter, Kristy, will remember our visit to Kenya when she was sixteen. Our all-night vigil at the water hole in a game preserve looking for the animals of the forest, our chase of giraffes in the Rift Valley, and our endless late night conversations as we commented on the quality of marriages, working relationships, and friendships we'd seen during the day.

Perhaps not every father is in a position to do something as seemingly dramatic as take a trip around the world or to the game preserves of East Africa. But do not be paralyzed with the suspicion that all memories have to be expensive or international in scope. It is not the place or the expanse of time; it is the quality of the time that is spent. That is never forgotten.

When the day comes that either Gail or I die, the other will always remember the traditions we have created together. The early morning news, walks through Lexington Center, walks in Switzerland, Sabbath days at Peace Ledge. These are legacies we've given to each other, markers on the road of reality that say we've been here or there. They are the graffiti that we'll always see and know punctuate our lives together.

Too many men are so busy that these legacies will never be formatted and handed on. "I never heard of a man regretting on his deathbed that he hadn't spent enough time at the office," we often hear. But the truth behind the familiar statement is too fundamental to ignore. As a man grows older and his private thoughts move closer to the subject of legacy, there will be a time to regret or a time to smile. It will depend on the memories he has stored up. And if the memories are there, so will be the cheer and the courage another generation will badly need.

7. MY LEGACY OF SOUL: WILL I HAVE POINTED THE WAY TO GOD?

Oswald Chambers wrote in *My Utmost for His Highest*, "Those people who influence us most are not those who button hole us and talk to us, but those who live their lives like the stars of heaven and the lilies in the field, perfectly, simply and unaffectedly. Those are the lives that mold us."

The theologian will question the usage of the word, but I want to give a few people the *bequest* of my soul. In other words, I want them to have known as much of me as is possible to know. I want them to have my heart, and I want them to meet God there.

The opening of the soul to the younger generation is an even more sacred concept although parallel to this. It has to do with telling my story to my children. How did I face life and for what reasons? Where did I succeed, and where did I fail? How did I feel as I passed through the various stages of life? Was I ever discouraged? Did I ever deal with the temptation to quit? What were the sources of my energy when the hard times came? And what principles and what lessons have I learned in the stormy moments? How have we managed to keep this marriage of thirty-five-plus years together when all around us were relationships that shattered again and again?

These are the stories our children need to hear from us over and over again. They live on far more powerfully than any amount of money we give to our children.

But most of all, I have this passionate desire that when I have opened my soul and displayed all of its "furniture," there will have been something that helps a few people in the next generation find God.

If my children read my journals (and I am not disturbed by this possibility), I want them to have seen a man who really did want to please his Creator. They will have a chance to determine for themselves how serious I was in pursuit of my mission in life: to devote myself to God, to develop the interior life, and to serve people by offering them hope, courage, enthusiasm, and wisdom. And as they explore, they will learn of fears and failures they never knew about. If they didn't know about the sleepless nights when I worried for them, the mornings when I exalted in their growth and achievement, they'll know it then. If they did not appreciate how much I depended on their mother and how great a role she played in whatever success I have enjoyed, they'll know it then. For my journals are part of my graffiti. They are an open door to my soul, as open as I can be. They are part of my legacy to them.

None of us are that proud of what is in our souls. We can only hope that as we pass on the legacy of the soul to others, they'll be gracious and understanding. And amidst the morass of dark stuff, perhaps they'll find a little light from which there can be profit.

James P. Lenfestey is a New York architect. Writing in the *Minneapolis Star Tribune* some years ago, he recalled an evening in his eleventh year of life when he and his father were catching sunfish and perch off the dock of the family cabin on a New Hampshire lake. It was the night before bass season was to begin, Lenfestey explains. Suddenly his fishing pole bent almost in two, a sign that there was something big on the hook.

The fish did not give up easily, and the father proudly watched as his young boy fought gamely and finally lifted an exhausted fish from the water. Lenfestey writes, "It was the largest one [I'd] ever seen, but it was a bass."

For some people this would have been a moment to start fiddling with truth. The father looked at his watch and noted that the time was 10:00 P.M., two hours before bass season was to open. Just two hours! So, what's two hours? Would the father shrug his shoulders and conclude that the timing of the catch was *close enough* to the start of the season? That would have been easy to do, don't you think?

But not for Lenfestey's father. "You'll have to put it back, son," he said.

No matter how strongly the boy protested, the father insisted that the fish be thrown back into the lake. One could not blame the boy if he looked around to see if there was anyone watching them, if there was anyone taking note of this decision. And there wasn't. Still the father was unmoved. There was a law and a corresponding principle of compliance in operation: the fish had to be thrown back. And back it went, with an unhappy boy saying repeatedly that he would never see a fish that big again.

"That was 34 years ago," Lenfestey writes. The cabin is still there, and today he takes his own children to the same dock where he and his father once fished. After all these years, the truth is that he never has caught a fish close to the size of the one that hit his line that night so long ago.

On the other hand, Lenfestey says, he has seen other kinds of fish, the kind that rise to the bait when there is a question of ethics in one's adult business life.

The man who once threw a huge bass back asks: "Do we do right when no one is looking? Do we refuse to cut corners to get the design in on time? Or refuse to trade stocks based on information that we know we aren't supposed to have?"

"We would," he answers,

if we were taught to put the fish back when we were young. For we would have learned the truth. The decision to do right lives fresh and fragrant in our memory. It is a story we will proudly tell our friends and grand-children.

Not about how we had a chance to beat the system and took it, but about how we did the right thing and were forever strengthened.

James P. Lenfestey is describing for us a legacy, in this case the one passed on from his father to him and now to his children and grand-children. "How much do you think he left?" someone asks when a wealthy man dies. Well, how much did Lenfestey's father leave when he died? I don't know if there was a dollar amount, but this story suggests that there was a huge amount in terms of a spiritual legacy. More than one life has been changed because of a tiny scene on a New Hampshire lake one night when a father gave his son the greatest gift a boy can receive: a legacy that included guidance, integrity, courage, a perspective on how to live life.

In my fifty-seventh year I think a lot about legacy in my private thoughts. I want to leave a lot when the time comes to go to be with God. A lot of encouragement and affirmation, a lot of challenge, a lot of insight, a lot of modeling of the noble life, a lot of soul.

A Memo to My Grandsons: An Old Man's Private Thoughts

To: Lucas Gordon and Ryan Mark
From: Papa

I dare to have this vision that one day in an idle moment one or both of you will be looking at a shelf of books in your homes, and you'll see a copy of *When Men Think Private Thoughts* with the name MacDonald on the spine. If you have nothing better to do, you just might take it off the shelf, look at the jacket, and see that the author is indeed your old grandfather, the man you've always called Papa. "Wonder when Papa wrote this?" you might ask yourself. The date will tell you that it was about the time Bill Clinton was president, American troops were in Bosnia, the Dallas Cowboys had won a Super Bowl or two or three, the Dow Jones averages were in the mid-five thousands, and Internet was a fairly new idea.

Those days were a great time to be alive. You guys and your sisters had made your grandmother and me the happiest grandparents there could ever be. Your mothers placed each of you in our arms within an hour of your birth. I lifted each of you to God and prayed a special blessing on you. In the next years while you were still holdable and huggable, I loved to gather you into my arms and whisper over and over again into your ears, "Papa loves you, Papa loves you." You see, I had this conviction that if I said the words enough times, they would spiral their way down into your deepest memories, and you'd never forget what I said.

Now, fellows, you're going to look at your old grandfather—if he's still alive—and you're going to wonder if he ever knew anything about life as you think you know it. If he's still around, you'll probably see him sitting quietly off in some corner perhaps listening to symphonic music or jazz (I like them both), reading a book, and typing a record of private thoughts into his laptop—all at the same time. All men play the "Midnight Games" with private thoughts, and don't you dare forget that older men are no exception.

I'll probably be thinking about the past; older men do that sometimes. Remembering when Guya (your grandmother) and I met and got married. How we struggled those first years to complete graduate school and get started on our life track. Ryan, I'll be remembering when your dad was an athlete, and I loved watching him score goal after goal on the soccer field. And I'll be thinking of your mom, Lucas—the times when we'd walk the neighborhood and talk about the ideas swirling about in her private world.

My private thoughts will be about what I've learned through life, how faithful God has been, how much living Guya and I have been privileged to do in various parts of the world. How much more there was to be done. A few regrets, of course; a few smiles for stupidities and naiveties; a few praises for things that were more like miracles.

But if you see me thinking private thoughts over in that corner, please know that they're not just centered in the past. There will also be thoughts of the present and the future. I'll wonder about how I can encourage young men like you, how I can offer (when asked I hope) any counsel or wisdom from the years. By the time you get around to reading this memo, my heart (the spiritual dimension, that is) will have accrued seven decades of experience. I'd like to give a portion of that heart to each of you. You'll simply have to ask. And my private thoughts will also include the hope that you'll share your souls with me: your questions, your dreams, your beliefs.

What about your private thoughts? Every young man wonders about his father and his father's father. Sooner or later both of you will look back to the men who made up our family line (as I look back to the men of earlier generations, all the way back to Thomas of the early 1800s) and ask what heritage they have left for you. Perhaps I can help just a bit.

We MacDonalds have been a strange bunch. We've got engineers, preachers, writers, and businesspeople in our DNA. Each of us has had some incredibly bright moments, and each of us has had some real downers. We've known laughter and awe, tears and grief. It's hard to think of anything that men face that we MacDonalds haven't faced. So we have enough of almost every kind of experience, good and bad, to pass on down to the two of you. Sorry for the bad; hope you hold on to the good. As Nehemiah repented of his sins and those of his fathers, so I repent. And as Job prayed for his sons and daughters—that they would not curse God—so I pray for you. That's what an older man does.

But there is nothing in the line of heritage that I want to pass on to you that's more important than this: the fact that one day I (and my father and my father's fathers) made a personal life-defining choice that I'm hoping you guys make. No kidding here; this is serious.

Years ago, when a young man as I now imagine you both to be, I made a life-defining decision. I decided to organize my life around Jesus of Nazareth. I've come to call that decision by the term *Christ-following*. Because that's what it's all about, following Him wherever He wants to lead.

You see, I'd grown up on the stories of Jesus, and I'd been deluged with information about Him and those who claimed that He was the Son of God. But there came this moment in my life when I could no longer coast on the strength of the stories, no longer lean on the life perspective of my father or his father. I had to make my own choices.

The choice to become a Christ-follower was a defining moment in my life. In some ways it would have been easy to reject my father's perspective because all young men like to do that. To make the same choice was to say that he knew something before I did. But it was worth the risk, and one evening during my college days, I made a conscious decision to wrap my life and its direction around the call of Jesus to follow Him. I had no idea what I was getting into.

That was thirty-six years ago. I'm still following. Oh, I've fallen seriously behind on several occasions. I actually fell flat on my face at one point, and there were some who doubted if I'd ever get up. But because I had the help of people who loved me, I did. Now I'm old enough to connect the dots and calculate the results of several decades of following Jesus. And I want you two young men to know that it's been a great trip. I only regret that sometimes I didn't follow more closely. As I get older, I'm determined to catch up and get even closer.

You young guys need to know that this decision to be a Christ-follower is *the choice that drives all other choices*. When I made mine, it seemed at first to be so easy, like getting married to your grandmother was relatively easy. Incidentally, she was one gorgeous bride. The wedding was a no-brainer. It was the living after the wedding—the keeping of the vows, the challenge to be a servant, the polishing of rough edges—that was the big item. Even as I write this memo to the two of you, I'm still working on that one. Bottom line: following Jesus is a lifelong learning, growing, serving, celebrating process. And I dearly hope that the two of you have been smart, humble, and decisive enough to get on the journey. Although we can make this journey with you, we cannot make the journey for you: not your fathers or your grandfathers or any other man in the horizon of your lives.

This book ought to demonstrate that your grandfather was an average man whose few successes really depended on a kind God. That as he got older, he grew less and less reluctant to acknowledge his weak sides, his dreams, his struggles, and his fears. You'll figure out that he got real tired of being part of any system of spirituality that put on airs or refused to acknowledge the fact that life is an uphill battle, winnable only if you keep humble, prayerful, cheerful, faithful, and transparent before God and others.

Now a couple of more things. You probably look at your old grandfather and grandmother (if we're still around, mind you), and you see us as two old dottering folks who are sort of out of touch with things that are important to you. You can't imagine that we're ever been tempted to defy God, fight with each other, or want to do things that are out of keeping with the good Christian life. Take another look.

By the time you really read this, Papa and Guya will likely have moved well past our fiftieth wedding anniversary. Unless, of course, one or both of us have (as your grandmother has always put it) croaked. But if we haven't yet croaked (wherever did she get that word?), please be sure to know that life is as full and real for both of us as it is for you. We love each other dearly and mercifully. We've not stopped believing that every day offers possibilities to grow, to serve, and to discover more about God's world. We'll still be plugging along like Caleb of the Bible "who served the Lord wholeheartedly" and was challenged by big dreams and great visions. And I suspect you'll find that's true of us.

I'll still be reaching out to touch your grandmother and expressing myself to her in code words of affection that no one else can decipher. I expect to still be thinking of new ideas for books and sermons even if no one wants to read the books or hear the sermons. I'll be turning ideas over in my mind and relishing the good changes that are going on in this world. And if I have my legs and my mind, I'll still be wanting to work and make a difference in someone's life. That, after all, is my personal mission.

I've enjoyed my life, Lucas and Ryan. Becoming a noble man through these years has been my greatest challenge. It's an elusive goal I'm still pursuing. Like the men I've described in this book, I have had many, many nights of private thoughts. Some of those thoughts I'd be embarrassed to share. But other private thoughts have taken me on to experiences of insight and achievement. On balance, I have only a few regrets and lots of delights.

Finally, if you see me sitting quietly deep inside my private thoughts, please know that a lot of them are centered on the two of you. That you will be virtuous men, listening intently for the signals of God, serving your generation with vigor, bearing in your character the image of God. Go into the days of your manhood, Lucas and Ryan. Go with the knowledge that the men in your family line are proud of you, that we believe in you, that we love you. Go on with your dreams, and don't play dead for anyone. Be tender, gentle, strong, wise, and character-driven. In your private thoughts be purposeful; in your public lives be men of God.

And I say now what I told you I used to whisper in your ears when you were cuddling size: Papa loves you. That's among the best private thoughts a man can think.

BOOKS TO NURTURE YOUR SPIRIT.

The Life God Blesses

This gracefully written book navigates seldom charted depths and steers you toward the disciplines, convictions, silence, beauty, and spirit that feed and prepare the soul to recognize and receive God's blessings.

0-8407-9155-0 • Hardcover • 256 pages
0-7852-7610-6 • Audio

Rebuilding Your Broken World

Many men and women are apparently dropping off the edges of our horizons because of deep personal tragedy or even dramatic failure. Sometimes silently, sometimes loudly, they cry for help, and they're not heard in or out of church. *Rebuilding Your Broken World* offers the strength and compassion of biblical hope to those who struggle with these problems.

0-8407-9576-9 • Paperback • 240 pages

Renewing Your Spiritual Passion

Do you feel stressed and exhausted when you wake up? Are your goals confused and your performance inconsistent? Are you faced with a relentless barrage of choices? Do you feel utterly impotent because you can't keep a promise? Learn what is happening, why it is happening, and what you can do about it.

0-8407-9564-5 • Paperback • 240 pages

Ordering Your Private World

The Scriptures say there is a private inner world that each of us possesses—and that the inner life can be ordered and regulated. Where people live with disorder within, there is anxiety and little growth. But where the private world is constantly realigned and regulated, there is remarkable personal development and Christian witness. Anniversary edition. Over one million copies sold.

0-7852-7602-5 • Paperback • 228 pages